Don't Turn Away

Don't Turn Away

STORIES OF TROUBLED MINDS IN FRACTURED TIMES

PENELOPE CAMPLING

Elliott&Thompson

First published 2022 by
Elliott and Thompson Limited
2 John Street
London WC1N 2ES
www.eandtbooks.com

ISBN: 978-1-78396-650-9

9 8 7 6 5 4 3 2 1

A catalogue record for this book is available from
the British Library.

Typesetting: Marie Doherty
Printed by CPI Group (UK) Ltd, Croydon, CR0 4YY

This book is dedicated to those struggling with severe mental health problems who find themselves unable to access the support they need and deserve; and to those mental health workers who continue to give their all in very difficult circumstances.

And in memory of Dr Steve Pearce, who died too young after a long illness, one of the kindest and the best.

AUTHOR'S NOTE

This book and the stories within it are based on my clinical experience. Some people have generously agreed to appear in these pages, but the book covers many years and it has not been possible to trace everyone. I have therefore changed details of people and incidents, trying to remain true to their essence, but mindful of the need to protect confidentiality and privacy.

~

The stories in this book touch on some difficult and distressing topics. If you are affected by any of the themes covered in these pages, you can call Samaritans on 08457 909090 or visit the Samaritans website to find details of the nearest branch.

Many mental health trusts now operate a central access line for acute problems. You can find the number by visiting your local trust's website.

CONTENTS

INTRODUCTION

I am worried about Prabha. She is a happily married, successful doctor with no history of mental health problems – and yet she's increasingly preoccupied with the thought of suicide. For many months she has been working in an intensive care unit with Covid-19 patients. She is deeply exhausted and finds herself wishing it would all stop. Images of ending her life keep intruding into her mind.

'That must be frightening. Can you tell me a bit more about what you've been imagining?' I ask gently.

'Just stuff,' she says in a tiny voice, after a long delay and avoiding my eyes. She looks painfully embarrassed, like a child caught stealing. She shakes her head rapidly from side to side as if she's trying to free herself of the pictures insistently pushing through to the surface. She is ashamed of these thoughts; they feel alien and she assures me she would never act on them. Over and over again, she tells me how well she functions in ordinary times. Like many clinicians working in ICU, Prabha has a deeply set belief in her own resilience. Asking for support is not something that comes easily but she is frightened at how little control she has over her mind at the present time. I'm a bit frightened too. The incidence of suicide is higher in doctors than in the general population, and anaesthetists like Prabha are thought to be particularly at risk – we both know that with so many drugs at hand she has the means of killing herself at her fingertips.

Later that day, Tom, another senior ICU doctor, sits head in hands and tells me he feels crushed. He used to love his job but now dreads coming to work. He knows he's not functioning well and might make a mistake. But despite being more exhausted than he ever thought possible, he also knows that the staffing shortages have become so acute that standards are dropping to a dangerous level and he can't bear the thought of taking time off and leaving his colleagues with even more pressure. He is having fleeting self-destructive thoughts while driving, enticed by the idea of oblivion rather than actually killing himself. Somehow, I need to help Tom rediscover his sense of agency, but his burdensome circumstances weigh heavy and it would be easy to be infected by his sense of helplessness.

Working with ICU staff during the pandemic brings home the precariousness of the healthcare systems that are there supposedly to help us in our hour of need. Having endured my own experience of trying to hold a mental health team together through bad times, there is something about watching another service under severe stress – once removed as it were, in relative comfort as therapist and witness – that makes me want to shout about it and make people listen. It makes me think about the fragility of progress and how easy it is for things to go into reverse.

~

I started my career as a psychiatrist nearly forty years ago at the Towers, one of two Victorian asylums in Leicester. It was a profoundly flawed institution where I encountered patients who had been locked away and forgotten for years – institutionalised, infantilised, their individuality eroded. Some of them had originally been admitted decades earlier for no better reason than they'd had an illegitimate baby. And yet I began that first job full of optimism. We all knew that change was under way: plans to close the Towers were already in place, and the generation before us had taken huge steps towards humane care, reforming the Mental Health Act and breaking down the barriers between the asylums and the community. We believed in progress. It was an era filled with hope.

Just six months later, I moved on to a brand new mental health unit attached to the General Hospital. It was a hugely significant change, one that reflected the reforms taking place throughout the country, indeed throughout most of the richer countries in the world. The building itself seemed to embody a new and hopeful chapter in the history of psychiatry. At the time it felt as if I was part of a great leap forward, playing a small part on the right side of history, my future career glittering in my imagination with grateful patients, exciting discoveries, and a palpable sense of progress.

And indeed some things did improve. We now understand a lot more about the human mind and have a growing evidence base informing us how best to help people who are struggling. There has also been a sea change in attitudes to mental health more generally. People are more open about their feelings, and mental health problems are no longer the taboo they were a generation or two ago. Celebrities – even royalty – talk publicly about their battles with mental illness. Mental well-being and mindfulness have become part of everyday language and therapy is increasingly seen – in some sections of society, at least – as a normal, healthy thing to do. Public health campaigns reassure us that there is no shame in sharing feelings of despair and thoughts of suicide and remind us that mental health problems will affect as many as one in four of us at some point in our lives.

But despite all of this, mental health services have not thrived in recent years. Morale is desperately low on the front line. People with serious mental illness are likely to die on average fifteen to twenty-five years earlier than those without SMI, largely from preventable diseases such as heart disease and diabetes.[1] Report after report has confirmed what every mental health worker knows: that the service is in a terrible state and that the shocking chasm between what is needed and what we are actually resourced to provide is getting larger, leaving an increasing number of vulnerable people and their families in dark and desperate states of mind. The theme tunes seem horribly familiar as the potential for depriving, brutalising and dehumanising mental health patients re-emerges in different settings. To my great sadness, we seem to be moving backwards: the progress made during my early career steadily eroding.

Now we have services where desperate patients wait for months to see a psychiatrist or therapist; where the bed shortage is such that we end up sending severely ill adolescents hundreds of miles away from their families; where traumatised refugees are housed in detention centres that are more like prisons than care facilities. Why, at a time when we seem so much more comfortable talking openly about mental health and have so much more knowledge than previous generations, do we put up with sparse, inadequate and sometimes dehumanising services? There seems to be some sort of paradox here: a shadow as dark and gothic as those lunatic asylums of old.

Funding is, of course, a huge issue. Health ministers talk recurrently about 'transforming' services and promise more money, but action doesn't seem to follow the rhetoric. Despite all the positive talk, the gap between what we spend on mental health care and the level of need in our society has been growing steadily since the 1950s. The proportion of healthcare money spent on mental health has also declined. There are still excellent teams and individual clinicians working in mental health but there are simply not enough beds, not enough staff, not enough therapeutic opportunities.

Now in the wake of two years of Covid-19, things are worse than ever. Isolation has affected us all. Many have suffered from the social and economic consequences of the pandemic and are left with ongoing uncertainty and fear. Others are struggling with grief and loneliness, some of them haunted by thoughts of their loved ones dying in cruel circumstances. There is talk of collective trauma and much speculation about the effect of the pandemic and social distancing on, especially, the development and mental health of children.

This has exacerbated an already perilous situation. Just how much mental health services had lost their way was brought home to me in the first few weeks of the pandemic. The edict from NHS England was to discharge as many inpatients as possible. Clearly the risk of infection was real, but the mental health charity MIND has recently published research suggesting that in some cases this was done with no review of ongoing mental health needs and worrying outcomes for the patients.[2] Our local mental health trust, among others, discharged the majority of its outpatients at the beginning of March 2020, giving them instead a central crisis line number to ring in an emergency. Cutting off ongoing support at a very frightening time to those already identified as mentally vulnerable seemed utterly outlandish to me. It showed no understanding that encouraging people to use support to pre-empt crises is a fundamental premise of mental health work, and that abruptly terminating an ongoing therapeutic relationship is likely to be disturbing.

There has been a lot of talk in recent years about 'parity of esteem', treating mental health on a par with physical health, but these decisions seem to show just how low down the ranking order mental health services themselves see their patients. Compounding everything else, the pandemic has presented the country with a mental health crisis. But extraordinarily, rather than stepping up, it seems that mental health services were stepped down. One or two of my ex-colleagues ignored this edict, I'm proud to say, and continued to make contact with their more vulnerable patients, but it was months before they were allowed to restart the online group therapy sessions that were such an important part of help-ing patients through, of getting their lives back on track, indeed of managing the risks they faced or, much more rarely, presented to others.

Such a stark example of a whole organisation turning away from the mentally vulnerable patients it was responsible for, at the worst possible time, has given me the impetus needed to explore my thoughts on the uncertain progress of psychiatry over the last forty years. Patients and their families, and psychiatrists themselves, are deeply frustrated that the systems in place are increasingly focused on how to deny people care instead of helping them to access it.

How has it happened that we value our patients and our attempts to help them so little? How has it happened that we have drifted into an exclusion culture, in many ways as harsh and neglectful as I encountered in the institutions of old?

Perhaps the truth is that severe mental illness is just as frightening, just as stigmatising, just as much a taboo as it always has been. Our relationship as a society with mental disorder is not straightforward. How we think about the mentally ill, how we relate to them, how we manage the feelings they evoke, whether we see them as deserving of serious investment, even where we house them – none of these questions seems to get easier, however much progress we make in other areas. We do not want to face the reality of the suffering of those with more serious mental health problems, nor to fund their care adequately – or perhaps we simply don't know how. It is easier to tranquillise, restrain, separate, lock them up or ignore them than it is to engage properly with their needs and their pain.

The reality is that being up close with mental disturbance is difficult and discomforting. There will always be a degree of ambivalence. Connecting with others in severe mental distress can jolt us into facing our own vulnerability and hook into fears of dependency and losing our own sanity – fears that are often deeply buried. And the fact is that mental well-being is not something any of us can take for granted, as my work with ICU doctors made clear to me. Adverse life events can push most of us over a threshold where vicious circles – a complex mix of social, psychological and biological factors, all interacting and amplifying each other – start to take hold. Before the pandemic, very few of the clinicians I've been seeing had considered or ever imagined they would need any form of therapy or counselling but as the horrors of Covid-19 at its most destructive have unfolded, over a hundred have come knocking at my door.

In the twenty-first century, mental health problems are not about the 'other', but about you and me, our families and friends. Most of us know families struggling with a parent with severe dementia, a child with autism or an eating disorder, a teenager with obsessive compulsive disorder or severe drug problems, a young person who has just been diagnosed with bipolar disorder or schizophrenia, a mother with post-natal depression. These conditions and many others are commonplace but can have a devastating impact on the individual and their family, and lead to a significant cost for society at large.

I want this book to reach patients, clinicians, politicians, and 'ordinary people' living in a society where mental health problems are escalating; to bridge the distance between us and those in severe mental distress. Keep in mind that mental health services are expected to take over where family love, friendship and community support can no longer manage a person's disturbance, where patience has worn out and understanding has turned to bewilderment – or even worse, terror, anger or rejection. We professionals are invited in – or sometimes are duty-bound to intervene – when people are losing their grip on reality, when their brains are playing maddening tricks or when extreme emotion threatens to overwhelm them. We are privileged by society to see and to try to help people at their most desperate, frightened and exposed.

Bridging the world of psychiatry (the branch of medicine interested in ailments of the mind) and psychotherapy (the interpersonal process of healing the mind) through the last four decades, I am in a position to take you up close: to share my experience with patients and show you what is involved in genuinely struggling to connect with the psychological suffering of others. The seeds for such relationships to go wrong are always present. There's a constant danger of finding oneself invaded by hopelessness and helplessness. There's always the risk of falling into an us-and-them-type relationship – into an 'othering' dynamic. It's only too easy for care and protectiveness to turn into control or even abuse.

I've tried to be honest about the way these dynamics can creep in and to help the reader understand how they can further complicate the relationship we have with mental ill-health as individuals and as a society. As we shall see, they can arise in all sorts of situations, good and bad, though they are much more likely to take root at times – like the present – when staff are overstretched, undervalued and feel forgotten.

We desperately need to find a way to rebuild faltering services. There are no easy answers here, no simple mantras. I don't want to guilt-trip anyone or suggest the problems would go away if we were all a bit nicer. But I do invite you to care about these people, to take them and the often awful experiences that have befallen them seriously. Sadly, such experiences are often the result of all-too-common inhumanities and shortcomings in our society. Facing up to these things is difficult but such understanding is vital if we are to build enough momentum to move things forward. The more open we are to thinking about mental ill-health in all its complicated, disturbing reality, the more in touch with ourselves we shall be. And the more in touch with ourselves we are, the better able we are to promote safe relationships, build strong and healthy communities, support mental well-being, and effectively lobby for better mental health care.

We need to think radically. The scale of the problem has always been too big to be left to specialist mental health staff alone. Encounters with mental distress – in a loved one, a neighbour, a stranger, a patient, or in society as a whole – can feel too difficult to bear, too weird and frightening, or just too bloody misery-inducing. In a way, it is understandable that so many of us turn away and leave it to others. But we have a choice and if we do turn away from people in distress and abandon our mental health services to their steady decline, there are serious costs for us all.

1

OUT OF SIGHT,
OUT OF MIND

I have vivid memories of my first weekend on call as a junior psychiatrist. It was the long August bank holiday weekend, 1983.
I was twenty-five and the only doctor around in a neo-Gothic
building, the size of a small village: the Towers Hospital, one of
two Victorian asylums serving the population of Leicestershire.
Set on a hill in extensive, well-landscaped grounds, this outwardly
grand building had been built over a hundred years earlier to stand
imposing and isolated. Having six hundred beds, it was small in
comparison to many such institutions, but still seemed gulpingly
big to me.

It is hard to convey just how cold the corridors were: I soon
learned to take my coat with me, even though it was high summer. The blue-tiled floors and high ceilings amplified any noise;
the strip-lighting paled people's faces; the heavy church-like
doors on to the wards were almost always locked. The worst

passage was outside the kitchens where it was hard to avoid the sound of cockroaches crunching under my feet. A handful of patients frequented this corridor, seemingly preferring it to sitting around on the wards. One man, Eric, would spend all day, every day, walking up and down with his hands behind his back, jutting his head up and down rather like a pigeon, completely oblivious of my presence. Every few minutes, he would start to wail, a chilling eerie sound that I found harrowing, particularly when I was there on my own. 'Sweet Pete' was a more welcome feature of that corridor, dressed in a smart suit jacket, tie and trilby hat, carrying a brolly in one hand and a briefcase in the other. Pete would pace intently from one end of that corridor to the other, over and over, as if he were late for a business meeting – rumour had it he had once been a bank manager. There was nothing frightening about Pete, who would doff his hat as he passed, offer a cheery greeting and then mutter that he was late and hurry off. He was presumably preserving an islet of dignity in his otherwise damaged mind. Sadly, his legs – decked out in pyjama bottoms – gave the game away.

Most Victorian mental asylums were built a few miles outside their home city, close enough to serve the population but not so close as to encroach on citizens' consciousness, the fear of madness that they might engender kept a safe distance away. During my childhood in the 1960s, such institutions were referred to as 'loony bins'. I can still remember the hushed and fearful tone of voice that my parents used whenever we drove past the gates of our local asylum. A decade or two later, a series of media investigations laid bare the brutal way some of these institutions were treating their vulnerable inhabitants.

Although it avoided national attention, the Towers was no exception when it came to maltreatment. Scandal was rife, but whispered rather than publicised. It's difficult to get any perspective on the history we embody, especially when we're young. As a medical student, I had read books by the famous sociologist Erving Goffman about asylums, outlining the theoretical dangers of large institutions that were closed off to the outside world, but at this early stage in my career, I hadn't really applied these ideas to myself and my colleagues.[1] Nothing had prepared me for the casual brutality and nihilism I was to encounter on some of those wards, the wretched condition of some of the inhabitants for whom this squalid institution was their only home.

A brand new unit on the General Hospital site was due to open in six months' time, but that would only be for people with acute problems. Others would continue in the Towers for many years and it is the treatment of these patients that this chapter focuses on. Some of them, I was beginning to discover, had lived there for over half a century, everyday decisions being made for them, their lives organised by others and predictable in every detail, any sense of autonomy a far-distant memory, their individuality crushed by years of being treated the same as everyone else.

～

On Saturday morning, I was called by a nurse from one of the wards that housed these patients who were seen as chronic. We called these 'back wards' – derogatory enough – but 'forgotten wards' would have been more accurate. These were people who were not expected to get better and had spent many years in the hospital, too mad and too vulnerable – or, as we were beginning

3

to understand, too institutionalised – to cope outside the asylum. Would I pop over and have a look at Sylvia? She had started refusing drinks, which was unlike her, and the nurse was worried she would become dehydrated.

It took me twenty minutes to locate the ward, which was up a winding staircase in one of the towers that gave the building its name. I was intrigued at what I would find as I'd already discovered that each ward had its own culture, largely determined by the personality of the lead nurse. As with many asylums, it was usual for staff to be recruited from the local neighbourhood, with closely knit nursing teams and stories going back well before the war when someone's grandad had been the ward manager and someone else's aunt had been a nursing assistant.

The nurses on Sylvia's ward seemed kind, and she had been allowed to put her best dress on for my visit, a dress she had brought with her when she'd been admitted thirty years earlier. It was a cotton summer frock patterned with yellow roses, the full skirt gathered at her waist with a golden satin sash and a heart-shaped neckline. It looked very like a party dress I'd had when I was a little girl, but I knew the style had been popular with adults in the fifties. Sylvia was sitting in a standard hospital armchair covered in tatty red plastic, but draped with a beautiful cream lace shawl, similar to the one she was wearing over her shoulders. She was perched on the edge of the chair, sitting with an impressively straight back, tatting with an antique ivory pointed shuttle. Tatting is a type of lace-making that, luckily for this encounter, I'd happened to learn as a child at my grandmother's knee, so I was able to make informed and appreciative comments about the neatness of her 'cow hitch knots' and 'picots' that quickly established a rapport.

Sylvia bent her head towards me confidentially, speaking in not much more than a whisper.

'I'm so sorry, doctor, I would have liked to wear my best jewellery but due to a number of unfortunate experiences, I don't trust the hoi polloi in this vicinity of the city. They have their hands in everything' – eyebrows archly raised as she swept her gaze around the room, before nodding at me complicitly.

I asked her where she'd come from. She was silent for a few seconds, then said, 'Bath is a beautiful city. Have you ever visited the pump rooms?' She then poured, as if from a teapot, and lifted her hand to her mouth as if she was sipping a cup of tea – little finger properly crooked, of course. It seemed we were in some genteel pretend game. I played along – rather self-consciously I have to admit, worried that I was being watched and would seem ridiculous, not at all sure what was expected of me.

Sylvia was the first patient I'd met from a chronic ward. How were we expected to behave with these institutionalised people? There seemed to be no expectation that we explore their long-term problems, find out what first brought them into hospital, or indeed do anything to change the status quo. While I was sipping my pretend tea, I tried to move the conversation on to the reason for my visit, why she was not drinking more. She simply smiled sweetly and asked if the tea was to my liking.

Later, I chatted to the nurses, wondering aloud if she might be frightened of wetting herself. I was right. She had been incontinent recently and that had preceded her refusing to drink. I could imagine that wetting herself had been horribly humiliating for someone like Sylvia, so desperately trying to hang on to her dignity, against all the odds. I ordered a urine test, preferring not to wonder how the nurses would get a sample from someone so fastidious. Sure enough, a urinary tract infection was eventually diagnosed and I started Sylvia on antibiotics. But how to get Sylvia drinking properly again? Rather to the surprise of the nurse on duty, I brought in a little teapot with old-fashioned bone-china teacups and saucers that I'd noticed in the resident doctor's room and, to Sylvia's delight, we sat down to another tea party – this time with proper tea.

Sylvia had been admitted as an involuntary patient in 1949, in an era when once you were admitted to an asylum, there was little expectation of getting out again, indeed little sense of the potential to recover from a mental illness. Compared with the amount we are expected to document these days, there was very little written in her file. The last entry was nearly four years old and described a rash she'd developed on her hands. Her admission note was particularly sparse. A one-sentence letter from a GP: 'Please admit this post-partum young lady who has been acting in a crazy manner since she gave birth 3 weeks ago.' And a few more lines from the admitting psychiatrist: '22-year-old lactating woman . . . gave birth to a healthy boy weighing 6lbs 2ozs at 5 o'clock on 15th June 1950 . . . has developed a condition of deep melancholia . . . prescribed ECT.' There was no background history or any information about what had happened to the baby. For that I had to read through a handful of letters included in the file.

It seemed that Sylvia had fallen in love and married an ex-soldier, who had recently returned from Thailand where he had been a prisoner at the end of the war. It transpired that this young man – presumably very damaged from the experience – already had a wife and two children in Scotland. Sylvia discovered that she had married a bigamist who, once this truth emerged, quickly moved back to Scotland, leaving Sylvia to face the shock, the shame and the pregnancy alone. No surprise that with this social and psychological disruption in the background, the rapid changes in hormones in the first weeks after giving birth had tipped her into some sort of mental breakdown. How severe was not clear from the notes, but there was nothing to suggest the start of what we would think of today as a serious mental illness: 'agitated weeping' and 'attempts to escape the hospital' were the main symptoms documented. I could only imagine Sylvia's rage and despair.

Her medical notes, typical of their time, were written in an almost illegible scrawl. It is true we were probably better at deciphering other people's handwriting in those days but, nevertheless, there was little sense in the psychiatric documents of this era that doctors were expecting anyone else to read them or felt the need to account for their decisions. This was to change with the 1959 Mental Health Act which was designed to abolish the difference between psychiatric hospitals and other types of hospital, and make it easier for treatment to be voluntary and informal. Compulsory treatment became dependent on a formal medical decision and legal framework that held psychiatrists to account for detaining someone against their will. This was progress indeed, and the start of a decline in the numbers shut away in asylums. But it had had little effect on Sylvia, who, like so many patients of her generation, had become dependent on the hospital for her basic needs: her food, her warmth and shelter, her medical care and her clothing – a victim of the 'total institution'.

In October 1983, two months after I'd started in psychiatry, another Mental Health Act was passed, which tightened up the law around 'sectioning', making it harder to detain, assess and treat someone against their wishes. This meant no one could be brought into hospital against their will without the formal assessment of a legally approved and specially trained social worker, as well as two doctors and the signed consent of a close relative. It also offered more clarity about the nature of disorder where detention was deemed appropriate – the concept of 'treatable condition' was important – and held professionals to account through a system of appeals and tribunals. (The term 'section' refers to the particular Section of the Act involved.) Looking back, the timing of the new Act was fortuitous for me. It meant I spent two training days, right at the start of my career, immersed in mental health law and history, and engaged in a prolonged lively debate alongside psychiatrists, social workers and solicitors with decades of experience and widely differing views. There were some cynical voices, as you'd expect with any major change, but most people saw it as progress and spoke enthusiastically about the changes it would bring. When I look back on this time, I'm struck by the optimism around, our belief in ourselves and the strong sense of being part of a movement forward. To some degree, this mitigated the everyday grimness.

~

I have always been fascinated by the question of what it is to be human and psychiatry seemed a very obvious specialty to choose, but I was discovering that madness can lay you bare in very desperate ways and the urge to turn away was immense. The back wards at the Towers were full of people like Sylvia with their heartbreaking stories locked away inside themselves, scantily sketched in medical notes that nobody seemed to read, and lost even to the nursing teams who cared for them. The core symptoms of mental illness were often worryingly absent when people were admitted and, tragically, illegitimate pregnancies and homosexuality not uncommonly the main reason given.

Others had bizarre neurological symptoms, poorly under-stood at the time, that made them extremely difficult to nurse. I remember one man with a severe and interesting version of Capgras syndrome. He was convinced not only that the nurses were impostors but that the ward itself was a fake. His demen-tia was such that his psychotic beliefs were incoherent and often changing, but at times he was convinced we were the 'Bosch' and he was being held in a Colditz-like castle. At the time, we tried to understand this psychoanalytically, while the nurses tried to talk him out of it: 'Stop being silly, Ernie. You know perfectly well I'm no Kraut!' We know now that Capgras syndrome is common in the type of Alzheimer's disease where there is damage to the right parietal lobe – the area of the brain that is responsible for spatial and facial recognition. I'm not sure if knowing this would have helped the nurses manage Ernie's frightened state. He was quite obviously terrified of us and very afraid to walk through a door or even to cross the room.

I'd like to tell you that I spent hours with these long-stay patients, getting to know them, but this would be indulging in wishful thinking. In truth, I neglected them like everyone else. I was a bit frightened of them, although I wouldn't have admitted this at the time. Perhaps disturbed is the better word. There was certainly a dark side to their madness, with occasional scenes of gothic lunacy – ripping clothes off, screaming obscenities, lashing out, biting and scratching at anyone who got in their way – that could have sat comfortably in the pages of a Brontë novel. They were not all like Sylvia, clinging so determinedly to her modicum of bourgeois gentility – dear Sylvia, who a few months later gave me a beautiful handmade lace shawl. Today we rarely see such extreme outward expressions of madness because patients are medicated with modern drugs from an early stage. Many in the 'critical psychiatry' movement would argue that they are just being put in chemical straitjackets, the underlying psychotic beliefs not much changed.[2]

I had loved my psychiatry placement as a medical student, fired up by the academic learning, the applied philosophy and the more prolonged contact with patients, but we'd been kept well away from the asylum and sheltered by particularly humane enthusiastic consultants. My experience at the Towers could not have been more different. The consultant I now worked for seemed to find my presence an irritant, shaking his head anxiously whenever I spoke, raising his eyebrows quizzically whenever I dared give an opinion. He had a few patients with whom he worked psychoanalytically. It was months into the job before I discovered that I was supposed to steer clear of these 'special' patients. It was as if by talking with them I'd been found doing something inappropriate and intrusive. Again and again, I found myself tripping over unwritten rules that made no sense. Everyone but me seemed to be 'in the know', but the culture somehow made it difficult to ask questions. I realise now that this sense of alienation, of being outside the group, is a classic scenario in institutions. At the time I just lost my bearings a bit.

I was spending a lot of time doing things I hated: prescribing ever higher levels of horrible drugs, doing depot (long-acting injection) clinics and administering electroconvulsive therapy (ECT). No one seemed to value the fact that I talked with patients. In fact, I was often expected to write up medicines without even seeing the person. Sometimes I was asked to 'counsel' a particular individual, which sounded more promising, but it turned out this meant I was supposed to 'give them a good ticking off' – the threat of increasing their medication implied – because they'd refused to eat their dinner, or pinched their friend's doll, or tried to bite one of the nurses.

On one occasion, though, reading through someone's notes going back over fifty years, I was surprised to come across a very different type of psychiatrist. It was his beautiful looped handwriting that first grabbed my attention, but then I was drawn in by the narrative. His description of his conversations with this particular patient, Hester May, read like a detective story: a working-class girl made pregnant by her upper-class 'sweetheart', she had refused to submit to the pressures put on her to disappear quietly and have the child adopted, which had eventually led to her being categorised as a 'moral imbecile' and incarcerated. (The category of 'moral imbecile' was eventually abolished in the 1959 Mental Health Act.)

A classic story but no less painful for that. The psychiatrist seemed fascinated by the patient's story, enraged by it, unable to let it go, and I had a growing sense of encountering someone a bit like me. But his notes, which started in 1942, lasted only two years, then abruptly stopped. I felt I'd made a friend, then lost him. Who was this humane psychiatrist, kicking against the system back in the 1940s? Why wasn't he part of the 'war effort'? What had happened to him? After that, if I was seeing elderly long-stay patients, I always turned to 1942 to see if he had been involved. I was mostly disappointed. There were a handful of scripts by him in other patients' notes, but short and to the point.

When I was asked to see this lady who had so fascinated him, more than forty years later, Hester May was very elderly, struggling with heart failure, and adamant that her symptoms had been caused by Ethel, another patient on the ward, casting a spell on her. She was particularly upset by her swollen legs: 'Fred used to tell me I had beautiful ankles,' she'd say, just as if it was yesterday rather than forty-five years ago. 'I always knew she was jealous and would find a way to spoil them.' Fred, I assumed, was the 'sweetheart' of her story. When I tried to explain to Hester about her heart failure and why I'd prescribed her diuretics, she'd cackled with painful laughter: 'Don't you go telling me about me old 'eart, me duck.' Then, gasping to get her breath, 'There's nothing you can tell Hester May about a broken 'eart.'

I had become a psychiatrist because I was interested in people's stories. I wanted to understand what made them tick. I wanted to find ways to connect with them. At the time my pretend tea party with Sylvia made me feel confused and ridiculous. In retrospect, however, my attempt to get alongside her reflects what my career has been about: a search to engage therapeutically, a quest to build and sustain empathy in a very non-empathetic world. I like to think my doctor with the beautiful handwriting would have understood that.

~

My friend, Marie, has had an impressive career, working for the Red Cross in some of the most dangerous, impoverished parts of the world. But she is quite clear that one of her worst experiences was her first placement as a student mental health nurse on an elderly ward at the Towers, where she was unlucky enough to encounter an outbreak of salmonella infection. The ward was put in quarantine, so what was meant to be a nine-hour shift turned out to be seventy-two hours: three days and three nights imprisoned on the ward nursing severely demented patients through a serious bout of gastroenteritis. She still has nightmares about the sheer force of the explosive diarrhoea and projectile vomiting happening around her and the utter wretchedness of those already frail old women. She had never seen anyone die before, but by the end of the three days she'd laid out four bodies.

Body waste and continence is an issue on all hospital wards, particularly elderly wards, but the stench of those at the Towers in the early 1980s was much worse than anything I've had to deal with before or since. It was hard to get away from excrement on these wards. It wasn't just the smell: it seemed to always be there, defining our relationship with the patient, leaving little room for any other part of their story. Millie, for example, was known as 'Mrs Teapot' because she used to mould her faeces into tiny little beads, hide them away and then, when no one was looking, post them down the spout of the teapot. Needless to say we were repulsed, but no one thought to try to understand or help her communicate the feelings lurking beneath this behaviour.

I experimented with visiting the wards at different times of day, but it made no difference. There simply seemed to be an acceptance that elderly people who were losing their minds could sit around in their own shit. It was this nihilism, I think, that made it so different from medical wards where the smell of pathological waste products and decaying flesh can be equally or more abhorrent but attracts scientific interest or heroic action from the staff around. Here the sight and smell of faeces seemed to express the hopelessness and horror of bodies outliving their minds, the despair of people judged as beyond dignity or respect.

As a doctor, I was spared the worst of it. I tried not to judge the nurses who were stuck on one ward for their whole shift and were earning less than I was, despite their many years of experience. I remember once walking past one of the student nurses and noticing she was looking rather grim. I asked if she was all right and she thrust a bowl towards me with a load of nail clippings. 'Smell them!' she said, holding it up near my face. The smell was so disgusting and so unexpected that I gagged. Apparently, cutting the patients' faeces-encrusted nails was one of the jobs the students hated most. Some of the nurses were brilliant, of course, as repelled by the environment and some of the more inhumane rituals as I was. One or two were already involved in the design of a new unit, still years away, which they would go on to lead. But there's no way to sugar-coat it: some of what I witnessed was vile.

I remember arriving on a male ward to find a queue of old men, standing in their greying underpants, waiting to be shaved. On another occasion, on the female ward, I came across two nurses systematically going around washing the women, one carrying a bowl of grimy-looking water, the other the flannel and hairbrush: 'Come on, me love, open your legs for me, let's get the dirty parts done.' And then on to the next woman: same bowl of grimy water; same filthy flannel; same hairbrush.

The bathroom had two baths in the middle of the room and on the shelf above the basins was a row of twenty-four sets of false teeth in unmarked jars. One poor woman used to masturbate so violently in the bath that the nurses had to hold her down. Like most people faced with such encounters, I felt embarrassment, disgust and perhaps a bit of fascination. Mostly, we just pretended it wasn't happening. It is easiest to deal with this uncomfortable mix of feelings with shocked disapproval or mirth. But the masturbation I was forced to encounter at the Towers wasn't predatory in any way, and 'lust' doesn't really capture it. It was more comfort-seeking than attention-seeking and when I look back at it from the safe distance of middle age, my heart goes out to those patients who had found perhaps the only way of being in touch with themselves.

I was also shocked to discover that there were still a handful of patients with neuro-syphilis or GPI (general paralysis of the insane) slowly dying in the Towers. Syphilis is a bacterial sexually transmitted disease that attacks the brain tissue in its tertiary stage, causing severe psychosis and dementia. It can be treated in its early stages with penicillin, so had become less common. Despite doing an infectious diseases job as a house officer, the nearest I'd come to the tragedy of this infection before doing time at the Towers was in the pages of Karen Blixen's novel *Out of Africa* and watching a production of Henrik Ibsen's play *Ghosts*.

Of all dehumanising diseases, tertiary syphilis must be one of the worst. Oozing sores become foul-smelling ulcers and abscesses that can spread across the face into bone and other organs. One of the men in the Towers had a disfigured chin with raw open flesh where his bottom lip should have been; another had half his nose missing. It was hard not to flinch with repulsion as well as pity and I had no difficulty understanding why victims of the disease had been shunned and isolated, the repellent necrotic symptoms read by previous generations as a sign of sin. Even in the first half of the twentieth century, prior to the establishment of the NHS, health insurance schemes did not cover self-inflicted conditions, so treatment for venereal disease was often withheld.

Penicillin had been available since 1943, but somehow these stragglers still around in the Towers in the early eighties had gone undiagnosed and untreated for years while the necrotic damage progressed. In the past, they would have died within a few months. Now we had the means to stop the disease progressing, but they literally had holes where brain tissue should be and there was little we could do to help. There was often severe frontal-lobe damage, which meant they were particularly disinhibited and difficult to nurse. I remember one man forever stripping off his clothes, underwear and all, and singing a crude version of a sea shanty – the first two lines over and over again.

Most distressing was the pain. I was called on a couple of occasions to see one man who seemed particularly tortured. His ravaged face and throat and brain disease made words impossible. But he tossed in agony and keened, a sound between a frightened squeal and a howl, more like an injured fox or a cat, the scream of an animal in the throes of death, which was desperately distressing for everyone around him. Bone pain is particularly difficult to bear and hard to alleviate. He was already on a large dose of morphine and a too high dose of tranquillisers, which I didn't dare increase. All I could do was make impotent soothing noises drowned out by his agony and sit for a while with the nurses before returning to my bed. It was hard to get back to sleep.

I don't want to give the impression that everything about the Towers was bad. Once off the long corridor and on the other side of the big heavy doors into the wards, I found little empires of their own, the regimes varying widely. The acute wards had a much stronger link with consultant psychiatrists and some of them were humane, progressive and pushing hard for reform. Nevertheless, much of the Towers exhibited the worst characteristics associated with what Erving Goffman described as a 'total institution', with most of the inhabitants – including many of the nurses, whose home was the nurses' residence – living and sleeping in the place, and institutional needs taking precedence over patient care. A particular problem for such institutions was their tendency to become inward-looking and to not question their own practices. I found it extraordinary that tea was served in huge metal pots, the milk and sugar already mixed in. And surely anybody could see that giving patients their final meal of the day at 4.30 p.m. followed by a mug of Ovaltine and bed at 7 p.m. was treating them as if they were children? But although these were issues I could moan about with other junior psychiatrists, none of us thought to challenge the powers that be. It was a hierarchical culture that was all-embracing, that could twist one's moral values and actions. Cut off from outside scrutiny, the staff had enormous power over the patients and there was always the potential for such power to be used abusively. The loss of liberty and social isolation from family and community left the patients pretty well at the mercy of however the staff chose to behave.

It's easy to work for a short time in a total institution and produce a satirical analysis of those whose lives were so narrowly defined. Easy for the junior doctor, always the visitor, always moving on after six months, always the outsider. So different for the nurses, leaving their late shifts at 9.15 p.m., back in for their 'earlies' at 7 a.m., long hours cooped up on one ward, day in day out, year after year, their lives entangled with their teammates and their disturbing patients. And as for the long-stay patients – wearing cheap, ill-fitting clothes bought by the nurses in a batch at a knock-down price in a sale; sleeping in dormitories with the next bed a hand-hold away; washing themselves in bathrooms and defecating in toilets with unlockable doors; eating bland, monotonous food served at times to suit the institution – they were a textbook example of the way total institutions are prone to putting people's needs second to those of the institution, demeaning and degrading them in the process.

But I was affected as much as anyone in my own way. It wasn't the grown-up temper tantrums, desperate though they were, that upset me most: at least in those cases there was still a person there, feeling something tangible. It was more the number of people who had totally retreated into their heads, completely mute, their personhood eroded and locked away, meaningful human connection long since deemed hopeless. Some of the patients had holes in their forehead, a sign that they'd been subjected to brain surgery – a frontal-lobe lobotomy. One man had lost his speech completely during the operation, his attempts to communicate reduced to barking.

At times I felt I was coming up against raw need that had overwhelmed any sense of dignity and broken through any conventionally civil inter-human boundary. I can still remember my first experience of this, working in what was then Bombay as a medical student; the staring hungry eyes of people begging, the aggression, the injuries and disabilities that we were told, rightly or wrongly, were sometimes self-inflicted to arouse our pity – as if

our pity needed further amplifying. Pity is such a disturbing feeling anyway: the vast gap between oneself and the other somehow
dehumanising; the impotent compassion too painful.

It felt a little bit like this walking onto some of the wards at
the Towers, with a chorus of 'Gimme a smoke!' emanating from
half a dozen or so voices, their sense of desperation condensed
down to the task of procuring a free fag. Not aggressive exactly but
certainly persistent: bodies sidling up to me, grabbing my hand,
pawing at my hair, dropping ash on my clothes.

Nowadays, I have a whole repertoire of psychological models
to help me make sense of how some of these patients made me
feel: an understanding of 'projective identification', for example,
whereby we unconsciously attempt to rid ourselves of overwhelming primitive feelings by projecting them into another person, to
such an extent that the other person feels them as their own. I
can look back and see that the patients' emotional experience of
having their personal space violated was being put into me, projected, communicated in a very direct skin-to-skin way. Or, less
fancy, simply that living in such an institution for so many years
had made it difficult for them to respect the personal space of
another person.

But, at the time, it was just how it was. Something to be
reacted to rather than thought about. No one seemed to want
to help or offer me advice on how to manage myself. The only
response from the nurses was to rather half-heartedly 'tell them
off': 'Gertie, leave the nice young doctor alone, you naughty girl!'
in a tone that made it clear they didn't expect anything to change.

I should say at this point that I was pregnant at the time, feeling nauseous and more protective of myself than I might normally

be. But nevertheless, it was the way I hid my vulnerability during these six months that stands out all these years on. Like most of my young psychiatry colleagues, I was desperate not to reveal my naivety, not to show how lost I was really feeling, certainly not to ask for help. My aim was to appear cool and streetwise. For some reason I tried to act as if I'd seen it all before, which, of course, I hadn't – how could I have?

Being institutionalised is not something many of us choose, although it sits more comfortably with some than others – perhaps when the need to belong is overwhelming. It's certainly not a process that many of us enter into with our eyes open. My point is that this was my version of being institutionalised, one that I couldn't see at the time, but one I think was common among junior psychiatrists, certainly of my generation. It was our way of responding to an institution that was deeply entrenched in its ways, where we were clearly outsiders to be moulded and manipulated; an institution surrounded in mystique, where we stumbled upon unwritten rules wherever we went but where expectations of our own roles were anything but clear. Oh, we could be so wise about the 'institutionalised' nurses, laughing at the way some of them infantilised their patients (encouraging them to play with their dolls) or ran the ward like a military operation (dressing the patients in identical cardigans). And we were scandalised by the behaviour of some of the older consultants: Dr X, for example, who took his bulldog with him to ward rounds, threw women staff wearing trousers off his ward, diagnosed anyone who cried with 'malignant discontent' – a trigger for ECT – and put all his new patients on his famously punishing 'milk-only diet and pyjamas regime'.

But when it came to ourselves, we just couldn't see it. Why did we never talk honestly about how shocked we were? Why was it so difficult to show how passionate, enraged, disillusioned, touched with pity we were? Why was it so difficult to ask basic questions? Why this need to look unfazed at the very beginning of our career? It seems we could talk about everything except our own vulnerability.

The redeeming feature of this time for me was the camaraderie among the staff. This was before the days of community care so mental health services were mostly hospital-based rather than devolved across the county. Inadequate in many ways, this did at least mean that there was a stable group of staff in one building. For all its faults, I had joined a community of sorts. So far, I have focused more on the dark side: the erosion of individuality, the pressures to collude, potentially toxic projections on the 'outsider' and the sanctioning of nihilism and brutality. But there was another side: a sense of being part of an institution where everyone had a role to play, where most people recognised you, knew who you were and had time to exchange a pleasant word or two; the sense of a joint mission, with shared stories, insider knowledge and easy gossipy conversation. The warmth and welcome and interest of people who became good friends.

One of the things that charmed me when I first arrived was the tradition of psychiatrists sharing a sandwich lunch together in the library: time to catch up, discuss a film, read the paper and put the world to rights. It was also an opportunity to chat informally about difficult patients, the dreaded membership exam, and – depending on who was around – the more philosophical and political aspects of the work. This sense of a slower pace, having time to reflect, time to look out for each other, time to think how the work fitted with wider issues, was what had attracted me to psychiatry as a medical student.

Am I contradicting myself? Of course I am. But I think anyone who has been part of a community, whether a workplace, a close-knit village, a church, club or political party, will recognise that there are two sides of the coin: the pressure to fit in versus the comfort of belonging. In a 'total institution' such as the Towers, these aspects of community are more extreme, dangerously so, but that doesn't mean the positive aspects – just glimpses for me as a junior doctor, moving on to a new post every few months – should be denied.

~

When I started at the Towers in the eighties, each scandalous exposure of abuse within an asylum was treated as if it was an isolated phenomenon, shocking to the public, but seen as the fault of a particularly corrupt group of staff and confined to the particular institution. But as scandal followed scandal – not just in the UK, but across Europe and the USA – evidence was growing that maltreatment was widespread. Clinical and political opinion was changing and the model of housing large numbers of mentally disordered people (in the USA some of the state mental hospitals had 10,000 beds and were surrounded by electric fences) in an enclosed environment, set apart from the rest of society, was being questioned and upturned. In the UK, asylums were being phased out across the country. Hospital beds for the mentally ill were to be attached to general hospitals to avoid stigma, and care in the community was to become the norm.

Five years or so later, when the Towers was finally closing for good, patients who'd been incarcerated for decades were gradually moved into various levels of supported housing in the community and some of their personal stories re-emerged – Hester May, for example, was still going strong, despite her heart failure. A few of my contemporaries became 'rehabilitation' specialists, applying their compassion and intelligence to view these long-stay patients as unique and interesting individuals with the potential to live fuller lives. It was heart-warming to hear their accounts of the work become increasingly animated as they witnessed some of these seemingly intractable institutionalised patients build up networks in the community and recover some sense of autonomy. The elderly wards were moved to a new thoughtfully designed unit attached to a general hospital, where most patients had their own rooms, the environment smelt fresh and clean, and specialist staff did everything they could to mitigate the fear of dementia and make them comfortable.

As the doors of the Towers closed for the last time, we were full of optimism, confident that we could do things better than a previous generation, hopeful that the worst in psychiatric practice would be left behind. Looking back today, this hope feels rather naive. Did we really think that so much that was bad could simply be left behind in those buildings? That the stigma, cruelty and neglect that have always infected society's dealings with the mentally ill would disappear thanks to our proximity to the General Hospital? But the idea of helping people to live 'ordinary', more meaningful lives alongside the rest of us in the community was inspiring. And I was as hopeful as anyone. Idealised it might have been, but I have to say that, for me, at the time, leaving the Towers felt like a liberation – for me and for the patients.

2

THE CABINET
OF CURIOSITIES

Being a psychiatrist is a complicated business. I think back to medical school and the way we stereotyped the various professors and others who tried to teach us. Psychiatrists were seen as crazy, eccentric, absent-minded, all-seeing and all-knowing; as weaklings who couldn't cope with the blood and gore; or failures who'd really wanted to be surgeons. So many psychiatrists have a story to tell of disappointed parents ('Why psychiatry, not a proper doctor?') or patronising surgeons and physicians ('What a waste when you've got the brains to be a . . .').

At the same time, psychiatrists are seen as powerful and manipulative. Colloquialisms such as 'shrink' and 'trick-cyclist' suggest a fear that we are able to read and interfere with minds. There is no doubt that psychiatrists are powerful. The Mental Health Act allows us to detain people against their wishes and to make judgements that affect their human rights, depriving them of liberty, placing them in seclusion, and intervening with potent treatments that can alter their mood, affect their memory, change their very sense of being and distort their experience of the world.

Yet psychiatrists can feel very impotent. Despite all the advances in neuroscience over the last thirty years, we still have to rely on informed guesswork much of the time. There is no equivalent to measuring blood sugar, reading a chest X-ray, looking at a biopsy under the microscope or identifying the bacteria doing the damage. The struggle to temper our sense of power or impotence, the temptation to give in to grandiosity or helplessness, is always there. No surprise that views are strongly held and arguments intense. No surprise that our insecurity as scientists leads us to inflate our sense of certainty. And no surprise that our quest for scientific truth can override our commitment as doctors to 'do no harm', humiliating and demeaning our patients in the process.

These dangers had been only too obvious on those back wards of the Towers in the early 1980s. In fact, they were increasingly writ large for all to see as undercover journalists graphically exposed the callous behaviour of some doctors and nurses behind the walls of one huge psychiatric institution after another across most of the rich world. But I was disappointed to find that among the new therapeutic activity groups and the refreshingly more open culture, some of the rituals I had most disliked at the Towers had been unthinkingly transposed to the new unit in the General Hospital.

As I found myself standing by yet again while a group of nurses pinned a patient to the floor and injected a drug he didn't want in order to control his behaviour, I began to wonder how much this violent practice reflected our inability to relate to the disturbed patient rather than anything resembling 'clinical need'. The potential for brutality is always there when we work with the mentally ill and it's not just a simple matter of closing down the asylums. I was starting to understand that there is a fine line between good and bad practice, where mental disturbance is concerned; and that mentally ill patients are vulnerable to exploitation, whatever the setting. It's not inevitable that we give in to these feelings, but it is important to realise that they are inherent to the issue of how mental illness sits within society. This is a troublesome dynamic that each generation – including our own – has to find a way to manage.

~

There are many ways to demean a patient. The fear of madness is such that we will go to great lengths as individuals and as a society to see the mentally ill as 'other', as essentially different from ourselves. We have a deep-seated need to separate ourselves from madness, to look at it over there rather than close to, from the outside rather than the inside. Placed at a distance, we can then observe it: an object of fear, horror, curiosity, revulsion, even comedy. We have a long history of exploiting the mentally ill as exhibits when they are at their most vulnerable, of treating the 'insane' as curiosities. Excited by their exotic symptoms and 'otherness', we've rationalised the need to expose them as exhibits for scientific scrutiny and, even more cravenly, set them up as comic entertainment.

In the seventeenth and eighteenth centuries, for example, the public paid money to be allowed to gawp at the 'lunatics' in the Bethlem hospital in London – a weekend amusement not unlike going to the circus, attracting crowds similar to those who would gather to watch a public hanging. Visitors would chatter and point excitedly as they passed people strapped to their beds or chained to the wall naked, shivering in the freezing temperatures believed to have a calming effect. Lunatics in those days were generally seen as subhuman; most of the medical authorities at the time argued that they did not feel physical discomfort and therefore did not suffer. At a time when beliefs such as demonic possession and bestial states were common, mad people were simply not seen as human by the majority of society.

Artists in residence at the Bethlem drew pictures of the inmates, both out of scientific interest and for commercial gain. Interestingly for us, three hundred years later, many of these pictures survive and show some of them adopting odd postures, consistent with a condition known as catatonia. Catatonia is a mental disorder with very obvious physical manifestations that can trigger disturbing dissonant feelings in those around them. Patients often present in a stupor, mute and unable to move. A particularly bizarre manifestation is a symptom known as 'waxy flexibility' where the patient stays in the bodily position you put them in, however strange the posture. For example, if you lift their arm, place their hand on their head and then let go, the arm will stay in that position. Catatonia is now understood as a symptom of an underlying psychiatric syndrome such as schizophrenia rather than an entity in its own right, and with earlier diagnosis and treatment, the condition is now rarely seen. But once upon a time our asylums were full of patients with this condition and there were still a handful around in the Towers in the early 1980s.

I remember well the spell of excited fascination that their condition seemed to cast on us all.

Whether or not those eighteenth-century paying visitors to the Bethlem were allowed to manipulate the catatonic patients into different positions, I don't know. I can tell you that it's an eerie sensation being able to move someone's body around with no resistance at all. The complete lack of tangible agency in the other gave me an uncomfortable but seductive sense of limitless power – a whiff of prurience even. There was also a regressive quality to the interaction, not unlike playing with a doll. And then there's the messianic potential, the possibility of being able to breathe life into someone, to raise someone from the dead. No wonder that some staff were protective and possessive while others gave free reign to their supposed 'scientific' curiosity.

Mental health workers are not immune to the need to observe and poke at madness from a safe distance. Consider, for example, the classic case conference or the weekly ward round, both ostensibly worthy projects to understand and work out how best to treat a mentally disordered individual. The reality, however, was deeply traumatising for many patients.

The case conference has roots going back at least two hundred years into medical history and was the weekly ritual that I used to dread most as a junior psychiatrist. It took place every Friday, between 12 noon and 2 p.m., alternating between the imposing, wood-panelled conference rooms at the Towers and Carlton Hayes. A patient of particular interest would be brought in front of the whole medical establishment, for teaching, debate and the supposed betterment of us all. Everyone was expected to attend, right through from medical students to Sidney Brandon, the professor, usually about sixty people. We juniors took it in turns to 'present' the patient, with a detailed history of their psychiatric problems, their childhood and their personal life. Then the patient herself (it was usually a woman, and no one ever questioned why that was) would be brought in by one of the ward nurses. It wasn't uncommon for them to be in night clothes in a wheelchair and, to my mind, either terrified or completely deranged. The assembled throng would then start directing their questions at the patient, interested not just in their story, but in what is known as their 'mental state' – the way they spoke, their body language, any evidence that they were hallucinating, signs of disordered thinking or disturbed mood.

The 'best' patients for case conferences (the best exhibits, you might say) were considered to be the floridly mad, with 'impressive' signs and symptoms – the poor young woman I mentioned with her 'waxy flexibility', for example – or 'cases' that were an interesting problem to diagnose or treat. I remember attending a case conference as a medical student where the clearly manic patient thought he could fly – indeed he'd already been rescued from a number of dangerous improvised launch pads. True to form, he threw himself onto the audience and we found ourselves gingerly passing him carefully over our heads, just as if he was crowd-surfing at a rock concert – long before crowd-surfing was a thing. He also exhibited a symptom called 'clanging'. This is a type of thought disorder, an extreme 'flight of ideas' that produces very rapid pressured speech, impossible to follow because it constantly takes nonsensical tangents, the only thread being the rhyming words.

Humour can be problematic in psychiatry. There is a fine line between 'laughing with' and 'laughing at', a fine line between kindness and cruelty. There is no doubt mad people do daft things. You can find yourself in the most unimaginably bizarre situations where it's impossible not to laugh, even if you might want to cry at the same time. I can remember the first time I laughed out loud at a manic patient. It was as if his elated mood, totally ungrounded in reality, had reached straight into my gut and produced a great belly laugh. He appeared utterly ridiculous, singing and dancing round the room, making no sense at all, and it was impossible not to laugh – even if the professional in me felt guilty.

Any temptation to laugh at the case conference, however, was stifled by pressure. The setting was extraordinarily tense and serious. We were desperately anxious about eliciting the right signs, documenting the telltale mannerisms, counting the 'first-rank symptoms' that had to be present for a diagnosis of schizophrenia, and trying to pre-empt the questions that would be fired at us later in the proceedings. For, once we'd had our fill of the patient and exhausted our scientific curiosity, she would leave the room and the spotlight would be turned on us, starting with easy questions for the medical students, then more difficult ones as we progressed through the ranks of the doctors present. We believed our future careers depended on how we performed in this bizarre theatrical setting. What we appeared less concerned about was the patient herself: what she was thinking and feeling, the trauma we were putting her through, our duty of care towards her.

At least Professor Brandon, who usually chaired the proceedings, always addressed the patient with kindness and respect. These were the days before management reforms had changed the face of the NHS, and the professor of a department (for there was only one such role) was all-powerful. Sidney Brandon looked a bit like a jolly little gnome: short, round, white-haired and energetic. He always wore a colourful bow tie and conveyed a sense of sharp intelligence, energetic determination, and a wry sense of humour. He'd been appointed early on in the inception of Leicester Medical School and had played a big part in the design of the curriculum, generally agreed to be very progressive for its day. He was quite something, and although, like all powerful leaders, he was often the butt of much exaggerated gossip and criticism, we were mostly proud and somewhat in awe of him.

I imagine that for Professor Brandon the case conferences had played an important part in developing Leicester psychiatric services into a unit fit to be part of a teaching hospital. There was certainly a sense of the 'establishment' being dragged into the modern world, and for Sidney's generation this meant putting psychiatry onto a firm scientific footing. He would have seen the case conference as a forum to question practice, to introduce the idea of an 'evidence base', although such a term was not yet common parlance. The powers that be had decided to site a new medical school in Leicester as health spending in the East Midlands had been way below other parts of the country. Because the school brought in a new source of money, Professor Brandon had been able to appoint a number of young consultants, go-ahead and enthusiastic in their outlook, but all approaching psychiatry from different angles and often disagreeing intensely with each other.

So this was the backdrop to our case conferences: a new academic department determined to ensure intellectual rigour and prove the training in Leicester to be as good as anywhere in the country; eager young alpha-male consultants and their protégés wanting to impress and outdo each other; cynical old codgers snorting with derision in the background; some rather bewildered medical students; and a very anxious group of trainees waiting to have their ignorance laid bare, or just used as sport by the various factions in the room. I tried to hide at the back, avoiding eye contact, but almost every week I would be asked to describe the 'patient's gait', or their 'mental state', or list the 'differential diagnosis', or, worst of all, come up with a 'formulation'.

It wasn't the actual questions that threw me, but the Jeremy Paxman style of firing them at you, and the ease with which the room could be manipulated to ridicule. The whole thing seemed utterly alien: first, exhibiting a vulnerable patient as a spectacle, which often made me want to cry; then the aggressive, male combat ritual, trying to prove oneself right and win by showing off – often humiliating another in the process. So often we became entrenched in polarised arguments over the specifics of a diagnosis, hung up on categorical distinctions: was the patient's psychosis due to schizophrenia or manic depression? Were they mentally ill or personality disordered? It was classic, old-fashioned medical-model thinking: treatment options depended on getting the correct diagnosis and good clinical outcomes would follow if the treatment was right. Unfortunately, the complexity of mental disorder cannot be so easily reduced. Some of the distinctions that were debated most furiously – 'endogenous' versus 'reactive' depression, for example – have long since been consigned to history. Perhaps my diffidence undermined my competitive edge. Perhaps I just found the whole thing a bit of a game, and one that I couldn't get excited about, another male arena that didn't resonate with reality as I saw it, and a process that jarred uncomfortably with my own sensibilities. Even in those early days, I was coming to the view that open reflective discussion was much better suited to solving psychiatric problems than dialectic debate.

~

The weekly ward round was another potentially humiliating ritual where patients were required to expose themselves in 'all their illness'. These events dominated my life as a junior psychiatrist, an unquestioned part of the routine on an inpatient unit. The ward round could be attended by up to twenty staff members: the consultant, a senior registrar, one or two junior doctors, the ward manager and a deputy ward manager, at least three other nurses, a psychologist, a social worker, an occupational therapist, possibly an art therapist, and any student that happened to be on placement – usually at least two medical students and two student nurses. It was my job to go methodically through the huge pile of notes stacked up in front of me to give an update on each patient. This was followed by the nurses offering often a very different perspective, then an open discussion with anyone else involved, or wanting to be involved.

The consultant would then decide whether or not he wished to see the patient, who was often hovering anxiously outside, dreading the ordeal ahead if he was called in, but also anxious about being sidelined in his own care if he was not called. Most of the patients were well aware that this was the forum where they would have to answer questions in front of the consultant and the whole team; and where, as a result of this 'performance', important decisions would be made about their treatment, including medication changes and discharge plans.

Most commonly, the decision was made to see him, and the patient was summoned and directed to the vacant chair to be interviewed by the consultant. The rest of us sat back, watching the drama from our circle of comfortable armchairs, the patient often showing visible signs of stage fright, sometimes freaking out completely and running off. Not surprisingly, many of the patients hated this ritual and were consumed by anxiety in the days leading up to it, begging me to intervene in some way on their behalf. Other patients were too deranged by their illness to care, but I couldn't help thinking it was exploitative to expose them in this way. It was certainly not something the patient was asked about or a matter of 'consent'.

I soon gathered that there was a good deal of intelligence around in the patient peer group about the questions that might be asked and the best answers to give; just because you're on an inpatient ward doesn't mean you're stupid. There were even occasions when my advocacy role with the patients outstripped any loyalty to the consultant, and I would coach the patient on what to say, for example, if she wanted her medication reduced. The idea that we were observing the 'authentic' patient, or exposing some sort of 'scientific truth' that we could use to make important decisions, seemed outlandish to me. It wasn't uncommon for consultants to use the ward round to lecture the patients about their 'bad' behaviour – as if this was simply under their control and a public 'telling-off' would make any difference. We doctors might be enacting a ceremony that made it clear who held the power on the wards, but patients had their ways of gaming the system.

I've never really understood why this feature of general medical life was transposed in such an unquestioned way into psychiatry. Apparently, it is still enacted in many places today, although staffing on wards is so reduced that such rounds don't have anything like the sense of theatre that they did in those days. Maybe it's something about our need, as doctors, to hang on to our medical identity among all this disorder. Or perhaps the controversial psychiatrist R. D. Laing was right and it's all about control. I know now that there are better settings to assess patients, better ways to teach junior staff, better forums to establish a team identity. At the time, I just knew it felt all wrong.

Our capacity to see mad people as so essentially different from ourselves that we used to pay to see them as entertainment seems shocking in our modern era. But are we really any better? This question has niggled away at me. It is easy to cast a critical eye back over history; much harder to face up to it in the present.

I can still remember the creepy, seductive fascination that I felt with that catatonic woman, the sense of her utter helplessness in my all-powerful hands. It seems to me that such extreme dependency, helplessness and need will always be in danger of attracting a sadistic reaction. There is no reason to think that we experience such basic responses any less or any more than previous generations.

After all, while the Bethlem closed to tourists in 1770, and most of us these days would like to think we don't see an unbridgeable gap between ourselves and someone with a mental illness, there are still forums for us to observe and ridicule those in need. Modern media, from reality TV to social media platforms, can often entrap the vulnerable in an abusive world, their flaws exposed and derided as they face booing crowds or a barrage of cruel online comments and trolling. It disturbs me that our instinct

to be entertained as a crowd by the exposure of mental disturbance and psychological vulnerability is as alive as ever.

At a personal level, I'm anxious that I'm writing here about
patients, that I'm exploiting them by exhibiting their stories in this
book. Of course I've consulted with them, wherever possible, and
taken great care to disguise identities, but I still worry that I'm
using them in some way, expropriating their stories. I've thought
about it at length and discussed it with people I trust – fellow clinicians, patients and friends. I very much want to share what I've
learned in my work, because I think there are lessons there that, if
we allow ourselves to think about them, can guide us into better
practice, better services and better attitudes towards people with
mental health needs. But writing about patients still makes me feel
a bit queasy if I'm honest. Will a future generation judge me for
writing this book in the same way that I judged those responsible
for exhibiting vulnerable patients in case conferences?

Scientific progress depends on a capacity to stand back,
observe and share our findings, but we should never let this diminish a patient's humanity. We need to learn better to be alongside
the mentally disturbed, and to value this as much as we value
scientific objectivity.

All those years ago, I hoped so much that the change of geographical location as we moved from the Towers would shift
attitudes and make it harder to disregard the patients' need to be
treated with dignity, respect and common human kindness. As we
settled into the new building attached to the General Hospital, I
could see clearly that many things were going to be different: more
openness demanded from the staff, less stigma for the patients.
Above everything, I longed for an environment in which it would

be easier to forge authentic, therapeutic relationships with the patients. I imagined myself listening respectfully and attentively to their stories – but I had no real idea how deeply disturbing those stories would be.

3

TERRIBLE SECRETS

When I first met Sally, I was particularly struck by her clothes: smart blouse and jacket, nice earrings, immaculate make-up and pristine hairstyle, but oversized tracksuit bottoms, scruffy trainers and a very incongruous 'My Little Pony' handbag. The disconnection was disconcerting. Who were we talking to? Sally was a hospital secretary, apparently good at her job, but she had been off sick since a recent overdose, after which the psychiatrist who had assessed her had uncovered an underlying eating disorder and referred her to the team I was now working for.

When I meet people for the first time, I like to explore the good things in their lives – their strengths and talents, whether they have any good friendships or people they trust, their achievements or things they're proud of – rather than just homing in on the things that have gone badly wrong. Sally had no problem talking about her achievements at school and in her career, but otherwise she seemed evasive and it was hard to make sense of her suicide attempt.

Eventually, I made a gentle comment about her appearance.

'I'm struck by your clothes, Sally. It's like they don't quite fit together. I'm wondering about that – wondering if something went badly wrong, something that doesn't fit well with the rest of you?'

The competent, self-confident secretary disappeared in an instant and was replaced by a frightened, curled-up ball of misery, almost mute. Eventually, she managed to convey that bad things had happened when she was a child but she couldn't say any more. It took many months for her to tell her story and even then she was terrified to name the men who had abused her, fearful of repercussions, fearful of not being believed.

I've encountered so many patients like Sally over the course of my career, the fears always the same: the impact of the truth, terrifying; the exposure of such darkly held secrets, a threat to their families, their communities and sometimes their very existence. I first saw Sally early in my career when such revelations were rarer – not because sexual abuse didn't exist, but because society, including most psychiatrists, didn't recognise it.

~

Back when I was a junior psychiatrist, I was lucky to work for a team which was ahead of the game in realising how frequently sexual abuse coloured their patients' life stories. Dr Palmer – Bob, as he liked to be called – was one of the bright young consultants Professor Brandon had successfully attracted to Leicester, a quietly spoken academic with shoulder-length brown hair and kind, inquisitive eyes. He worked closely with a senior social worker called Rhoda Oppenheimer who embodied experience and wisdom; a sense that she'd seen it all and couldn't be shocked.

The members of the team were experts in eating disorders, at a time when anorexia nervosa attracted little specialist interest in most parts of the country and was usually just lumped in with the job of general psychiatry. Bob had just written a paper entitled 'The Dietary Chaos Syndrome: a useful new term?', one of the first publications to describe the cycle of dieting, binge eating and self-induced vomiting that later became officially classified as bulimia nervosa.[1] The idea that people of normal weight could suffer from an eating disorder was new at this time. Most professionals were simply not tuning in and asking the relevant questions – either about bulimic symptoms or about sexual abuse.

The founder of psychoanalysis, Sigmund Freud, had uncovered child sexual abuse in the material from his early female patients. Notoriously, he moved from hearing them as accounts of real-life events to a belief that they were fantasies created by the woman to explain strong feelings of love and hate towards her father. Decades later, the majority of the psychiatric and psychoanalytic professions were still stuck in this position. Childhood sexual behaviour was not an area of inquiry and those patients brave enough to tell their stories often found them dismissed as fantasy or a sign of hysteria.

Accounts of the history of psychiatry often labour the physical interventions that seem so abusive to our twenty-first-century sensibilities – dunking people in ice-cold baths, insulin coma therapy and the use of straitjackets, for example. But it's equally important to ponder the omissions: the paucity of empathy, the failure of imagination, the lack of interest and respect for the patient's story, the complacent arrogance that leads us to dismiss and pathologise a story that doesn't fit comfortably with our world view.

Bob and Rhoda were pioneers. They exuded energetic curiosity and compassion, took their patients' stories seriously and encouraged juniors like me to do the same. What we were hearing appalled and upset us, but there was also the sense of excitement that accompanies a new discovery – albeit a discomforting one. Linking these stories together, a hypothesis began to emerge that an eating disorder was an expression of an unconscious wish to reclaim one's early childhood, sometimes as a result of sexual abuse – the wish to regress to a prepubertal state. It was easy to get carried away, but Bob was an academic through and through, and grounded us with his insistence on proper research. We soon realised that a history of sexual abuse was not confined to patients with a diagnosis of an eating disorder and, of course, that many people suffer from eating disorders who have never been abused.

My friend Debbie took up a year's research post with Bob to see how common such abuse was in female psychiatric patients. She was shocked to discover that the prevalence was high across all diagnostic groups. Fifty per cent of the patients she interviewed had suffered some sort of sexually abusive experience, and patients with eating disorders reported no more sexual abuse than people with other diagnoses. So much for our hypothesis. Debbie did find that the more severely disturbed the patient, the more common were accounts of child sexual abuse, and the more severe the sexual abuse described. Later, the same research questionnaire was used with patients in general practice, and after that with a randomised group of students from the university. The results continued to shock us. It felt as if we were discovering histories of child sexual abuse wherever we looked. It was a world a big part of me just didn't want to know about; a world of wickedness and savagery and perverse, pitiful weakness. It's hard to communicate the awful unease we felt but we also knew there was no retreat: the only way was forward.

Debbie found her research position took a toll on her. She had to gain permission from each of the consultants to administer her questionnaires to their patients, and where sexual abuse was reported, follow this up with a more in-depth interview. Many senior colleagues told her frankly that the research was a waste of time at best. Why risk upsetting people by asking such questions? Why put the ideas in their heads? Worse, some of their suspicion extended to Debbie herself. What was she up to, getting involved in such a project? Other consultants who were open to the idea that their patients might be holding such secrets increasingly simply referred them on to Debbie, washing their hands of them in the process. They became 'Debbie's problem'. She felt isolated and swamped. It was as if she herself was beginning to take on the burden of carrying such secrets. Like her patients, she was discovering that exposing these uncomfortable truths could split the family – including the professional family. And, like the patients, she was discovering how easy it is to be scapegoated. I was aware that it was undermining her confidence and making her miserable, but I didn't really understand the toxic dynamics or grasp how bad this was for her until years later.

At the time, this field of work was so new that there was little knowledge of the impact on the staff involved. Over the next decades, as my experience grew, I contributed to a growing list of publications on this topic[2] and highlighted the importance of supportive supervision. But for Debbie, working largely on her own, the experience was overwhelming and cast a dark shadow over her for some time.

Many years later, when she was an established consultant specialising in the care of the elderly, Debbie rang me, upset and angry. She had recognised the name of a new patient with early dementia in her outpatient clinic. He was a man who had regularly violently raped his young daughter, Breda, made her pregnant at thirteen, and condemned her to years of psychological torment, including severe anorexia and self-harm. Both Debbie and I had been involved with Breda's care. She was the sort of patient with whom it was almost impossible not to feel intensely emotionally entangled. We were frequently pulled into crisis situations and rescue attempts. After many years on the psychiatric intensive care unit, Breda had eventually succeeded in killing herself.

Debbie had already done the right thing professionally in asking a colleague to take on this now rather pitiful old man with dementia, Breda's father. But just seeing his name on the letter had put her back in touch with the awful feelings of outrage and impotence that had so coloured our relationship with Breda.

As much as we'd tried, it was difficult to give women like Breda anything like the help that they needed. I remember a well-presented young woman called Cheryl who used to clean out her vagina with Dettol and a toothbrush. By the age of twenty-five, she'd managed to persuade overenthusiastic surgeons to remove her ovaries, fallopian tubes, uterus and half her bowel and a previous psychiatrist to give her ECT. By the time I saw her, she had three volumes of medical notes. Not one

44

person had thought to inquire about sexual abuse, despite the pattern of sadomasochistic relationships that she was so clearly driven to recreate with those trying to help her. Even when we did know, it was one thing to recognise her compulsion to repeat the abusive relationship, but quite another to help her break such destructive dynamics.

In my six months working with Bob Palmer, I saw two women who each eventually told me that their teenage pregnancy had been the result of incest. One of them was trying to look after her son but constantly punishing him inappropriately when she saw flashes of her father in him. We spent a lot of time together in the team agonising our way to difficult decisions and clumsily trying to help highly stressed family members speak to each other. Driven by a powerful urge to rescue these poor women, we were aware that we were making it up as we went along and going through a painful process of learning from our mistakes. This was before the days of formal child protection procedures. If we even considered involving the police, we quickly discovered that they weren't interested, which left us feeling deeply frustrated and a bit impotent. We could see clearly that our little service alone was nowhere near able to help these women enough, let alone bring their abusers to justice, or protect vulnerable children still in danger.

Shaped by much passion, those two or three years seem a lot longer in my memory. Perhaps the early years in a challenging profession always do. But it was a particularly intense time, with these previously unimaginable, agonising dramas unfolding in our clinics, compounded by difficult, frequently lost arguments with consultants (usually male) determinedly blind to the fact that sexual abuse often underpinned their patients' problems. I was full of righteous indignation and swung to and fro between feeling silenced and doing battle, never feeling comfortable in either position.

Of course, there were others across the country who were beginning to face up to the reality of child sexual abuse and, like us, taking tentative steps to try to help. But there was no email, let alone Twitter, in those days, so finding out who they were and making links took a lot of time and energy. Then, in 1986, Esther Rantzen, presenter of popular consumer TV show *That's Life!*, presented a programme on child abuse and later launched a helpline for children in danger or distress: Childline. Controversial at the time, it felt like a huge step forward for those of us in the field. It put the work with survivors of abuse on the map, bringing us in from the margins and somehow making it more respectable to ask the pertinent questions.

Meanwhile, finding like-minded folk struggling with the same clinical issues was deeply supportive. From our different positions, we were realising that most of these patients needed us to adapt our therapy techniques. Cognitive behavioural therapists were starting to recognise that a directive approach could be experienced by the patient as intrusive and potentially abusive, while psychodynamic therapists were noting that patients needed a more structured approach. I realised pretty quickly, for example, that periods of silence were extremely threatening, sometimes triggering flashbacks of the abuse, and that I was being experienced as absent and oblivious to their hurt. These attempts to adapt our techniques as we learned from the patients paved the way for more formalised hybrid models that would become the mainstay of treatment in the future. If I had to pick one lesson that stayed with me from all these developments, it is the importance of making therapy feel *safe* for the patient.

~

Much of my work over the subsequent thirty years has been with women and men who have been severely abused as children. Many of them attracted a label of emotionally unstable personality disorder and were referred to the unit where I would become the lead consultant a few years later. I always disliked the label and preferred the more empathic concept of complex post-traumatic stress disorder.* I have to say, I have a lot of sympathy with survivor groups who protest at any type of label that includes the word 'disorder', wanting instead to affirm the strengths that the word survivor implies. But, label or not, for those of us wanting to help, it is important to be clear just how fundamentally a history of sexual abuse can affect people.

Severe trauma at a tender age disrupts and distorts relationships at a time when a child is still very dependent on others, which is why psychotherapists often think of them as struggling with what are called attachment issues. For very understandable reasons, such patients struggle with a profound mistrust of other people that, in many cases, affects every aspect of their lives. Very often such abused patients have turned to other ways of coping with overwhelming feelings such as rage and self-hatred – for example, self-medicating with drugs or cutting themselves

---

* As from 2022, complex post-traumatic stress disorder is formally recognised in ICD11, the most recent classification system of the World Health Organization.

– which in turn become problems: habitual, high-risk and hard to break. All of this can make a therapeutic relationship difficult to sustain. The work can be difficult and is not suitable for an inexperienced therapist unless they are well supervised.

Having worked in Bob Palmer's team early in my career, I had thought that nothing more could shock me. But my appointment as a consultant psychiatrist in Leicester in 1992 coincided with the trial and conviction of Frank Beck, who was sentenced to five life terms for sexual and physical assaults against more than a hundred children in Leicestershire children's homes and a further twenty-four years on seventeen charges of sexual assault, including rape. I was to meet many of his victims over the next few years as they struggled to get their lives back on track, some of them helped by the therapeutic community where I was based.

Frank Beck's trial was a landmark in many ways. There had been previous convictions for pervasive sexual abuse of children in Cleveland in 1987 and Orkney earlier in 1991, but both of these were controversial. The evidence presented in the Leicester trial was extensive and incontrovertible. Beck literally goaded the children in his care to lose control, provoking temper tantrums and thereby, in his sick mind, creating opportunities to exercise violent physical restraint. Children were restrained using a towel around their neck, choking them to the edge of unconsciousness as they were beaten, buggered and raped. Prior to the trial, few police officers and indeed members of the public had believed that such widespread and systematic abuse was possible. Details were extensively reported and promoted a breakthrough in public consciousness, with Beck receiving one of the most severe sentences in British legal history.

Sadly, Frank Beck's regime was not a shocking one-off case. Over my career, patients' life stories continued to impress on me the human capacity for depravity. I heard about a convent where children were called by number rather than name, locked in cupboards and forced to eat their own vomit. I heard about a ring of paedophiles, part of a large extended family where abuse went back for generations and terrorised a whole housing estate. I heard about a boarding house full of prostitutes and their children dominated by a tyrannical sadistic pimp who first forced the children to watch their mothers at work and then forced them into prostitution themselves. I heard about a cult where young children were involved in macabre rituals including animal sacrifice. About a church where 'naughty' children were seen as possessed by the devil, who had to be beaten and starved out of them. About ritual gang rape in a boarding school. And a residential child and adolescent mental health system (CAMHS) unit where the children were sexually abused.

Although I became something of a specialist, it is important to recognise that the link between childhood sexual abuse and psychiatric illness is not confined to one particular diagnosis or collection of symptoms. Abused patients will turn up in every psychiatrist's caseload, whatever their specialty. We know that the psycho-physiological effects of severe trauma impact on the brain while it is still developing and can become deeply ingrained and difficult to reverse. What's more, someone who was abused as a very young child may have disturbing sensory memories but lack the language to understand or express what happened to them. One or two of my patients over the years have said they don't remember the first time they were sexually abused; they were so young, it was just always part of their lives. There is now plenty of evidence in the public domain of babies as young as three months being sexually abused, the crimes acknowledged by the perpetrators in court or captured on videos. One can only imagine how this might affect an infant's developing brain and experience of the world.

~

So sexual abuse of children can lead to many different outcomes. And the concept encompasses a wide spectrum of predatory behaviours from inappropriate touching to the type of hideous institutionalised crimes experienced by the victims of the likes of Frank Beck. Abusers can be of any gender and can be anyone: older children, strangers, respected members of the community, family members or organised criminals. The age of abuse victims can be anything from babyhood up to the age of consent – sixteen in the UK – though, of course, sexual abuse happens to vulnerable adults too. Some will be relatively free of mental health symptoms, perhaps suffering from manageable anxiety and depression. Others – who knows? – may have locked the abuse away in an inaccessible part of themselves and present with a psychotic illness or apparent autism. A small number become abusers themselves and we meet them as both perpetrators and victims.

It's well to remember that a great many people across all walks of society have suffered child sexual abuse. Years ago, I was lecturing a cohort of medical students on the topic and one of them ran out of the room in great distress, later returning and confiding to me that she had been abused. After that, I made sure while introducing myself to acknowledge that the topic might affect some of them personally and to give contact details for anyone needing support afterwards. But why had I been taken by surprise? Immersed in the subject as I was, I still couldn't quite relate the high prevalence in the population to medical students – 'ordinary professionals' like me.

Clearly people who have experienced abuse present themselves in a variety of ways and contexts, and there is no way of working that is right for everyone. For some it's enough to acknowledge that abuse took place, to break the awful secrecy, to be reassured that they are not alone and that they were not to blame for what happened, but they have no desire or need to go into detail. Others may need many years in intensive therapy, some of it spent facing and reliving the traumatic events.

For many patients it is the sense of grief that is so difficult to put behind them: the awareness that their childhood was sabotaged and can never be recovered, the loss of innocence, the constant sense of fear that made concentration at school so impossible, the terrible secrets that separated them from their peer group and made normal childhood play meaningless. Child abuse, always manipulative, always an exploitation of power, is also a terrible robbery and corruption of innocence.

Not surprisingly, some of these patients have to grapple with the unleashing of hateful feelings, particularly the envy they may feel towards those – including therapists – who, they believe, haven't experienced such traumas. I try to convey a sense that I'm tough enough to hear and cope with the most disturbing facts and feelings but also a sense of kindness and sensitivity. Hopefulness is important but not if it comes across as glib positive thinking; if our patients are terrified and despairing, they need us to be sufficiently there with them. It often feels as if I'm getting it wrong, but I've learned that being vigilant and staying with what comes up tends to move things forward in the end.

We know so much more now than we did about how to help people face up to the traumas of the past in order to minimise their stranglehold on the future. It's hugely frustrating that miserly funding doesn't allow for a comprehensive and skilled service available to all without a long wait and unrealistic limits to the number of sessions allowed. I worry that as 'treatment' becomes more formulaic, there seems to be less and less scope to tailor therapy to a particular person's situation, symptoms and personality. We increasingly rely on volunteers, trainees and people who are prepared to work for less money, with less training, less experience and fewer skills. Surely, as a society, we owe something to people who have been abused as children and should want the very best for those who have been brave enough to seek help? This has to mean a thorough assessment and sensitive accommodation to each person's needs.

It's not just the NHS that is overwhelmed with too few staff with too few skills. Over the last few years, child sexual abuse has hardly been out of the news and one of the outcomes has been that more victims are making official allegations. Investigating historical abuse is time-consuming and far from straightforward; it requires detectives with sensitivity and courage as well as specialist forensic aptitude. Such people are thinly spread. Too many of my patients have put themselves through a process of exposing and raking through painful details of their abuse only to be told, after years of waiting and inept investigation, that there isn't enough evidence to proceed.

I wish I was more convinced that the culture around sexual abuse has really changed. Despite an escalation of guidelines, bureaucratic procedures and multi-agency meetings, I continue to pick up patients who have languished for years in the system, the underlying abuse ignored or its meaning dismissed. It is common now for mental health professionals to ask about child abuse. However, not enough of them have sufficient training or – given rising caseloads – the time to help the patients understand the impact on their lives and relationships, let alone the skills to help them manage terrifying flashbacks and the destructive acts of self-harm that are so often linked. I prefer to ask the questions in a more oblique way when I first meet someone. Do you remember feeling frightened by anyone when you were young? Did you ever have a sense that a grown-up was doing something that didn't feel right? This gentler approach invites a reflective response, whereas a direct question about abuse can so easily be refuted in a defensive, unthinking sort of way, or be experienced as an assault in itself.

Nowadays, patients with such histories of abuse are usually referred for psychotherapy but have to spend months or even years on a waiting list. In my geographical area, the referral process can take over two years and an increasing number of referrals are now sent outside the NHS to a charity, where they are seen by volunteer counsellors, often trainees. It's not right to expect people to do this sort of work unpaid. This is not to say that some of these counsellors are not good, but they are relatively inexperienced and don't have experience of serious mental health difficulties and the wider care system. Nor indeed the skilled support they need. The patients themselves are often bewildered by being passed on by the clinician who is caring for them to someone else. They don't experience the abused part of themselves as separate – it is part of who they are, all tangled up with their mood swings, eating problems, suicidal impulses, feelings about their body, problems sleeping, difficulties trusting other people and their issues with their own children. Good psychotherapy should be about integrating all parts of the person, not splitting off the needs of the 'abuse victim'.

~

Thirty years after Frank Beck was convicted, we have at some level become accustomed to news of extensive organised abuse of society's most vulnerable children. But at the time the Leicester trial was deeply shocking: it uncovered crimes never before described and hardly imagined by the majority of people. We thought of it as a one-off, a malignant regime centred around a particularly skilled psychopath, something that should never happen again. It contributed to a change in policy for children in care who were subsequently more likely to be fostered than left in a children's home. Ironically, it was thought that they would be safer, but this belief has too often proved naive.

As a society, we can no longer turn a blind eye and deny that child sexual abuse is an issue. There have been too many high-profile scandals for that. But we seem unable to move forward effectively with this knowledge. True, a national enquiry was set up in the UK that has been limping along for years. But we don't need to wait for the results of an enquiry to improve our response to patients wanting therapy and litigants wanting justice. We just need more therapists, more detectives, more courts, and more accessible good-quality training.

Back in the 1980s, we were ignorant of the highly organised, industrial levels of abuse that have been reported more recently in some of our cities. But the dynamics surrounding abuse haven't changed very much. As these stories emerge, it is evident that there are always one or two workers who can see what is happening before it becomes public knowledge. Invariably, they end up being silenced or denigrated in some way. It seems that the only way most of us can manage sexual abuse is to turn away, box it off neatly and locate it elsewhere. The true scale and pervasiveness of the problem remains a dirty secret that as a society we can't quite face. This comes at a huge cost to the children who desperately need protection and the adult survivors who need professional help.

~

Sally, whom we met briefly at the beginning of the chapter, had a difficult journey through therapy – much of the time frightened out of her wits – and eventually through court proceedings where I would also have to give evidence. The trial went on for weeks and Sally was put through days of cross-examination, all the time having to defend herself against suggestions that she was crazy or lying. Eventually seven men from the paedophile ring that had trafficked Sally and other children into prostitution were found guilty and received heavy sentences.

When I saw her a few weeks after the trial – no 'Little Ponies' or baggy tracksuit bottoms this time – I couldn't help feeling proud that we'd helped her become the person she was always meant to be. She was now a woman who could stand up tall, a woman with a powerful voice who could face the world straight on, knowing that she had endured prolonged terror but had stood up for herself and been active in bringing justice to bear.

4

EXPERTS BY EXPERIENCE

During the Second World War, thousands of soldiers returned home mentally damaged by their experience. The sheer numbers overwhelmed psychiatric services. One solution was to capitalise on what the soldiers could teach each other. Having been through similar experiences, it was felt they were well placed to provide mutual support that could be healing. So, instead of wards, 'therapeutic communities' were created where they were encouraged to live together co-operatively while sharing their traumatic memories and the feelings that so disturbed them in therapy groups. This touchingly simple, humane concept fitted well with the straitened circumstances of post-war Britain and the approach became influential in other areas of psychiatry.[1]

Therapeutic communities have struggled to survive more recently in our increasingly risk-averse and bureaucratic healthcare culture. Nevertheless, the fundamental questions the approach seeks to answer about the treatment of mental disturbance are as pertinent as ever. What's more, all organisations and environments can be seen on a spectrum from toxic to therapeutic; reflecting more on this can only be helpful. After working for the eating disorder service for six months, I was lucky enough to 'rotate' as a trainee to a therapeutic community called Francis Dixon Lodge, where – unbeknown to me at the time – I would later return as the consultant. The concept underpinning a therapeutic community might be simple but, in practice, I found the work as complex and fascinating as it gets. On a personal level, the work has left me with a lasting confidence in the capacity of ordinary people – including people with mental health problems – to help each other recover and take back control of their lives, given the right frame of support.

~

For most people, the memory of their first day spent in a therapeutic community becomes etched vividly in their mind. My memory is cloudy – in the literal sense, because people are chain-smoking and there are no open windows. I find myself sitting in a group of about thirty young people, all eyes on me. Some are sitting back in their chairs, smoking nonchalantly, the scarred arms and strangle-marked necks the only glimpse of psychological disturbance. Others sit forward – vigilant, afraid –clearly used to being in environments where being on your guard is the key to survival. One or two seem to stare at me with intense expectation and longing, a desperate look I am starting to get used to working in psychiatry, a kind of silent 'rescue me' scream.

I am asked to introduce myself by a very competent and personable chairperson. I have been told (or, rather, warned) that the meetings are chaired by patients (known as residents in a therapeutic community). Have I got that wrong? I feel disorientated, unsettled. Questions follow quickly: Why did I choose psychiatry? What sort of psychiatrist do I want to be? Have I worked for Dr X and what do I think of him? I am well used to the daunting sense that I am being weighed up as the new doctor but it is made very clear to me by that group in those first few minutes that I have to earn their respect as a *person*, as a member of the group. I realise there is precious little in my medical or psychiatric training that I can use to impress them or hide behind. I feel utterly deskilled. And there is no road map. Starting work in a therapeutic community is like being parachuted into an exciting but dangerous country without knowing a word of the language.

The discussion moves on to events of the previous night. I am surprised to find that in addition to the timetabled community meetings that sandwich the working day, crisis meetings can be called at any time of the day or night if a resident is feeling overwhelmingly self-destructive or suicidal. Encouraging people to talk together, and therefore to think about their feelings rather than to act on them, makes a lot of sense for people who have a tendency to be impulsive. It emerges that a meeting had been called for Sadie at two in the morning and everyone had piled out of bed to try to support her — some more enthusiastically than others. The meeting had been called by Michelle who had discovered that Sadie had bought some razors. She'd agreed to hand them in before they all went back to bed and it had also been agreed that Michelle and Rachel move into her room and spend the rest of the night with her. How is she feeling this morning, the chairperson asks kindly. Is she still wanting to cut herself? Sadie doesn't reply. Michelle then wonders aloud if Sadie has any more razors hidden away. She sounds suspicious and to my mind slightly superior.

'Well, you should fucking know. You seem to know everything about me!' Sadie says angrily, suddenly finding her voice. She hasn't slept a wink. She didn't want 'fucking minders' in her room. It just proved everyone looked down on her and didn't believe her. 'You're supposed to be my sponsor, not the fucking police,' she shouts at Michelle. 'You've had it in for me from the first day!'

Michelle looks unabashed and makes a gesture to the group with her hands: *See what I have to put up with!*

Rob, one of the nurses, then asks Sadie why she thinks it was difficult to sleep with other people in the room. After all, that was arranged because it was felt she needed support. He wonders if it felt more as if she was being imprisoned than being cared for.

'Why do you always have to bring prison into it?' Sadie responds sharply before he's even finished.

Rachel then says that she's not slept well either. Someone asks if she feels angry that yet another crisis meeting was held for Sadie in the middle of the night.

'I don't think so. It's just that I'm struggling so much not to cut. I don't want to give in, but it's really hard. It makes me feel really unsafe to know that Sadie might cut at any time,' she says thoughtfully. Others murmur agreement.

The chairperson says he needs to move the meeting on. Has anyone got anything more important to say about last night? After a bit of other business, the meeting is eventually brought to a close bang on 10.30 a.m. and I am ushered away with other members of staff for what's called an 'after-group' – a sort of reflective debriefing session – before joining the residents for coffee and the biggest pile of toast imaginable. To my surprise, Sadie is busy spreading the jam, seemingly relaxed and chatty.

I leave my first day in that fuggy, smoke-filled room knowing already that this is a placement where I will learn easily as much from the patients as they will learn from me. Rather to my surprise I realise that beneath the stirring of anxiety and excitement there is a strong sense of calm and resonance, a sense of coming home, a sense of finding – at last – a place in psychiatry where I can be authentic, use my creativity and be the sort of doctor that I want to be.

~

During the Second World War, one of the first therapeutic communities evolved at Mill Hill Hospital in London through the attempt to help soldiers with what was known then as 'effort syndrome' – 'shell shock' in the First World War. These soldiers exhibited a collection of symptoms similar to what we know today as post-traumatic stress disorder (PTSD). Four types of symptoms are common: intrusive memories, such as flashbacks and night-mares; anxiety, fear, hypervigilance and avoidance of situations that trigger reminders of the trauma; negative changes in mood and thinking, for example, sadness, irritability, helplessness, hopeless-ness and despair; and changes in physical and emotional reactions, such as a startle response, a panic attack, or a sudden onset of rage or sense of catastrophe.

Panic attacks are terrifying and can be seen as physiological vicious circles triggered by fear – often, but not always, in response to a 'flashback' of an aspect of the original trauma. The experience of anxiety causes a sudden rise in adrenalin – the 'fright, fight, flight' hormone. This affects various organs of the body and can cause symptoms that include an increase in heart and respiratory rate, chest pain, a dry mouth, pins and needles, dizziness, nausea, stomach cramps and difficulty thinking. The symptoms often start suddenly, which can feel particularly frightening. Fear triggers more adrenalin: hence the vicious circle. Many people think they are having a heart attack and are going to die. They often turn up reluctantly to mental health services, desperate for help but convinced the problem is physical, not mental: 'It's real, doctor, not in my head.' Real it certainly is, but of course body and mind are much more entangled than we like to think.

Consciously minimising fear should be a goal in any environment that sets out to be therapeutic, from ICU to psychiatric ward. Over the years, I must have spent hundreds of hours explaining to very frightened individuals the link between psychological processes and physiology. I try to speak in a reassuring, soothing tone while I draw diagrams of the vicious circle that links anxiety with such overwhelming bodily symptoms. The hope is that knowing what is going on will stop symptoms escalating. This reframing of a problem, plus some help with relaxation techniques and advice about breathing, can be sufficient help for some people, taking the edge off their fear and giving them back a sense of control. Nowadays, such psychoeducation tends to take place in groups, partly because it's cheaper but also because people tend to feel encouraged by meeting others with similar problems and the camaraderie that comes with forming a peer group.

This is exactly what happened at Mill Hill during the war. Lectures about the physiological basis of the symptoms gradually led to more open discussions, the more experienced patients giving information to newer patients, and a less rigid demarcation between doctors, nurses and patients. It was soon realised that the interaction that went on between group members was as important as what they were being taught by professionals. Sharing their experience with each other in groups could be a powerful and cathartic experience and taking responsibility for themselves and each other, organising the day-to-day running of the place and learning to live comfortably with each other – the 'living–learning experience' – was as important as the formal group sessions. The idea took hold that it is the life of the community itself that has the potential to contain and heal severe emotional disturbance. Because the community is seen as the agent of change rather than individual therapists, the primary task is to analyse and make conscious the dynamics of the organisation and engage everyone in the work of maintaining a healthy community.

A fundamental principle is that all involved are encouraged to be curious about themselves, each other, the staff, the management structure, psychological processes, the group process, the institution and everything else pertinent to events and relationships within the community. This is known as the 'culture of enquiry' – an openness to questioning, so that understanding is owned by all and not seen solely to reside in professionals. A typical day starts and finishes with a community meeting such as the one I encountered on my first day. The agenda is driven by the attempt to make as much information as possible accessible to as many people as possible, creating a culture where secrets are discouraged, where individuals can check things out, and paranoia is minimised.

Of course, this sense of safety was always being threatened. It was hard to break the familiar patterns of neglect and abuse that were such a feature of our patients' histories. Many of them had spent years protecting others from their rage, instead directing it at themselves. Breaking such entrenched behaviour patterns involves a dark and messy therapeutic journey as inner wounds are explored, and hateful – indeed murderous – feelings come to the fore and demand expression. There were many times over the years when I felt we'd failed people and wondered if it was worth all the effort. But far more often I'd find myself awed yet again by the paradox that putting a lot of potentially dangerous people together can create something strong, safe and therapeutic. I'd love to see all mental health staff work for a stretch in a therapeutic community, just to show them what is possible.

One of the key factors that makes a therapeutic community feel safe is that everyone has a stake in running the place, with residents chairing the meetings and organising daily chores such as cooking and cleaning. Every month a new group of senior residents is elected to take on the various roles. A difficult decision, such as whether someone who has messed things up big time should leave, is usually put to the vote. And the rules themselves are constantly up for review. Some are non-negotiable, such as no illegal drugs on the premises and no physical violence, but others are owned by the community and give the individuals involved an important taste of responsibility. No token gestures here. Even the most diffident discovered quickly that their votes mattered and, in general, voting was approached with a touching seriousness and always after long discussion. This is how it should be.

Today, at a national level, with a drop in polling rates in many parts of the world and an ill-thought-out referendum in the UK, we have seen the results of lazily taking the concept of democracy for granted. We have been reminded that democracy is hard work requiring the complicated labour of engagement; that sustaining a sense that everyone has a stake in society is a dynamic struggle; that citizenship has to be nurtured, thought about and practised. These types of discussions take place in a therapeutic community almost every day as new residents explore such concepts, test out their limits and discover for themselves how to create a micro-society that is safe and functional.

~

I was fascinated to first see the voting process in action when, later that day, I spent the afternoon with a small group assessing a new patient. The residents always have the majority vote, which I found intriguing. Psychotherapy assessments are difficult, especially with patients who are at risk of harming themselves or others. How can they be sure the residents will make the right choice? The applicant in question, Pauline, had made two suicide attempts and much of the assessment was focused on whether she really wanted to change her behaviour and start taking responsibility for herself. After about an hour, she was asked to leave the room and a lively discussion ensued. In the end, three voted for offering her a place and two against but it was a wide-reaching and respectful discussion.

The sophistication of the process amazed and thrilled me. I was sure that I would not have got as much out of Pauline if I'd seen her on my own. Later I discovered that a research study from another therapeutic community showed that groups of patients tend to make the same selection decisions as clinical staff. But I needed no persuading. That one day convinced me of the healing potential when a group of damaged people have a genuine stake in the treatment process and real involvement in their own and other people's therapy.

There was one occasion, however, during that first six-month stint when I felt very troubled by the way the community voted to discharge someone. Libby had an unusual story. She had been brought up in America in a strange, sect-like extended family and had been forced to participate in a complex system of cruel punishments. The one that had affected her most was when she had been made to kill a beloved pet. To her credit, she eventually managed to break away, move to the UK, put herself through college and qualify as a teacher in what was known then as a special school. She had an empathy with the children she worked with and found her job fulfilling but she had kept away from close relationships, had an ongoing eating disorder and hadn't been able to stop cutting herself. When this was discovered, she was immediately put on compulsory sick leave. Her work had clearly been holding her together and without it she rapidly regressed, made a serious suicide attempt and was admitted to an acute psychiatric ward.

On the ward, she continued to harm herself and make attempts to end her life and the staff were clearly relieved to pass her on to us. She'd seemed to take easily to the therapeutic community regime – perhaps because in some ways her family had resembled a commune – becoming an impressive and vocal member of the resident group, quick to confront and support others. Some of the group felt she saw herself more as a member of staff than a patient and there was a growing unease around her and perhaps some envy at her seeming emotional literacy. Usually, residents were encouraged to take their time, to build up trusting relationships before they talked in detail about things they found shameful. Not so with Libby. Pressure was put on her to share more of her own story, even though she'd been in the group for only six weeks.

The details she shared, both about the extent of her secret self-harm and the things she'd been forced to do as a child, were hard to listen to, but the story of being forced to kill her baby rabbit was particularly terrible. She'd been worried she would vomit, which would attract further punishment, so perhaps no surprise that I felt nauseous as I listened. It was a story that got right inside me and didn't sit comfortably. Looking round the group it was clear that others too were finding it hard to digest, some of them looking distressed while a few had clearly distanced themselves.

Libby shared her story in a small therapy group and, as was the custom, the contents of the small groups were summarised and read out in the community meeting the following day. The write-up of Libby's group was not done particularly sensitively and one or two important details had been missed. She was obviously feeling vulnerable and exposed, and after complaining that it was a poor account of what she'd said the day before, refused to say any more.

'There's no point,' she kept repeating, rather despairingly. 'Just leave it.'

Someone then asked her if she was confused about what had actually happened. She was only seven after all, and it did sound very bizarre. He sounded concerned but it was a badly judged question and the timing was terrible. I was just mulling over how to intervene when Libby stood up and chucked her coffee cup high and hard so that it cracked a mirror hanging on the wall. She headed towards the door then turned back, grabbed the broken mirror off the wall and flung it against a cupboard, where it smashed into pieces. She left the room, still in a frenzy, throwing aside a chair that was in her way and starting to cut into her arms and face with a jagged piece of the broken mirror. Later she said she hadn't felt any physical pain despite the deep lacerations. She spent most of the rest of the day in the emergency department accompanied by two other residents.

In the community meeting the following morning, the incident was unpicked in forensic detail as the community was split over whether or not she should be discharged. Both sides felt strongly. If she'd threatened a person it would have been a clear-cut discharge, but violence against property and self was more of a grey area. Libby did herself no favours by claiming she couldn't remember much about what had happened the day before and her apology was half-hearted. Was it possible she'd been so dissociated that she really couldn't remember? There was a lot at stake. It felt as though Francis Dixon Lodge had been her last chance if she was to have any hope of resuming her career and no doubt her suicidal feelings would be amplified if she was discharged against her will.

One or two of us argued that she'd been traumatised by what she'd talked about in the group, overwhelmed by what she'd experienced as a child and the intensity of feelings that had surfaced. But we were lone voices and it soon became clear that the majority of the community had been affected very differently by the incident: they didn't feel safe with her around. They were more irritated and frightened by Libby the erratic professional than moved – as I was – by Libby the helpless abused seven-year-old. She was discharged that day and told she could reapply in six months.

I didn't sleep that night, tossing and turning, worried that she'd kill herself, feeling frustrated with myself for not arguing her case better, feeling angry with the community for being unable to empathise with her, and cross with more seasoned staff who seemed comfortable with a 'win some, lose some' attitude. In staff discussions, the safety of the group and the importance of clear behaviour boundaries were reiterated and I felt my feelings were being put down to naivety.

I continued to feel aggrieved on Libby's behalf and it was hard to shake it off. It was as if I had been left carrying the 'hurt child' part of her and I would find myself having soothing conversations with her in my head. Even weirder, I found myself re-running a fantasy community meeting, where I played a much more heroic role in arguing her case and bringing the rest of the community round to my way of seeing things.

Eventually, I plucked up the courage to confess to Dr Spaul, the consultant, how preoccupied I still was with the incident. To my relief, he was warm, unsurprised and understanding. He helped me disentangle my sense of guilt and overblown responsibility for encouraging her to talk about the abuse she'd been part of before she or the community were ready. His gentle philosophical reflections helped me understand how important it was that the group had the power to make and enforce the rules if it was to function well and that it was never anyone's 'last chance'.

His psychoanalytical insights helped me understand how different aspects of a personality can be picked up by different people in the group and that given so few had empathised with Libby's hurt inner child, it was no surprise that I was holding that part of her so intensely. At his suggestion, I wrote her a letter, sharing my hope that she would reapply to the therapeutic community in six months' time. She didn't respond. I never saw her again and never found out what happened to her.

The incident left a lasting impression. Years later when I became the consultant at Francis Dixon Lodge, I changed the rules: the community could vote to advise that someone be discharged but, as consultant, I had the final say. Many of my colleagues thought I was wrong in this and saw me as watering down the therapeutic model. But this was the 1990s and the role of psychiatry and attitudes to risk and professional accountability were changing. In fact, I very rarely needed to overturn a decision made by members of the community and was well aware that it undermined their sense of responsibility and my alliance with them when I did.

In Libby's case, I was concerned that a scapegoating process had occurred. In the Bible story, sins are symbolically attached to a goat, which is then sent into the wilderness. Scapegoating is a constant danger in groups of any size from family to nation. It is a way of ridding ourselves of the disturbing. It is often an unconscious process or involves 'turning a blind eye' to our own 'sins' and projecting our unwanted disturbance on to an individual or subgroup. At a national level, for example, some would lead us to believe that immigrants are the cause of all our woes; in the debate about whether Libby should stay or go, there was a strong sense that her rage would destroy the group, that the community would be safe if it wasn't for her, that the rest of them were peace-loving and conflict-free. The fact that many in that group were also struggling with violent feelings was not evident that morning. It had been frightening to experience a seemingly composed member of the group erupt into a frenzy. But perhaps the most disturbing fear it triggered for many in the group was the fear of their own aggression and the potential for their own rage to overwhelm and destroy relationships and a community that they were coming to value.

Libby's experience illustrates many of the difficult dynamics that I was to struggle with over the years. So often the sharing of a particularly disturbing story seems to bring the emotional drama alive in the present, not just for the individual but for the group. It's almost as if the narrative gets inside the group and we all unwittingly get embroiled in an enactment. Libby's story was of a terrified, vulnerable child forced to sacrifice her baby rabbit in a perverse punishment ritual. In some weird kind of parallel process, after hearing about how this terrified, vulnerable child had been forced to sacrifice her pet it felt that Libby had been sacrificed by the community. At the time, I would have found such an interpretation too far-fetched, but over the years I was to participate in and observe so many similar re-enactments that I came to agree that there must be some unconscious process driving such a phenomenon. This is an elaboration of Freud's observation that unless we remember, we are doomed to repeat. In these re-enactments in the therapeutic community, the potent act of sharing the memory somehow transferred and became part of the complex dynamics in the group.

The psychotherapy literature is full of descriptions of such phenomena and technical terms that attempt to make sense of the process. More recently, neuroscience has contributed to our understanding, with the concept of 'mirror neurones' and the latest technology (functional MRI scans) showing corresponding parts of our own brain being activated when we are in the presence of another person in a disturbed state of mind. But on the front line, away from the textbooks, I never fail to be awed by the extraordinary unconscious links between a deeply conflicted individual mind and the interplay of characters within the group. Again and again, the dynamic is so powerful that it takes me by surprise and can be understood only in retrospect.

Libby's story illustrates the interplay between the two important philosophical models that make up a therapeutic community. The first is psychopolitical: creating and sustaining a culture where power and responsibility is shared, where authority is earned, where everyone has a voice and a vote and – if all goes well – a growing sense of agency. The second is psychoanalytic: a commitment to standing back in order to try to make sense of what is going on, where stuff is allowed to happen but everything is a focus for reflection and understanding, where knowing oneself better, it is hoped, leads to greater integrity and emotional containment.

More generally, I became an advocate for involving patients in as many activities related to the service as possible – 'experts by experience', long before this term was in popular usage. I used to drag them along to teaching sessions: the patients nervous and the medical students uncomfortable to start with, but then everyone reluctant to leave as the patients found their voice and the medical students felt free to be curious. The patients were heavily involved in our staff-recruitment process: the design of the assessment day, chairing a large group question-and-answer session, and as advisers in the formal interview. (I went against their advice only once and ended up really regretting the appointment we made.) We involved them in the early days when there were threats to stop funding the service and I remember well how moved the chairman of the health authority was when they explained in eloquent personal detail how much the unit meant to them. We used to take them along to speak at conferences and even persuaded them to take up an invitation to speak on *Woman's Hour* on Radio 4.

I can't pretend I wasn't nervous for them at times, wondering how they'd manage, worrying that it might interfere with their therapy, and, on a more basic level, praying that no one would 'cut up' or get drunk. But they were given lots of support by other members of the therapeutic community and there were reserves on standby if someone didn't feel up to it. I can honestly say to any sceptics that they nearly always rose to the occasion, enriching the experience for everyone involved, and growing in self-esteem in the process.

Therapeutic communities are not perfect – no treatment approach is – but in my career I have seen them play a hugely positive role in the lives of many patients. These days their existence and influence have waned, a trend I find disappointing – and a mistake. The therapeutic community model emerged during the Second World War at a time of great need, driven by the economic situation as much as by ideology. Since the pandemic and consequent lockdowns, many more of us have had to face up to mental health issues; some have been pushed over the edge, and the impact on the mental health of children and young adults is likely to have long-term consequences.

We have to rethink how to address this overwhelming demand. The work of therapeutic communities shows the value of bringing together the resources and strengths of patients themselves in the process of healing. For so many reasons, it would be crazy not to build this into our response.

5

LOCKED IN

All psychiatrists work with people who are potentially dangerous. We make difficult decisions about 'mental capacity' – whether or not a person can be held accountable and responsible for their actions, while assessing risk and deciding whether detention using the Mental Health Act is warranted.

Our forensic colleagues are responsible for patients with the most obvious potential for law-breaking violence. They work with very disturbed people with a dangerous psychosis or reckless impulsivity or – much more rarely – cold, sadistic personalities, sometimes so lacking in fellow-feeling that they can leave one feeling chilled to the bone. I have a great respect for colleagues who specialise in forensic psychiatry, but early on I realised I was more suited to a career in psychotherapy. Even so, like all psychiatrists, I encounter criminals in my caseload, interview people in prison, and appear in court on occasion. The burden of responsibility involved in considering whether patients pose a danger to themselves or to others is one that continues to weigh heavily on me. Deciding whether to use compulsory powers to detain someone is not always clear-cut – particularly in my field of 'personality disorder' – and often involves balancing the short-term alleviation of immediate risk with the longer-term consequences of depriving someone of their liberty.

When I first started my consultant job, a regional medium-secure psychiatric hospital, Field House, had recently opened, only a few hundred metres from Francis Dixon Lodge. I knew most of the forensic consultants that worked there and attended the same management team meetings as their clinical director. The unit ran one of its wards on therapeutic community lines, so there was some understanding of what we were about. It was relatively easy to pick up the phone and ask advice or even move patients between the two units. All this was to change and much more formal care pathways and systems were later introduced, but it was a bonus to have this easy exchange on hand for the first year or two. It meant that our two units, one where patients were ultimately free to come and go, and one where they were locked in, could work together to get our response to the particular patient right.

~

My first visit to Field House was to see Geraldine, an ex-veterinary student, who'd been admitted there for her own safety. This was before strict admission criteria had been introduced, but even in those days it was very unusual to admit someone to a secure unit who had not committed a crime, which says something about the degree of anxiety she had created among those in the mental health system with whom she'd had contact. So determined was Geraldine to kill herself before her twenty-first birthday that, in addition to overdosing, she'd tried cutting her neck with a razor, tying ligatures around her neck, even injecting herself with sour milk, and she had repeatedly self-harmed by banging her head so badly that she'd given herself a subdural haemorrhage that had needed surgery.

Geraldine's story was something of a mystery – she would never reveal the full details of the abuse she had suffered as a child. All we could get from her was a story of being held prisoner in a dark cellar along with another child. She still heard her screams in her nightmares. The only thing she was very clear on was that she had to kill herself before she turned twenty-one in order not to fall back into 'their' clutches for the rest of her life. Geraldine didn't want to die but she was even more terrified of the consequences of not dying, consequences that she'd been fixated on for many years, ever since the abuse started when she was about six years old.

It was hard to know where to start with Geraldine, but I'd allowed the whole afternoon for my assessment. I didn't want to be rushed into a precipitate decision. By the time I saw her, her birthday had come and passed. Whether or not she was suffering from a paranoid psychosis as a result of an underlying schizophrenic illness was clearly an important question, and exploring this question had been part of the rationale for admitting her to the secure unit. But there was nothing to support this possible diagnosis other than the terror she seemed to be experiencing. I don't know why, but reading Geraldine's story I'd imagined someone flighty and superficial. But the person I encountered greeted me with direct and enquiring eyes, had a surprising level-headedness about her, and was very much in touch with the seriousness of her situation. The diagnosis of hysteria seemed unlikely. Perhaps even more important, I was already warming to her. I reminded myself to be cautious: this woman had violently harmed herself repeatedly and hit out aggressively at nursing staff trying to stop her.

'It's not easy to go into reverse when you're halfway down a slippery slope,' I ventured.

'Tell me about it!' she'd responded wryly. No problem with metaphor, I noted to myself – always useful to know more about how an individual's mind works when you're trying to work towards a diagnosis and match them to a particular therapy.

Rather than push her to talk about the traumatic fear that seemed to have so destabilised her, I started by asking her about her experience at veterinary school, trying to establish a different sort of connection. I wanted to avoid getting locked into the 'Do you believe me?' question until we'd got to know each other a bit. There was no way I could begin to imagine what it would have been like to be abused and terrorised as a child – if this was in fact what had happened – but I could certainly be genuine and empathic about doing a challenging vocational course at university. As well as hoping to get a feel of her as a person, I wanted to get a sense of how much she was able to think psychologically for, whatever lay behind her story, she was going to have to work hard to extricate herself from her present circumstances.

Geraldine had passed her first two years at veterinary school easily enough but then things had gone from bad to worse during the summer holidays, with panic attacks and suicidal thoughts becoming increasingly frequent as her twenty-first birthday loomed nearer. Once she'd been admitted to the ward, matters had escalated very quickly as it dawned on her how easily they could detain her using the Mental Health Act.

'We don't want to have to section you,' she'd been told, 'but if you try to leave the ward, we'll have no choice.' The Mental Health Act shouldn't be used like this, but I've heard these threats from anxious ward staff quite frequently. In Geraldine's case, it had sent her into a frenzy. By the time I saw her, the system had 'pinned' her – physically restrained and injected her with a tranquilliser – many times.

I made a tentative suggestion: 'I'm wondering if perhaps your sense of being trapped on the ward hooked into an earlier experience of being trapped in frightening circumstances.'

She nodded thoughtfully, then said urgently, 'Please don't make me talk about it. I just can't . . . the childhood bit, I mean . . . I just can't.'

As we continued to talk, Geraldine became less coherent. When she started talking about needing to 'get away from them' it was difficult to know if she was talking about the people who had abused her as a child or the staff on the ward. I began to pen a formulation in my head: something unbearably frightening had happened to Geraldine as a child that she'd compartmentalised in her mind while she just about managed to get on with her life, but the approaching birthday and the nature of her contact with mental health services had destabilised this brittle equilibrium, triggering the symptoms that we were struggling to understand. But that had then been compounded by Geraldine finding herself locked away in a medium secure unit, her worst fears come to pass. All those walls, those electronically operated doors, must have been playing into her belief that she was destined to be locked away for the rest of her life.

I could just about understand why her previous psychiatrists had taken this course: she'd been weeks away from her twenty-first birthday and the self-destructive behaviour had been escalating, with collateral damage to the nurses who had tried to stop her. I wondered if the fact that she was a veterinary student had led to overzealous attempts to keep her safe. Whatever the reason, the decision to detain her in a medium-secure unit seemed as much about panic in the system as helping Geraldine, and my mind was screaming, 'Category error!' It seemed worth trying a different approach.

Tentatively, I started a conversation with Geraldine about a possible admission to Francis Dixon Lodge. No locks, just the psychological containment of being part of a group, knowing that you are held in mind, and that your behaviour affects everyone in the group. She grasped the concept quickly and responded positively, albeit cautiously. It was clear she didn't want to be locked in, but she wanted her abusers locked out. We talked through how she might use the community to make her feel safe from her abusers, and how she would need to make a commitment to try to talk to the group about thoughts of suicide or self-harm before acting on them in the heat of the moment. I made it clear that we would not try to physically detain her but neither would we put ourselves in danger; that she would need to take back responsibility for the part of her that wanted to self-destruct but that we would do everything we could to help her with this. Much of this conversation took place in a second meeting with one of the therapeutic community patients present. Taking Geraldine into Francis Dixon Lodge was a huge gamble and there was no chance of it working unless the resident community was on board. Everyone understood the risk involved but in the end they decided to give her a chance.

The gamble paid off: Geraldine responded as I had hoped. Rather than replay and amplify her fear of imprisonment, we were able to create a safe space for her to explore what had really happened to her as a child, so it no longer took her by surprise or had quite such a nightmarish edge. True, the first few months were difficult and required us all to hold our nerve but, given back her agency, Geraldine was eventually able to go from strength to strength. The last time we heard from her, she had just been awarded a doctorate degree and had a job doing cancer research.

∼

My clinical judgement with Geraldine turned out to be correct: being detained wasn't the best way to treat her. But there are some patients where there is no avoiding it.

One such patient was Wayne, a man in his early thirties, who we were finding very unsettling but couldn't put our finger on why. He had been a librarian but had retired due to chronic depression. He was intelligent, good-looking and could be charming. But the more we tried, the less we felt we knew him or understood what made him tick. It is not uncommon to get the feeling a patient is psychologically dodging one's attempts to help them face the realities in their life, but with Wayne we were all beginning to feel that there was something more sinister going on. He had not said anything that made sense of his marriage breaking up or his decision to leave the library service. Drugs? A secret drinker? Not as far as we could see. But things just didn't quite fit together and it was making us uneasy.

It is important to be aware of and interested in such 'gut feelings'. In the general practice literature, for example, where decisions are made after only a few minutes with the patient, there are numerous stories of doctors acting on a hunch that something was very wrong, despite no objective evidence, and later finding that their hunch was correct and that acting on it had saved the patient.

There is a rather extraordinary but elegant German research study that tries to explore this issue. It is focused on psychiatrists' reliability at assessing patients for risk of suicide.[1] All the patients in the study had made a previous suicide attempt and the psychiatrists were asked to predict the likelihood of them making a further serious attempt in the future. At the same time, these assessments were being watched through a one-way screen by researchers who couldn't hear the content of what was being said, so were making their risk assessment just on the body language of the psychiatrists, particularly focusing on their facial expressions. The patients were followed up over several years with completed suicides mapped against prediction. To everyone's surprise, the risk assessments done by the observers who couldn't hear what was going on turned out to be of better predictive value (correct in 82 per cent of cases) than those made by the psychiatrists in the room (only 23 per cent). How could this strange result be explained? The researchers hypothesised that the body language – for example, a fleeting look of disgust or bemusement – was expressing the psychiatrists' 'gut feelings' and that reading these offered greater insight into the patient than the conscious verbal exchange. A sort of 'unconscious knowing' that psychotherapists like me find so fascinating. From the study, it looked as if the conscious verbal exchange was getting in the way and that psychiatrists would do better trying to listen to what their bodies already knew.

In Wayne's case, our 'guts' were ringing alarm bells. One day, I watched a look of panic cross the face of a student nurse as she arrived at the community meeting a bit late and realised the only seat left was next to Wayne on the sofa. When I asked her about this in the staff meeting afterwards, she looked genuinely surprised. She seemed to have found her flash of panic unacceptable and quickly shut it out of her consciousness, although when I later encouraged her, she was willing to dig it up and look at it. Of course, when you become aware that someone gives you the creeps, it's important to question it, particularly if the person is different in a way that feeds into common prejudice or perhaps reminds you of someone from your past. But this didn't help with Wayne. Maybe we were onto something or maybe we were just all becoming a bit paranoid.

The call came on my day off. Did I know Wayne had a gun in his room? (Of course I didn't.) One of the other residents had noticed something gun-like poking out of a suitcase under his bed. She'd worried about it overnight and challenged him in the community meeting.

'It's just an air rifle,' he said patronisingly. 'Nothing dangerous. Just been shooting a few birds! Nothing wrong with that! It's not against the rules as far as I'm aware.' The community erupted. One of the residents had been held at gunpoint by her ex-partner in the past; others felt passionately about animal rights, but, in truth, there was no need for a backstory to explain the fury let loose at the thought of a gun in this supposedly safe, therapeutic environment.

'You're talking about a poncy air rifle!' he kept saying, as if everyone was overreacting and he was the only sane person in the room. But the community was having none of it and demanded he let them search his room to see what else he had stored under the bed. To everyone's horror, the suitcase contained a collection of strange objects — a rather sophisticated garrotte, a selection of clamps, tweezers of various sizes, elastic bands, a tube of super-glue — that he eventually confessed to using to torture animals. Sinister indeed. By this time, Wayne's jovial facade was beginning to collapse. When did all this start? we asked him.

In a very flat voice, he eventually described an incident a few years earlier when a disturbed child in his village had been discovered to have caught a mouse and chopped bits off its tail. This had brought back forgotten memories of his own child-hood, when systematically torturing small animals had been an obsession.

The one fact every medical student knows about psychopaths is that cruelty to animals is often a feature of their childhoods.

Wayne adamantly denied ever having hurt a human being, but his response was not reassuring. 'Why do you think I fucking well left my job and walked out on my wife and the twins!' he had replied angrily to my question. It was all beginning to fit together, and my panic and fury were starting to subside and make a bit of room for compassion.

Our willingness to take a risk with Geraldine made it easier to ask the secure unit staff to help out with Wayne. I was able to arrange for a forensic psychologist to see him the very next day and he ended up making a transition from Francis Dixon Lodge to the secure unit within the space of a week, easily convinced by me that it was his best opportunity to get the specialist help he needed.

Not a chance of that happening these days. With occupancy rates running at over 100 per cent, long waiting times to be seen, and specialists' hands tied within bureaucratic systems, he would most probably be left to his own devices till he did something much worse. As far as we know, he had not abused a child, but the psychologist had no doubt about the potential danger he posed and feared he was heading fast in that direction.

Wayne left us all shaken. I was still finding my feet, worried about my inexperience and naivety, worried about the reputation of the service and how this story could run in the wrong hands. The 'air rifle' turned out to be a .22 rifle – a step up from an air rifle and not quite as poncy as he'd told us. He reputedly did well with the psychological therapy on offer at Field House. I don't know what happened to him after he left there but, at that point in his life, the forensic unit was the best place for him.

～

While our run-in with Wayne was undeniably frightening, at least he was able to recognise in the end that his behaviour was danger-ously perverted and was willing to accept that he needed help to change. That is not always the case: an encounter with a young man called Benny left me feeling spooked for some time.

On first contact, he seemed boyish, enthusiastic, keen to please, but as I got to know him, his sycophantic attitude started to make me feel uncomfortable and, after a few weeks, he had infiltrated my dreams. Underneath the pseudo-friendliness and superficial conformity, I sensed something cold, despairing and obsessive. We knew he had spent time in prison for burglary but were shocked to the bone when he described a period of his life when he had stalked his ex-girlfriend, living secretly for a time in her attic, moving her furniture and belongings around while she was out or asleep – just as the Stasi do in the film *The Lives of Others*. He recounted this story as a personal adventure, with his ex-girlfriend as the baddie who deserved to be 'shaken up a bit'. He denied wanting to send her crazy or even frighten her and couldn't see why we were upset by the story. 'It wasn't right that she could just get rid of me like that,' he kept repeating, as if that justified his subsequent actions.

A patient's history gives us vital information and is the most important predictor of future events, particularly when it comes to the question of whether they are a threat to themselves or others. That might sound obvious but when you're working up close to danger, it can be hard to keep in mind. Despite risk assessment systems that are now considerably more thorough than they used to be, it can be hard to hold together all the different, often conflicting, aspects of a patient. Dangerous people can also be vulnerable, needy, often the victims of violence and neglect themselves, even kind and caring. Our understandable desire to see the best in them, and work positively with their potential, can blind us to danger. It's as if it's too difficult for our minds to hold the vulnerable dependant alongside the cruel sadist in one being: too much cognitive dissonance.

In the wake of the 1995 'Falling Shadow' Inquiry (following the tragic death of occupational therapist Georgina Robinson, killed by a schizophrenic patient whose past history of serious threatening behaviour had never been clearly communicated to the hospital staff who were working with him at the time), a number of recommendations were adopted, including the advice that nursing and medical notes should be amalgamated. But bureaucratic solutions are never a complete answer, and the mushrooming paperwork and digitalised information produced these days can bury the important facts. Everyone is overwhelmed by the task of inputting information; few get the time to read what's there.

I was very aware that when you're working closely with someone it's easy to become blind to any risk they may pose. Consequently, we took Benny's story of hiding in the woman's attic very seriously, while at the same time thinking about whether it might be exaggerated or even a fantasy. There was something terribly sad about Benny and we realised quickly that any work we might manage to do with him was limited. Within a few weeks, he had taken a serious overdose. Challenged about this, it was clear that he had no hope or intention of addressing his problems. Eventually, it came out that Benny was committing minor robberies, 'in full daylight' as it were, hoping to be arrested and sent back to jail: 'It's the only place I feel safe,' he told us.

People like Benny feel so threatened by their own rage and inner demons that they long to be closely surrounded by brick walls and the comfort of a hefty lock: 'secure' in both senses. Forensic teams are skilled at working with people like this, some of whom, safe in the knowledge that others are mindful of their potential dangerousness, manage to take the psychological risks that therapy entails, gradually developing the necessary internal boundaries that will enable self-control.

Benny left our unit after taking another massive overdose that, to our relief and to his anguish, he survived. While he was on the medical ward, one of the nurses found a drawing folded away in a book that he had left lying about on a coffee table. It was an accurate replica of my house, drawn from the outside but still chilling. Like most psychiatrists, I tick the box on the electoral-roll form indicating my address should not be made public. How did he even know where I lived? I went to see him in hospital with the drawing and asked him directly.

'I just know,' he kept saying, his mouth a grimace, his eyes blank. I couldn't get any more out of him.

'You must have followed me home,' I continued. 'Why? What were you planning?'

He wasn't going to tell me.

I took advice from my forensic colleagues and informed the police, who just told me to let them know if I had any evidence of being stalked in the future. If it happened now, I imagine a multi-agency case conference would be convened and a contingency plan drawn up for everyone involved. But, at that time, there was little effective support for a psychiatrist being stalked – indeed, stalking did not become a criminal offence in the UK until 2012. The therapeutic community team was kind and concerned about me at the time, but before long Benny, who'd been with us only a few weeks, was forgotten and our attention at work moved on to a new cohort of patients.

But the questions niggled away at me for months. I was a single parent at the time and felt vulnerable and protective of my brood. As a psychiatrist, I'd been in more immediately risky situations, but there was something particularly personal and intrusive about the lingering threat from Benny. Sometimes I'd hear noises in the night that left me restless and fearful and, on two occasions, I rather sheepishly asked a friend to check in the attic, knowing really that no one was there. The police had offered to let me know if he was arrested but I'd heard nothing. After a year, the same friend who had checked the attic suggested I phone them. To my great relief and some annoyance that I'd not been told earlier, I discovered he'd been picked up for assault within a month of being discharged from hospital. He'd been safely behind bars all this time. My fears for myself had been unnecessary. But I still feared for Benny. He might now be 'secure', but I doubted he would get any therapeutic help in prison. And even if he was offered help, I wasn't sure he would be able to make use of it.

~

In society at large, the attitude to security has shifted considerably over the last forty years and not always, to my mind, for the best. You can see it in all sorts of surveillance technology that we're told is for our safety but that many find both intrusive and alarming. Psychiatry suffers from a similar trend within the context of a legal framework that has been evolving for many decades. Mental health legislation has always had to steer a difficult road between respecting a person's autonomy and the duty of a civilised society to intervene and protect the very vulnerable. But the 2007 amendments to the 1983 Mental Health Act enshrined a drift away from treating patients towards protecting the public. This was foreshadowed by a few high-profile cases of people with severe mental illness committing violent crimes, which fed into the increasing preoccupation with security as a society. It was hard to get across to the public – or, indeed, politicians – that killings by those with mental illness were unusual and the rate of such killings was declining.

The 2007 legislation was intended originally to replace the 1983 Mental Health Act, but provoked such opposition from stakeholders, including the psychiatric profession and mental health charities, that it ended up being much reduced and appended to the original Act. Of course all mental health workers should be mindful of the need to protect the public as well as the best interests of our patients, but there are situations when these motivations pull in different directions, and many examples where prioritising risk has undermined treatment.

When I meet junior psychiatrists, I am struck by their anxious preoccupation with assessing short-term risk, often, it seems, to the extent that they hardly have time to get to know the patient. Such a preoccupation can be counterproductive, for risk is best minimised in trusted therapeutic relationships where patients are able to communicate their most frightening feelings. If we don't spend enough time sitting down with patients such as Geraldine, we don't have a narrative for explaining what has led to them behaving as they do. This means we can't contextualise risk or exercise the understanding and empathy that can provide psychological containment, minimise dangerous behaviour and avert the need for legal detention. Similarly, if we don't get close enough to people like Wayne and Benny, we are likely to miss important, and dangerous, aspects of their personalities – to the detriment of the safety of others, and their own longer-term chances of something like recovery.

In 2018, work started on a new review of the Mental Health Act with a government white paper published in August 2021.[2] Refreshingly, the report is clear that legislation should be seen as part of the overall picture, and that the real challenge is to change the way we deliver care so that people do not need to be detained in the first place. The tone of the report is very different from that of the 2007 legislation. The changes recommended set out to rebalance the system to be more responsive to the needs of the patient, giving greater legal weight to people's wishes and preferences, and improving as much as possible the ability of patients to make choices even when circumstances make this far from easy. Acknowledging the rising levels of coercion used within mental health services in the UK, it demands stronger, more transparent justification for using compulsory powers. Perhaps most importantly, it attempts to tackle the rising rates of people being involuntarily detained, particularly the disproportionate number of people from black and minority ethnic groups.

Working in Leicester, it has been impossible to ignore the fact that people from ethnic minorities are so much more likely to be subject to detention under the Mental Health Act. And that, even among that group, black men of African and Caribbean origin are significantly over-represented. What's more, once members of the latter group are detained, they are more likely to be diagnosed with schizophrenia, more likely to be put in seclusion, more likely to be sent to the locked ward, and more likely to progress to a secure unit. These statistics have been known for decades, reflecting many factors, including, of course, the profound inequalities and racism in our society.

It is a mistake to think of the problem as starting with the decision to legally detain someone – by the time this point is reached, it is often the only way forward. What is more important, as survey after survey has highlighted, are the inequities in access to treatment and experience of care. The best way to improve the care and outcomes for those with severe mental illness – whatever their ethnicity or cultural background – is to actively engage with them, try to understand them, and to provide early intervention that genuinely helps them turn their lives around before detention even becomes an issue.

For this reason, I was personally more worried about the under-representation of people from ethnic minority communities in our psychotherapy services, including the therapeutic community, than the high number on the wards of the secure unit. We tried to address the issue by encouraging referrals from disadvantaged groups, but change was frustratingly slow.

It is too easy to blame this dynamic on a fear of stigma within particular communities themselves. There is evidence that people from ethnic minorities anticipate that they will meet discrimination if they engage with mental health services and particularly fear being admitted to a mental health ward – dreading that the hospital will worsen, rather than improve, their mental distress. Tragically, there have been incidents of abuse and deaths on psychiatric wards. Such events have compounded the lack of trust that is a product of being disadvantaged by institutional power dynamics more generally. The result is that needs remain unmet, mental states deteriorate, and admission is precipitated by a crisis further down the line. Too often, this happens in a way that patients feel strips them of dignity and respect, thus perpetuating the fear and stigma.

From the clinicians' point of view, there are studies that show how racially prejudiced our perceptions of dangerousness can be, reminding us that unconscious racism can affect our clinical judgement. Geraldine was of mixed heritage: her mother was white

British, and her father, also British, was from a black Caribbean community. I always wondered how much this had affected the decisions that were made about her care. She was a big, strong woman and I can remember once sitting in a group where I thought she might seriously lose her temper, feeling anxious about how we would handle that. I don't know if my anxiety was higher because she was black, but given what we know about unconscious bias I cannot rule it out.

~

We admitted Geraldine into the therapeutic community, sharing the responsibility for keeping her safe with her until she was ready to take it on herself. Psychological containment is always the best option if at all possible but it often involves a degree of therapeutic risk-taking in the short term and the capacity to hold one's nerve.

Every psychiatrist has dangerous people in their caseload. The challenge is to identify which of them – a tiny minority – will actually make a serious attempt to harm another human being, and then to decide what type of intervention will best help them hold themselves together and begin to face and manage their dark urges and feelings. These clinical judgements need to be supported by a system that is sufficiently resourced and flexible enough to allow staff from different teams, with different perspectives and skills, to communicate freely and co-operatively around a patient's changing needs – much as happened with both Geraldine and Wayne.

While the technology and 'tools' that help us assess risk continue to improve, they will never rule out uncertainty, nor obviate the need for psychiatrists to make difficult clinical judgements. Meanwhile, there is little capacity in the system to provide the type of therapeutic relationships that build the in-depth under-standing that is so important in minimising risk. Clinicians are overstretched and have too much of their time taken up by bureau-cratic tasks. Moreover, most clinicians do not have access to the type of facilitated reflective space, training and supervision that might encourage the questioning of assumptions and unconscious prejudices that drive judgements towards too much, or indeed too little, restriction of liberty.

There will always be a need to keep the most dangerous people locked in – mostly for limited periods, but in some cases for the long term or even for ever. However, most people will manage better in the long run as voluntary patients. It is to be hoped that the government white paper modernising the Mental Health Act – with its aspiration to once again normalise voluntary admissions – will eventually become law. In the meantime, the principles it embodies should influence funding decisions, guide good practice and challenge mental health professionals to think more rigorously about the way they use the power the state has devolved to them.

6

WHO'S IN CHARGE?

Power relationships in the context of mental health should demand ongoing vigilance: one person's power can mean another person's disempowerment; one person's need for control can undermine the developing sense of agency in another.

Most of the patients in the therapeutic community arrive with very little sense of personal authority. Their behaviour is reactive, impulsive, unreflective. They are driven by their emotions, which have them in their grip and overwhelm their capacity to think. They are trapped by their addictive behaviours, which often started as ways of coping with unbearable emotion. They are imprisoned by their histories, old patterns of relationship intruding, unwanted, into the present. Some of them experience auditory hallucinations, the voices, impossible to silence, denigrating them or instructing them what to do. The task is to help them develop a sense of agency, to help them move into the driving seat after being thrown around in the back seat for most of their lives.

If things go well, they leave with a sense of being on a meaningful journey, rather than just surviving and reacting to what life throws at them.

In therapeutic communities, the staff don't have automatic authority. They must earn respect like everyone else, and the patients have to start taking back responsibility for themselves and share responsibility for each other. This is so much more than a 'right-on', politically correct, ideological stance. The process of empowerment can take us through dark places as deeply buried rage and shame is transferred into the room, played out in the – we hope – safe enough environment provided by the community. It is a jagged, often painful process that can expose extreme vulnerability.

~

Despite the formal medical hierarchy and years of having junior doctors and medical students to teach, train and supervise, nothing quite prepared me for becoming a consultant myself.

The consultant in charge of Francis Dixon Lodge when I first went there in 1985 as part of my training and whom I succeeded six years later was George Spaul. Taking over from such a giant of a man was one of the biggest challenges of my career. The realisation that the buck stopped with me, that there was no one to refer on to if the problem seemed too difficult or the burden felt too heavy, was compounded by the level of mistrust people felt towards me as the newcomer in charge, and the hostility many expressed.

Dr Spaul was a larger-than-life character, hugely compassionate and wise, with a wonderful twinkle in his eye and a good ear for the absurd. He was a general psychiatrist with a love of psychoanalysis. No one knew if he'd had any psychotherapy training or been psychoanalysed himself, and no one dared even think of asking. He had set up a residential democratic therapeutic community in the 1970s, in a self-contained rambling old building, Francis Dixon Lodge, with twenty-five beds and a staff team selected for their interest in the psychosocial aspects of therapy. It was mostly occupied by people who would now tend to attract the label of severe personality disorder, the community having learned by trial and error which patients tend to do well and which patients tend to do badly.

Dr Spaul had a reputation for standing up to tyrants and eschewing authoritarianism. Learning the difference between being authoritarian and being authoritative is one of the most important lessons one should learn as a leader, particularly in mental health. More than anyone I knew, Dr Spaul knew and embodied the difference. Having said that, he was of his generation and enjoyed the entitled authority that men of that era inhabited so easily, despite the roles they took up challenging the establishment. He was beloved and revered and a law unto himself. By the time I did my second stint of training, he was semi-retired and working part-time. The community meeting would start at 9 a.m. but there was always a sense of treading water until Dr Spaul (which he insisted on being called, despite other staff in this flattened hierarchy being known by their first names) would make an appearance at about 9.30. 'Just carry on as if I'm not here,' he would say. As if!

Nowadays, when leaders change so often, it is perhaps hard to fathom the intensity and drama that can follow when a long-standing charismatic leader moves on. I was one of many 'second-generation' NHS consultants being handed on a legacy by the charismatic pioneers who had dared to actualise such a provocative, countercultural model in the first place, so my story, although it feels very personal to me, is not unusual. Nothing had prepared me for that move: becoming the leader and taking over from a legend. Nothing could. Therapeutic communities in this era were a way of life for many staff and attracted people who were emotionally and politically hungry and passionate. It felt as if I was fighting to survive, residents and staff alike punishing me for not being (or for 'killing off') Dr Spaul, who had been forced to leave abruptly because of serious illness.

Within the unit, one or two staff were very supportive of me, but there were significant subgroups that were hostile, colluding with the residents' relentless negativity about my leadership. These residents were now missing meetings, flagrantly breaking rules, crossing their arms and jutting out their chins as they jeered and constantly found ways to put me in impossible situations.

Luckily, there was a close and supportive network of therapeutic communities across the country and there were one or two colleagues working in other cities who'd been through similar 'initiation rites' and understood very well what I was going through. At times the patients' hostility made me hate them, although this didn't completely crowd out my compassion for the suffering that had brought them into intensive therapy in the first place. One famous academic paper that I've found very helpful is 'Hate in the Counter-Transference' by the paediatrician and psychoanalyst Donald Winnicott. In this paper, he bravely broke two taboos, comparing the hatred therapists sometimes feel towards their patients to the hatred mothers can sometimes feel towards their babies. Hate in these roles is inevitable, Winnicott tells us, even necessary; the important thing is to be aware of such feelings.

I determined to play the long game, and so we battled on. I realised that what was going on wasn't necessarily against me personally: I embodied a younger generation, a new era in the NHS, and – probably most problematic for them – I was a woman. We also tried to keep Dr Spaul's departure on the agenda, acknowledging that they must be anxious and missing him, and understanding that what was being played out was, in part, a grieving process. There was one man, Shane, who had been particularly dependent on Dr Spaul and whose hatred towards me seemed on another level. He would literally spit out his words, his face contorted and cruel. Spurred on by what had become an adolescent culture of bullying, contempt and provocative risk-taking, his language was becoming increasingly vile and his sentiments more violently pornographic. I tried to remember that he must be feeling at least as frightened as I was. Putting Dr Spaul on a pedestal, projecting heroic qualities onto him, had made Shane feel temporarily safe. But I knew only too well that idealisation has its dark side: splitting the world into good and bad, and directing so much unquestioning love onto one parental figure, meant someone else had to be denigrated. Some of the staff were urging me to discharge him, but although I was happy to stand up for myself, I wanted the community to take responsibility for this decision. Sure enough, his threats towards me gradually began to offend some of the patient group who were at last starting to debate what was and was not acceptable and take some responsibility for themselves. What had turned into something like a gang of thugs was becoming a working community again.

All this took months to play out. There were dire moments, much tossing and turning and agonising through sleepless nights, along with miserable spells of self-doubt. But I have to acknowledge that, despite the strain, I also found work during this time terribly exciting, drama on drama, my brain whirring at double speed and adrenalin levels similar to a heart surgeon's. Strangely, I didn't once question if I wanted the job. I was passionate about the patients, passionate about the model of therapy and optimistic about the developments we might make.

~

In the background to this messy period of succession, it soon emerged that several consultants in the wider organisation had been waiting for the moment Dr Spaul finally retired, eagerly plotting what they might do with the building and the money. It wasn't just my leadership; the existence of the therapeutic community itself was under threat.

This was the era of closing asylums and moving as many people as possible out into the community. A number of therapeutic communities across the country had closed, in one or two cases following scandals that inevitably tarnished people's attitude towards this way of working more generally. Even without such scandals, there had always been people who found the concept of a therapeutic community threatening. The 1990s have been branded the 'decade of the brain' in psychiatry because many of the leaps in innovation seemed to be in the realm of neuroscience and pharmacology, and there was a lot more choice in the drugs that could be offered. It is sadly true that this attracted more attention than the gritty problem of how to provide healing environments and intervene psychologically. Cognitive behavioural therapy (CBT) was on the rise and, with its easy-to-measure outcomes and quick time frames, was the perfect fit with the short-termism and fixation on markets and monetary cost that was beginning to colour the culture of the NHS. Twelve months of intensive residential therapy in a therapeutic community for a group of unpopular patients with a history of deliberately harming themselves seemed an excessive expense to a lot of people, and there was no shortage of ideas about alternative ways to spend the money. I had to show the outside world, first, that we worked and, second, that we were worth the cost.

The timing for all this coincided with the first major attack by Margaret Thatcher's government on the NHS, with the introduction of the 'purchaser–provider' split, and the importing of a certain kind of manager from the business world. Most of those who worked for the NHS had long seen it as a benign parent (if a rather sleepy one). Now it was becoming more cut-throat. Everything was changing. It wasn't just my patients who were turning on the consultant. In hindsight, this period was the start of a process of disempowering doctors and other professionals that continues to this day.

The one subject we didn't broach in much depth back then was the fact that I was a woman – an omission that now seems extraordinary. At the time, I just wanted to show I could do the job as well as a man. But I was learning very quickly that the anxieties around me, the lower expectations, the intrusive levels of personal scrutiny, the readiness to see weakness – in other words, the particular projections I attracted *as a woman* – meant that my experience of doing the job was very different from that of male colleagues. Much later, through reading and discussion and further training, it was affirming to realise that these observations and feelings I was struggling to articulate were commonplace.

Authenticity is a quality highly regarded in modern leaders, but so easily exploited in women. Research studies show that women leaders are particularly visible, with people noticing much more about our appearance – our clothes, our hair, the bags under our eyes – than they do about the appearance of our male equivalents. Compared with men, we also tend to feel and show our vulnerability more. The combination of the two has led organisation consultants to describe the 'visibility–vulnerability spiral'.[1] The phenomenon is amplified if you are part of a minority group, as was still the case for women consultants in the early 1990s. Later in my career, I promoted two black women to senior positions – a much smaller minority group – and was appalled by how much they were forced to struggle with this dynamic – exacerbated, of course, by racist projections.

The so-called glass ceiling that stops women going for the top jobs has been studied from many angles. One perspective that makes a lot of sense to me as a psychotherapist is the Madonna–whore dynamic: the notion that women are meant to nurture and that any move away from this role is seen as a betrayal of that ideal. I'm a naturally facilitative, nurturing person, but like anyone moving into a leadership role, I found there was less time for informal supportive chat with the individuals I now managed, less room in my brain to hold in mind each person's struggles. Stepping up, I was more distant, more preoccupied with the politics of the wider organisation, too concerned about the survival of the unit itself to always smile encouragingly or ask how someone's child was getting on at their new school. It seems from the research that, generally speaking, men are less concerned with their colleagues' everyday lives than women in the first place, and that people are more forgiving of such changes in men as they take up positions of authority, presumably feeling more comfortable with deeply embedded traditional gender stereotypes. In women, that change in role from nurturer (mother figure) to boss (father figure) can trigger a primitive rage, often unconscious and easily channelled into righteous contempt.

Perhaps too, as a woman brought up in a traditional family and subject to the same gender stereotypes as everyone else, I struggled to feel that I was right in the role. An irrational little bit of me felt I had taken it under false pretences: too young, as well as the wrong gender. Impostor syndrome had not entered common parlance in those days.

My lack of confidence was exacerbated by other people's reaction to the changing of the guard, a new generation taking the reins. Dr Spaul himself was very keen for me to succeed him, but assumed I would keep everything essentially the same, an extension of his own leadership rather than a leader in my own right. Once I started to make changes, it seemed that his attitude to me soured very quickly. Not such an unusual dynamic, but for many years he had been a warm and affirming mentor and the loss of his goodwill was painful – even though I realised by this time he was very sick.

Many years later, with Dr Spaul long since dead, we had to make the difficult decision to close the beds in the therapeutic community and become a day unit. It was a financially driven decision and, having established that there was really no choice, I addressed the task with positive pragmatism. Nevertheless, I found myself depressed and thrown back into an inner world of parental archetypes: sparring with a stern and disappointed Dr Spaul in troubling dreams, trying to persuade him that it was the right thing to do, the only thing to do, trying to win his understanding, even begging his forgiveness.

~

Therapeutic communities have never become mainstream. Given that we live in an age of supposed service-user 'empowerment', this is hard to understand. The situation might have been different if the government had been serious about sustaining their project to expand services for people with a diagnosis of severe personality disorder. A Department of Health project was launched in 2003 to great fanfare – but, as so often happens, this turned out to be little more than an expensive whim, with the central funding for projects stopped after three years and handed over to local commissioners and market forces to drive decisions about funding in the future.

For anyone not familiar with NHS politics, please note that there is very little link between so-called market forces in the NHS and what patients want and need. It is much more about prioritising – and placing in competition – different patient groups, and then initiating a bidding process between providers to see who can offer the cheapest service. For years, we had long lists of patients who'd been referred from clinicians outside Leicestershire, but we weren't allowed to admit them because they hadn't had funding approved.

Despite our fears, there were some benefits in moving from a residential to a day unit and the move was greatly helped by the careful use of mobile phones – by this time commonplace – to keep in contact with each other. Initially, it put many of the patients in touch with feelings of rejection, abandonment and even fear, but most of them came round to the idea, realising that as well as being less stigmatising, attending daily stopped them becoming overly dependent, allowed them to keep their accommodation, and avoided such a traumatic transition at the end of therapy. It also allowed us to set up a diverse selection of outpatient groups, trying to tailor the service to the needs of the population. Some, however, couldn't make the transition; they needed residential care and couldn't be safely contained on a nine-to-five basis. Many years after we closed, I continued to find it heartbreaking to assess such individuals then have to tell them we had nothing to offer, knowing full well that many of them would end up in prison or homeless, and that some of them would kill themselves.

To my mind, the most important wisdom to come out of therapeutic communities is a different way of thinking about authority and power relations. In truth, most of us have our breaking points, but it's all too easy in mental health organisations to overemphasise the difference between us and our patients. In so doing, we deny our own fears of death and madness while exaggerating the vulnerability in our patients, sometimes remaining blind to their strengths. Some patients will be comfortable with stereotypes of themselves as weak and helpless and the staff as powerful, caring and helpful as it gives hope to their wish to be nurtured and protected. Others fight against being dependent but often end up being labelled as 'difficult'. Ultimately, such projections deplete all concerned and make therapeutic change more difficult.

Good psychiatric practice involves flexible leadership styles. Of course, there are times when patients are at high risk or out of touch with reality, when we have to step up, issue commands and take control. In my experience, psychiatrists tend to be better at this 'command and control' end of things than they are at collaborative working with their patients – not surprisingly, given much of our medical education was about coping with emergencies. But the patients' recovery will suffer if we get stuck in this role. If we refuse to step back down from our pedestal at the top and fail to start nudging them to begin taking back some of their autonomy, they will remain disempowered. We need to find ways to renegotiate the power imbalance and consequent responsibility issues as soon as the crisis is over.

Failing to do so can lead to serious problems in psychiatry, in particular a syndrome known as 'malignant regression', where a patient and the staff in an inpatient unit can find themselves in a sometimes deadly battle for control. Anxious to stop the patient killing himself, the psychiatrist understandably takes increasing steps to restrict his freedom. For some very disempowered people, however, having the capacity to self-harm or make a suicide attempt is the only thing that gives them any sense of agency; it is the only thing left that they feel they can control. The more the psychiatrist restricts their freedom, the more obsessed they become with this ultimate action. In doing so, they end up – paradoxically – being extremely powerful, dominating the attention of the ward staff in their ever more desperate determination to die.

I once attended a case conference at Leicester Royal Infirmary about a young woman, Trish, who had run out of the A&E department, managed to dodge security and climb onto some scaffolding and had then thrown herself off. The cost of that meeting alone must have been enormous, with another psychiatry consultant present, as well as an A&E consultant, an orthopaedic consultant, no fewer than three executive directors from across two trusts, two senior nurses and a handful of nurses from the wards. But this was nothing compared with the cost of her treatment, which had included five weeks in intensive care followed by eight months on an orthopaedic ward, much of that time having additional one-to-one care from a psychiatric nurse as well as intense support from the orthopaedic team. Trish had tried to kill herself on many occasions. She did not suffer from schizophrenia, bipolar disorder, severe clinical depression or dementia. She was diagnosed as suffering from severe personality disorder and, because I was the specialist in personality disorder, everyone was looking to me to advise them about the way forward.

Trish was still in her early twenties, but she was already well known on the psychiatric wards, having taken her first overdose at the age of fifteen – the age her mother had been when she got pregnant after being gang-raped. I, too, knew her well: she'd been admitted to the therapeutic community three years earlier but had attempted to hang herself from a tree in the grounds after only a few weeks – a 'near miss' that had shaken us deeply. I'd continued to see her as an outpatient, trying to keep the other professionals involved with her calm and trying to avoid a hospital admission. But it couldn't last. And once she'd got herself admitted to an acute ward, things went from bad to worse very quickly, with a dramatic escalation in the frequency and severity of her suicidal behaviour.

What could I contribute to this discussion that would help? The orthopaedic surgeon was angry. His team had managed her at great cost on their ward. She would be able to leave his ward in two months' time when her injuries improved, although she would be wheelchair-dependent for the rest of her life and would suffer a lot of pain. 'It's your turn now. Just lock her away and keep her safe – why's that so difficult? She's obviously mad – just look what she's done to herself – thrown herself off the scaffolding just to get attention.' The other psychiatrist was relatively inexperienced, and I knew only too well how much he dreaded Trish returning to the ward, the inevitable regression, the high risk of suicide, the detrimental effect on his staff team and the other patients. All eyes were on me.

How could I usefully change this conversation? I thought back to patients such as Geraldine, who had done so much better once the system had changed direction and – rather than putting their efforts into fruitlessly restricting their autonomy – started to support them to regain control of their lives. As with Geraldine, it would be a risk, but it was clear from the faces of the people around me that other options had been exhausted. I took a deep breath and tried to explain that, technically, Trish wasn't mad and long-term use of the Mental Health Act would be problematic. I told them that there was research showing that people like Trish did particularly badly on general psychiatry acute wards. Although locking her away seemed the obvious solution, all the evidence from her own history suggested that restricting her freedom only served to focus her mind on this one act of desperation and made her suicidal behaviour even worse. I suggested that the discussion about whether or not she really wanted to die was not going to get us very far, as 'living' – 'being a person' – was intimately bound up with the ability to make choices, and that Trish had reached a point where the only meaningful choice she felt she could exercise was about self-harm and suicide.

I told them the story of a patient of mine with a terrible history of suicide attempts who had managed herself increasingly well by keeping razor blades tucked away safely in the cup of her bra – she found them a comforting reminder that she still had a choice about whether she lived or died, and it was this sense of agency that empowered her to make positive changes in her life. The therapeutic community tolerated this logic for a while, but eventually put pressure on her to give up the razor blades, a decision that, sure enough, resulted in a severe suicide attempt.

How do you explain that, for some people, harming themselves is the only thing that makes them feel alive, that suicidal behaviour is the only way they can imagine of having some sense of agency, of making an impact on the world? That the best way of reducing this risk is to help them feel more in control, not less. Like most people labelled as attention-seekers, Trish had never been able to attract the sort of attention that she really needed. Helping her think about this and addressing her basic practical needs – considerable, given she now had a chronic physical disability – might be the best way forward. Paradoxically, patients such as Trish respond badly to heroic attempts to rescue them, but sometimes do well with long-term care plans: realistic expectations broken down into manageable goals; low-key interventions; consistent supportive relationships with firm boundaries and a collaborative manner.

Doctors, nurses and NHS managers are not the best at paradox and the orthopaedic surgeon walked out as I was speaking. But to my surprise, enough of them grasped what I was saying. Trish was eventually discharged into the community under the watch of a very experienced social worker, along with physiotherapy and occupational therapy support for her physical disability. I agreed to supervise the social worker and support her with the risk management. It was far from straightforward: we just about managed to hold our nerve, and deal with the self-harm in a practical, matter-of-fact way, while not allowing her increased risk behaviour to hijack the care plan. The A&E consultant – who thankfully did understand what we were trying to achieve – agreed a special care plan for her when she self-harmed. She would be fast-tracked and seen as soon as possible by senior staff who would be kind and attentive to her injuries but move her on as quickly as possible. In this way, we hoped to cut out all the hours spent waiting around, trying and failing to get people's attention, threatening to run off or further damage herself, while, at the same time, absorbing mixed and sometimes hostile messages from busy front-line staff. This plan proved so successful that the two of us set up regular meetings to identify other frequent attenders where a similar package might be efficient in the long term.

Rather to everyone's surprise and relief – including my own – Trish's behaviour started to settle down. This was very much down to the hard-working social worker who had just the right mix of intelligent kindness, immense patience, and the courage to keep her eyes firmly on the long game and not be panicked into over-reaction. No one would choose to live life with a crushed pelvis but, for Trish, being disabled seemed to provide her with the type of regular practical attention she could just about manage.

Maybe the physical pain helped too in a way that is counter-intuitive and hard for most of us to get our heads around. Many people who cut themselves talk about converting psychological pain into physical pain and the relief that this brings, or how physical pain can break the sense of numbness and make them feel alive. There may also be something comforting about being *visibly* disabled, when you feel deeply, but invisibly, disabled by emotional scars. In my early days as a consultant, I unwisely persuaded a plastic surgeon to operate on the facial scars of a young man who had seemed to have made good progress in the therapeutic community and put the days of desperately lacerating his face behind him. To everyone's dismay, getting rid of the scars caused a massive regression to his old behaviours. Although on one level he had wanted the scars removed, at a deeper level he still needed this visible sign that he was damaged and far from well.

The process of empowering our patients can frustrate us with paradox at every turn. It is so easy to project our own prejudices and needs, so easy to think we're working collaboratively, while failing to listen properly, failing to understand from the inside.

~

Therapeutic communities are by no means the only movement to challenge the projections that can unhelpfully prolong the patient inhabiting the sick role – the Recovery Movement, for example, embedded in work done by survivor groups, takes a very positive stance to prognosis after a psychotic illness and sets out to identify and build on individuals' strengths. But it is therapeutic communities that have vigilantly unpicked the mechanisms of disempowerment at the level of essential day-to-day interpersonal exchange.

I came to picture the therapeutic community as a kind of living laboratory, an organisation that can be experienced and observed at the same time, with everyone involved trying to understand the power relations that are being enacted and, ideally, learning about and owning their own part in the dramas unfolding. It gave me invaluable insights into how we can take control of our lives and how others can facilitate or interfere with this process.

7

HOPE AND DESPAIR

Therapeutic communities are based on the age-old philosophy that we do better together than on our own; that the ingredients necessary for an individual to thrive lie within the matrix of relationships provided within a healthy community.

Some of us grow up within such a matrix. We learn that love can be more or less trusted, that people are on the whole dependable. We have a relatively secure sense of who we are and some confidence that we can manage our thoughts and feelings. As adults we build on this positive start, blessed with the fundamental interpersonal tools to manage more complex relationships and life events.

The people we try to help in therapeutic communities have been unlucky in their early experiences. The networks of relationships in which they've lived have been damaging. Connections with others have been sparse, overloaded with vile projections or abruptly and randomly terminated. And their inner connections are consequently jumbled and chaotic. They are fragmented: thinking one thing, feeling another. Their mood swings are violent and make no sense. Feelings and thoughts consume them but often feel alien. They have little sense of who they are, sometimes feeling as if they are a different person from one day to the next. Haunted by the past, terrified of the future, they find it hard to live in the present. Their capacity for intelligent trust is damaged, and many, disabled by their poor intuition and desperation for contact, flit from one abusive relationship to the next. In a desperate attempt to get some control, some hit out against the world with violence; others turn on themselves and come to rely on lonely, self-absorbed coping mechanisms, often ending up hooked into self-destructive patterns that take hold and seem to possess them. Many of our patients are trapped in a state of deep despair. For them, connection feels impossible, absent or severed, and the sense of emptiness and impotence is overwhelming.

The therapeutic community gives people another chance to make healthy connections. All groups of people will do better if there is a focus on getting relationships right. But in therapeutic communities, the aspiration is that such an experience will be transformative, have a lasting effect on the individual, kindle a more hopeful engagement with the world, even change the connections within the brain. This idea is at the heart of all psychoanalytic therapies: that good relationships can be internalised, connections within the mind strengthened; the 'self' (or 'ego' as psychoanalysts call it) emerging more defined, more flexible, more robust.

That's the intention – but sometimes working in mental health can feel very bleak; it seems that nothing we do makes any difference, especially with people who seem locked into mad and despairing inner worlds.

~

It is January 2002, about halfway through my twenty-year stint leading the service at Francis Dixon Lodge. We have just returned after the Christmas break. I've had a tiring but nourishing family Christmas. The children were upset when I left this morning and I would have dearly loved a few more days at home with them. But Christmas is always a difficult time in the therapeutic community so I didn't feel I could take any more leave.

Of course, Christmas is supposed to be about hope and new beginnings, a time of comfort and joy. But there is little of that evident here today. I sense the despair as soon as I walk through the door and can feel my spirits plummeting. The community meeting feels lifeless and empty from the start. Numbers are down as two residents have not returned after the Christmas break.

Lotti is asked how she is feeling. She was referred originally from the rehabilitation service after spending almost half of the last five years in hospital because her self-harming was so severe and life-threatening. Her progress over six months in the therapeutic community has been dramatic and she has shown herself to be a woman of strong principle and courage. But today she's utterly bleak. She asks for sleeping tablets: 'It's too much. I need to switch off . . . I cry and cry and cry and cry . . . it's not right to cry as much as this . . . it's never going to end.' She describes her experience of endless days stretching into nights, her thoughts of death and her preoccupation with suicide: 'It's like looking longingly into a sweet shop. I know I mustn't go in but I just can't drag myself away.'

As a very lonely child, Lotti had populated her inner world with characters absent in her life. She invented playmates – one loyal, one very naughty, a strong and brave father figure, a wise auntie. Over the years, these characters became so real to her that she'd been treated with antipsychotic medication – the dosage escalating very quickly as her self-harm became more danger-ous. When I first met her, it was impossible to do an assessment because she was so heavily sedated. From Lotti's perspective, the staff on the acute psychiatric ward had forced her, brutally, to say these characters weren't real. She experienced this as an unin-vited violation that had robbed her of any sense of meaning or, in her words, 'broken me' – hence the escalating suicidal behaviour. Three years down the line, a more enlightened rehabilitation con-sultant had realised how essential these inner-world characters were to Lotti and encouraged her to talk about them. As he lis-tened, he realised how much of her creativity, goodness and hope they carried. In an absence of flesh-and-blood connections, they had held her together and life without them seemed unbearable.

We suggest links to her lonely childhood but she just shakes her head. 'I didn't really think about being lonely,' she says. 'It was all I'd known, I just got on with it. My friends were there – I know they were pretend, but they really helped – and it was good in the cupboard together, the cupboard was safe.'

It's difficult to hear her because she speaks so quietly. I say this to her. 'It's as if you're speaking to yourself, as if there's no one else in the room.'

She nods her head in agreement. 'I'm utterly alone. Deep down I know nobody understands. I just want to sleep and sleep . . .' I seem to have captured how she is experiencing the group and this sense of aloneness is the only reality she's in touch with at the moment. She doesn't hear my all-important 'as if'.

The meeting darkens further as Alison describes dumping her boyfriend. She says he is the best thing that ever happened to her but she feels agonisingly anxious whenever she's with him. 'It's fucking ridiculous, farcical. I'm just a stupid cunt.' She carries on in this vein, her tone so contemptuous towards herself that I have a picture of her self-lacerating. The patient chairing the meeting asks if anyone wants to say anything to Alison but she asks in a way that is reminiscent of the type of boring business meeting where everyone wants to tick off the agenda items and get home as early as possible.

Alison suddenly yells, 'Of course no one is going to give me any fucking feedback. No one here gets me. No one's been through what I've been through.' Then, decibels rising, 'I'm a freak.' Then great shuddering sobs: 'I'm never going to have another relationship.'

Vague reassuring platitudes are uttered. Then, more helpfully, someone tries to link Alison's feelings towards Izza, her boyfriend – or rather ex-boyfriend – with her feelings towards her father who died of cancer a few months ago. Alison responds by telling us more about the death, about how her father would beg her to keep him warm and she would get into bed and put her arms round him, 'like a skeleton, his skin and eyes a ghastly yellow'. There is nothing warm or touching about the way she tells this story. It is followed by an uncomfortable silence. I realise that I too just want this awful meeting to end.

Adrian then tells us about Christmas with his mother. He was referred to us by the eating disorder team after two years as an inpatient being treated for severe anorexia nervosa. It is hoped that a spell in the therapeutic community will help him establish some independence from his neurotic and overbearing mother, but this morning Adrian seems unaware of this therapeutic agenda: 'I had a lovely time with Mummy'; 'Mummy was really helpful'; 'Mummy put little cards with the number of calories on all my food, so I didn't have to worry'; 'Mummy thought it would be a treat to watch our favourite Disney films together.'

'If you say "Mummy" once more, I'm gonna have to thump you!' Bill interrupts. There's a titter of laughter and I suspect everyone is thinking the same. Adrian looks crushed.

'Isn't that a threat to harm?' someone asks self-righteously.

'Whaaaat!' Bill responds, shaking his head in disbelief.

There follows a debate about whether saying 'I'm gonna have to thump you' is breaking the rules. Bill eventually gives a half-hearted apology. He insists that he didn't mean the threat to be taken seriously and that we all know that really. 'You lot crease me up! You're so bloody mardy!'

Well, that's an understatement, I think to myself. Bill is right; the whole debate feels like a distraction from the despair in the room.

In the staff 'after-group' we try to think in more depth about the group dynamics. We share our fear that we are losing connection with Lotti and acknowledge there is a heightened risk that she might kill herself. I become aware that I've been feeling anxious about the students: they seem so young to be amid such despair. I try to think of ways to explore these issues in a way they might relate to. I ask them if they've read the Harry Potter books? They haven't but they've both seen the film. Harry Potter is forced by his ghastly step-parents to live in the cupboard under the stairs, so I tell them how frequently cupboards appear in our patients' narratives. Sometimes the cupboard is the feared place of punishment, dark, cramped, airless and locked, but sometimes, as with Lotti, it is a safe and private place. If you're deprived of physical affection, curling up in a small place where you can feel the walls around you can offer some sort of comfort. One of the students, Martin, then manages to say how repulsed he is by the thought of Alison in bed with her dad. Alison is twenty, about their age. 'It just doesn't feel right,' he says, shuddering.

In the run-up to Christmas, the atmosphere had been different. There had been a lot of stories of hateful parents getting drunk on Christmas Day, sadistically breaking their children's toys, or worse – envious parents are at their most hateful on birthdays and festivals. For some of our patients, Christmas is remembered as the day they were first physically or sexually abused. Others had talked about being ignored and neglected by the grown-ups, then experimenting with cutting themselves in an attempt to rid themselves of the painful yearning, the burning resentment and the dreaded sense of emptiness. Harrowing stuff, but helpful links were made, the sharing was constructive, there was a sense of solidarity.

There is nothing like that sense of pre-Christmas camaraderie around today to relieve the gloom. Hope lies in making connections but the stark truth about extreme despair is that nothing seems to work.

Psychiatrist and psychoanalyst Professor Bob Hinshelwood, who also worked in therapeutic communities for much of his career, wrote about mental health work as follows:

The particular work that is required of psychiatric staff is 'anxiety work'. It means coping with high levels of psychological tension and it requires withstanding the intolerable. We must do first what the patient, his intimate relatives or his friends and neighbours, and other professional helpers cannot do – that is, to bear his experiences. This is a tall order, and it faces the service with the problem that staff must face unbearable suffering.[1]

There are more positive ways of describing the job, but on bleak days, these words get to the nub of the matter.

~

Group therapy aims to establish an ever-developing network of connections between people – where disturbance can be processed and thought about. This can happen only if the relationships formed are sufficiently strong and healthy to withstand the destructive potential of the disturbance being unleashed.

In the therapeutic community, we try to make things feel safe, with clear expectations and a robust structure to the day. Newcomers can find our adherence to the timetable a bit obsessional, but it is important for people whose childhood was spent in environments where supposedly responsible adults failed to protect them. A small child shut in a cupboard has little sense of time and fears she will be there forever. It is important to know that the community meeting will end at 10.30; that tea and toast will follow, whatever the conflicts that emerged; that there will be an expectation that they join an activity group later in the morning, rather than struggle alone with their pain.

Of course, none of this is straightforward. We are all of us complex beings, with drives taking us in contradictory directions. New patients arrive desperately wanting to change while at the same time clinging to their old ways of coping: the quick release of punching someone, the sharp physical shock of carving into their own flesh, the immediate comfort of bingeing on chocolate, smoking a joint or downing a bottle of vodka. Anything to avoid facing the emotional pain. Many of them experience the structure of the programme at the start of their stay as persecutory. They feel neglected. They so want to be understood, to feel better in themselves but instead feel resentful, angry and hurt, thrown back on old patterns of defending themselves.

'Stick with your feelings,' the more senior residents tell them. 'It gets worse before it gets better.'

At its best, the community will have a group of seasoned residents who have begun to experience the benefits. They too found the programme difficult when they first arrived. They too experienced the rules as rigid and uncaring and kicked against the boundaries. But they have been around long enough to see how the place works, to see that pouring out your feelings without any limits can leave one feeling overexposed and overwhelmed. They have debated, argued and perhaps voted for a change in the rules or a modification to the programme; so they have a sense of ownership, a sense that it is *their* programme, *their* rules. They speak with candour about their experience: the hardships they have suffered, but also their own weakness and misjudgements. They reach out to others with compassion while challenging wrongdoing. Beginning to know themselves better, they speak with heart and mind aligned. As they become more authentic, they grow in authority.

With senior residents like this, staff can relax a bit. But, like English weather, it never lasts for long. Change is so bloody difficult and psychological progress defies straight lines. There are long spells when the patient community seems weak. It is tempting to step into the gaps, but better to hold back, to leave the group members to find their way through and discover their potency – nudging them in the right direction rather than taking over. It would be easy for the group to become a place where one individual patient after another is directly helped by me and my colleagues – 'After all, isn't this what you're paid for?' It can be seductive for a short time, becoming the Person-Who-Really-Understands, but such idealisation is never trustworthy and often brings fear and envy in its wake. Far better to direct our interventions to the group as a whole and contain our anxiety as the group struggles to re-form and find its strength. It is then that tiny miracles emerge.

Often these start in the kitchen.

⁓

Kim feels sad for Lotti with her terrible bouts of bleak tearfulness, so decides to make her a special cake. She has not made a cake before but is part of the team responsible for menu planning this month and has been looking through recipe books. Julie offers to help her and spots a picture of a cake covered in smarties. It reminds her of a sweet shop and resonates with the bleak analogy Lotti used in the community meeting. All goes well at first: two cake tins full of mixture are safely put in the oven and the timer set.

An hour later, Kim is alone in the kitchen and, in her enthusiasm, starts to decorate the cake. The sponge is still warm and the smarties start to melt. Kim is now in a panic and scrapes off the

gooey smartie mix, some of the still-warm sponge coming away
with the melted chocolate and odd-looking bits of bright-coloured
smartie shell. The pristine sponge she was so proud of now looks
a sorry mess. I happen to arrive in the kitchen at this moment to
find Kim in a furious rage with herself.

'Fucking cunt,' she mutters, over and over. 'Fucking useless
cunt.'

She looks as if she might tip the whole thing into the bin and
is pacing around seriously agitated, still clutching the chocolate-
smeared knife. I spotted Julie watching TV in the room next door
as I walked through and beckon her over, then start making soothing platitudes about the cake and gently ask Kim to give me the
knife. She throws the knife on the floor but carries on pacing and
punching her face, contorted in hatred towards herself. I start
to tell her about a cake I'd made recently that went disastrously
wrong but I know she can hardly hear me. Kim, I know, was often
cruelly humiliated as a kid, and the depth of rage and shame she's
in touch with is frightening for her. I'm feeling frightened for her
myself and weighing up whether to leave Kim alone for a minute
while I gather some more help.

Julie bounces in: 'Smells fantastic!'

Then, taking in the situation: 'What the hell?! Why didn't you
wait for me?' I give her a look, willing Julie to take it gently. This
could go either way, I'm thinking. Then she looks at Kim, who
is now sitting on the floor, head buried under her arms but still
shaking. 'You idiot!' she shouts. There is a short silence, then she
bursts out laughing.

'I know I'm a fucking idiot!' Kim mutters, but the laughter
is getting to her and, to my relief, she realises Julie is laughing at

the situation, not at her. By the time Julie joins her to sit on the floor, sloppily fingering the gooey mess into her mouth, Kim is laughing too – well, I think she's laughing, it's difficult to tell as she still has her head buried.

'Here, Penny. Try some!' Julie says as she passes the plate over. 'Kim's invented a new type of chocolate cream!'

'We could make some butter icing,' I suggest later, and while Julie offers to go to the shop to buy some more smarties, I get a sharp knife and help Kim cut a thin, clean slice off the top of the now properly cooled sponge.

Making a cake might seem very ordinary, but our patients' lives have been sadly lacking in the ordinary. Creating the opportunity for such ordinary living–learning experiences is therefore essential. Good therapeutic community staff try to interact in an ordinary way while thinking about what's going on in the patient's mind and in their own mind and always remembering that they are there for their patients, not the other way round. This may sound simple, but in fact it's professionalism at its most sophisticated. The point is Kim has never made a cake, and never thought of herself as someone who could ever make a cake. Something has shifted and that is heart-warming.

And in some ways it's not ordinary at all. How extraordinary that it is Lotti's profound despair that inspires this kind gesture in Kim and Julie, this impulse to try to connect through food, through creating something both tangible and symbolic.

Despite the grim morning meeting, I leave for home feeling it's been a good day.

~

After I'm gone, the community gathers for the evening meeting. This is a chance to talk about tensions that have emerged during the day, and a chance for people to register issues that are bothering them and might bubble up during the night. If you are struggling not to take a razor to your thighs or battling with a craving for cocaine, it can be helpful that others are aware, holding you in mind, watching out for you – although, of course, such things can be hard to admit to yourself, let alone a roomful of people. Secrets are inevitable. At times people just want to be left alone with their secret behaviours, but at least we have a structure that tries to minimise these risks, that tries to make regression to old ways more difficult.

Julie and Kim have decided to talk about their cooking project. They'd presented the cake to Lotti earlier in the evening and her main response was bemusement. Nevertheless, she hadn't thrown the cake at them, as we'd feared she might, and had shared it out – albeit cutting herself a very small slice and carefully removing the smarties.

One or two people tell Kim the cake was delicious.

'You did a great job,' Bill tells her. He is particularly protective towards Kim. 'Can I put in an order for my birthday next month?'

'When's that then, birthday boy?' Julie asks, grinning.

Bill shakes his head vigorously. 'I can't believe I said that! No one knows when my birthday is. I never celebrate it.' He laughs ruefully and refuses to give a date.

Someone asks Adrian if he's OK. She'd noticed him hurriedly leaving the room when the cake was being shared.

'I'm fine,' he says. (Tim describes him to us in the following day's handover as 'smiling sweetly, but dangerously'.) 'I'm quite happy for you all to eat cake, I just don't want to watch it.'

'How do you think that makes me and Kim feel?' Julie asks, annoyed.

'That is not my business,' Adrian retorts smugly.

'Wanker!' Julie mutters to herself, but loud enough for others to hear.

'You do sound a bit angry . . .' Tim suggests to Adrian. Like me, Tim's not finding it easy to like this young man. 'I can understand you must have felt a bit left out. Maybe . . . maybe we'd forgotten that eating cake is a big deal for you?'

'A provocation and a torture is how I would put it, but no need for anyone to worry.' His diction is precise, but he means the opposite of what he says.

Ben, the chair, suggests Adrian talks more about it the next day, but Julie, having expressed her frustration, is now feeling generous. (She's on a roll today.)

'Well, I kinda get it. If someone cuts up in front of me, I feel really fucked off. It's like disrespect. It's like . . . like Too Much Pressure.'

'Perhaps Adrian would like to eat cake but doesn't trust himself?' someone else volunteers, a patient who also struggles with an eating disorder.

Adrian looks on, detached, as if the group is talking about someone else, and indeed, it is interesting that they have started to talk about him, rather than to him.

'Shouldn't we leave this topic now as Ben has already suggested?' he says, still sounding worryingly supercilious.

Julie goes back to muttering under her breath.

Tim feels for her. She's tried to reach out to Adrian, but it takes two to make a connection.

~

Sometimes it feels impossible to pull patients out of their despairing circular logic. Sadly, Adrian didn't change very much during his time with us. Whenever he got near to glimpsing his underlying problems, he regressed back into his eating disorder, replacing any tentative connection to us with an obsessive connection to food, weight and body image. After six months, his weight had dropped dangerously low and he returned to the eating disorder team.

A few years later, he is referred to our service once again. Reading between the lines, no one knows what to do with him. The eating disorder team, whom I respect enormously, has run out of ideas. None of us seems able to get him to a point where he can engage with the psychological conflicts that so restrict him. Nevertheless, it can sometimes be productive to cast a fresh pair of eyes over a long-standing problem and I hope this will be the case with Adrian.

I am shocked when I see him. He is still only in his mid-thirties but looks twenty years older than that. Where once his low weight had made him seem a boyish Peter Pan, he now seems middle-aged, his body frail, his face ravaged with furrows, his muscles starkly delineated. It is clear from one look at him that Adrian is feeling utterly despairing about his life: my task is not to persuade him otherwise, but to try to find a seed of hope deep within him and create the conditions where this might grow.

Since his mother died of cancer, he has struggled to look after himself. He has inherited his mother's house but effectively camps rather than lives there, not having managed to sort through her possessions and afraid to throw anything away. His distorted connection with food overwhelms any attempt to connect with people and increasingly occupies every bit of his conscious mind. It sounds like torture to me, the constant struggle to deprive himself, the desperate bingeing, the violent vomiting, all closing in on him in an ever-tightening circle. He talks about food in the way some misogynists talk about women, as if food has a mind of its own, always out to seduce him, trap him, get the better of him. He doesn't trust himself to keep food in the house so lives off ready-made sandwiches and the occasional pack of soup. He restricts the amount of money he takes out with him so he can't be tempted to buy more food, but then responds to urges to binge and often ends up stealing. Sometimes he'll rip open the packaging and devour a cake in the shop, then, disgusted with himself, puke into a bag as soon as he gets into the car.

I feel overwhelmed by the hold these behaviour patterns have over him and wonder how on earth I can help him. I don't feel hopeful. He desperately needs to make a meaningful relationship with someone if he is ever to relinquish his pathological relationship to food, but his motivation or capacity to connect seems minimal. I decide to ask Angie, one of our nurses, to see him for regular supportive psychotherapy. In the psychotherapy world, people get very heated comparing different models of therapy, but the one consistent finding that links to good outcome is the strength of the relationship between patient and therapist, what we call the therapeutic alliance. This in turn links to qualities in the therapist such as sensitivity and empathy.

Angie is down to earth, kind, straightforward. There is just a chance she will be able to get through where other therapists have failed. I also refer him to a social worker, wondering if it's possible to link him in to a community group or voluntary work.

I ask the social worker if he could check out the house as I have a hunch (later proved right) that it is in a terrible state.

Neither of these approaches makes a dramatic difference although they ease things for a while. Adrian does confide a bit in Angie and she is able to gently help him talk about his grief for his mother and the gap her death has left behind. But then, for no obvious reason, he stops coming. The social worker continues to see him but the news is that he resists all attempts to help and continues to lead a squalid existence in the shadows. Angie will keep the door open for him just in case he can make use of her in the future, but I'm not optimistic. To some patients, the idea of connecting with others in a way that would make life meaningful is just too threatening to their fragile sense of self.

It is difficult not to be engulfed by the hopelessness around Adrian and people like him, hard to process the sense of helplessness – futility even. Thankfully, there are many others who, despite being written off as hopeless cases by other teams, grasped the lifeline we offered them and are now leading productive lives.

Lotti did better than any of us expected. She gradually emerged from the state of deep depression she had been in over that Christmas. Over the next few months, she engaged more with community life, taking on various roles and responsibilities, reaching out to new residents. One of the nurses became particularly important to her. Lotti had never felt anything like this before. Her unrequited feelings were painfully consuming for a while but she was eventually able to talk about them; the process of working them through bringing about a shift from 'mind-fuckingly overwhelming' to 'just about manageable'. Before she left, she spoke thoughtfully about her stay at Francis Dixon Lodge, how the pretend friends that had populated her inner world for so long had gradually been replaced by attachments to real people in the community.

The period over Christmas was a dark shadow in her memory, but she mentioned the cake that Kim made her. It had clearly touched her more than she was able to show at the time. She started to cry as she told us how important we were to her and how frightened she was of leaving. I felt optimistic. 'You will carry these attachments inside yourself,' I thought. But I didn't speak this out loud; it was something she would have to discover for herself.

~

How do we evaluate psychotherapy; how do we measure change? This can be a difficult question for psychotherapists, but an important one. In therapeutic communities, it's not such a problem. Most people arrive noticeably disordered, their disturbance blatantly out there, in the public domain. One approach, therefore, is to look at the change in contact with services. We can add up presentations to A&E, nights spent on psychiatric wards, number of arrests or time spent in prison. We can even work out the monetary cost of such disturbance. At Francis Dixon Lodge, for example, we looked at 'cost-offset' in what happened to a cohort of consecutive admissions. We were able to compare the average cost to the NHS in the three years before admission to the therapeutic community to the three years after discharge. The savings far outweighed the cost of the inpatient psychotherapy. We were able to argue that a stay in the therapeutic community, while expensive, paid for itself within two to three years.[2] Our successful 'graduates' no longer sucked in expensive resources in a chaotic, reactive and usually unproductive fashion; they were better connected and able to make use of their support network.

On another level, it's easy enough to show changes in behaviour: often a reduction or ending of self-harm and violence, reduced substance misuse, better sleep and eating patterns. It's more difficult to measure interpersonal and intrapsychic change. How do we capture the journey from feeling alienated, through feeling lonely, to feeling genuinely connected? How do we capture the nuanced shifts in someone's inner world that can make all the difference to that person's well-being? There are many ways of answering this question. We live in a society and an era obsessed with data collection, so a whole industry has sprung up with tools to measure what we do, various questionnaires and complicated statistical analysis. I'm all for audits and attempting to evaluate what we do but have seen so many examples where the process of measurement has narrowed down our concept of change, closed down opportunities for connection and replaced curiosity in the therapist with persecutory anxiety. Like teachers, many NHS psychotherapists are required to show progress during each session – a ridiculous misunderstanding of how change occurs. We so readily forget that all such measures are a proxy and fail to factor in how much time they absorb or how they subtly intrude into the therapeutic relationship.

There are many things I miss about working in the NHS, but the pressure to tick boxes and focus on measurable outcome is not one of them. Working independently now and free from such scrutiny, I feel more present in the relationship in the room, better able to read the conversation, more attentive to the intricate signals that pass between us and more prepared to be surprised.

Psychodynamic therapy is not about imposing a particular interpretation of events onto the patient. It is about a deepening conversation where connections get made and new frameworks emerge in the space between two people. I might well have wise interpretations to offer but the art of therapy is not in presenting brilliant ideas, but in creating a trusting relationship where new ideas can grow and become part of us. Fancy concepts that don't connect with the patient are worse than useless. Sometimes, I suggest a framework of understanding that just doesn't fit or jars in a way that leaves the patient feeling disconnected from me, disappointed, furious even. It might be a question of timing, something we can come back to later, or it might be that I've got the wrong end of the stick, put things together in a way that shows I've not been listening well enough. The disappointment and anger towards me may be hard to say out loud. I need to read between the lines, note the slumped body posture, the lost eye contact, the tone of voice. Everything is grist to the mill: if I can articulate the disappointment and anger and make sense of that with the patient, then we can move forward again. The scientist in me is constantly at work, reformulating, trying to work out what is going on in the other person's mind, checking out a hypothesis, evaluating risk, carefully titrating my input in relation to the level of emotional disturbance in the patient. I am a relationship-focused therapist, so if I measure anything, it's the subtle changes of rapport in the room, the level of connection. A deepening rapport means I'm on the right track.

~

I retired early from the NHS a few years back, exhausted and not really sure of what I wanted to do next. After a few months of enjoying doing all the ordinary things that work and children had crowded out over the years, I realised I was missing the connection with patients, yearning for those private, permissive conversations that go so far beyond what we might say to our best friend. Was this a neurotic narcissistic need on my part? Was I just clinging to the familiar? Maybe. But the truth is I feel at my most creative when I'm doing this work. Hours can go by when nothing much seems to be happening, then an important connection is made, something clicks, a burden is lifted, the world seems a slightly different place. And so I started working independently.

One of my new patients is Rahim. This week it's Ramadan and I encourage him to tell me what this means to him. He starts shyly but gets more animated as he continues. He's been going to mosque every day since Ramadan started and is warmed by the welcome he receives. Rituals that once made him feel self-conscious and hypocritical now ease him into the calm of contemplation. To his surprise, he doesn't want the prayers to finish and leaves the mosque looking forward to returning the next day. It is midsummer and the days are long, but when I enquire about fasting, he brushes it aside:

> It is so much easier than you'd think. I've fasted, on and off, since I was a child so it's not a big deal. You feel so proud when you're younger. Everyone's doing it, so you feel part of something bigger than you, everyone focused on the same thing. And then breaking the fast together late in the evening, I can't explain, it just feels so special. I feel good, good about myself.

I'm touched. Being a Muslim is not straightforward for Rahim. His heritage is mixed and complicated. Rahim's mother was brought up in Leicester, emigrating from Kenya when she was eight years old; his father is from Bosnia, arriving in Leicester as a young adult. They have a complicated and troubled relationship, with cultural and religious differences, even though they are both Muslim. Rahim has no siblings and keeps a distance from his cousins, not comfortable with their more extreme religious beliefs. It was a lonely childhood as he deliberately kept himself apart from others in order to protect himself from becoming entangled in his parents' arguments.

He was made to feel the outsider at school, and to a degree in his family. As a teenager, desperate to belong somewhere, he joined a group flirting with radicalisation, allowing the easy certainties and sense of being part of something to go to his head for a few weeks. It didn't take long for him to see through to its destructive barbarism, but he has also learned to be cautious about his yearning for a sense of belonging, often retreating into his intellect, an agnostic through and through. He pushed to be allowed to study in another city but found himself embroiled in similar arguments with his fellow Muslim students, some pushing him to radicalise, others encouraging him to take his faith less seriously. The parallels with home were too much: he felt increasingly consumed by these conflicts, unable to study, anxious around other students, angry with himself, full of shame, a disappointment to everyone. His depression worsened until he couldn't get out of bed.

In therapy, he tends to make sharp observations about the world but I have to work hard to bring him into the picture, to help him focus in on himself. Today, he talks tentatively and thoughtfully about how he feels. He risks telling me something close to his heart. The rapport in the room deepens.

In the weeks that follow, he is more open generally. He now attends his sessions with me more regularly, no longer cancelling at the last minute because he 'can't get out of bed'. He's decided to apply to return to university, having dropped out first time round during the second year. He talks more openly about just how estranged he had become from his fellow students, working all night and sleeping during the day in an attempt to avoid meeting people. He has made two good friends at the mosque. One of them is an academic working on a doctorate and he offers to help him with his university application. The other, like Rahim, had also been tempted into more radical Wahhabism when he was a student and they talk together about this experience, the false certainties and opportunities for destructive heroism.

There is much to be thought about in therapy, including a history of ethnic violence, trauma and loss going back at least two generations on both sides of the family. None of this has been directly talked about and his father particularly is reluctant to open up, but Rahim is a persistent man and there have been enough clues for him to start conversations with other family members. As he pieces together his family history, he begins to feel that he fits more comfortably together in himself.

The prognosis for Rahim when we first met was not promising. He'd cut himself off from his university course, his friends and his family. For the first few months I was never sure if he was going to turn up for his therapy sessions. But suddenly things started to click into place. He developed a capacity to think about his own mind – a capacity we refer to as mentalisation – that will stand him in good stead in the future. Connections were made that helped him make sense of his past. Shared experiences, shared ideas, shared ideals challenged his enforced loneliness. And in therapy, he started to convey a sense of purpose, grabbing my attention, full of hope that something good would come from our conversations. Like Lotti and so many other patients who were in a state of bleak despair when I first met them, he is now able to think about the future with a degree of hopefulness.

8

FACING UP TO SUICIDE

It's a beautiful autumnal day in late September and I am at a funeral for Hina, one of my patients.

There are about ten of us in the chapel of Gilroes Cemetery, Jasmine and I from the mental health unit, a couple of people I recognise as past patients, and a handful of strangers. No one who looks like a relative. The minister talks in a kindly but rather general way about the battle with mental illness, not even trying to personalise someone he's never known. No connections made. Standing in this lonely space, the thought comes that this loneliness was Hina's day-to-day experience. I try to bring a more vivid picture of Hina to mind, her timid kindness, her tentative steps towards intimacy and exasperating explosions of self-destructiveness that appear to have finally ended her life a week before her thirtieth birthday.

The minister hurries through the prayers and the promise of eternal life, with no response from the rest of us. Was she even religious? I don't think so. She was Jainist by birth but alienated from her family and community. But why the Christian minister?

We stay around afterwards to talk with the two people I've recognised, Lee and Katie. Katie looks emptied out, black eyes staring out of an ashen face. We let them tell us the story we already know. Katie had called round at Hina's flat on the Friday evening for a pre-planned drink and was surprised, then worried, when there was no response. Eventually, the police were called and found her body, dead for three days and already foul-smelling in the August heat.

No one knows what happened. No suicide note or evidence that she had planned or prepared for her death. Post-mortem inconclusive because of the 'advanced state of decay'. She would have been finally starting at university the following week and, as far as anyone knew, was feeling positive about it. She'd certainly worked hard enough to get there, uphill all the way, having left school with no qualifications and a terrible conviction that she was worthless and stupid.

'She seemed so . . . so good about uni – the happiest I'd seen her,' says Katie, the effort to articulate the words battling with her sobs, the cruel irony hanging in the air.

'I can't believe this is real,' says Lee, angrily kicking some gravel. Both Katie and Lee have made suicide attempts themselves in the past.

How could this have happened? Was the success, the hope, too much for her? Katie is sure it wasn't suicide, but how else could it be explained? Like Katie, I feel protective of Hina's memory. I've known her since she was nineteen. How awful to jump to the conclusion it was suicide, just because of her psychiatric history. I

think of all that work she'd done trying to put her violent persecutory childhood behind her. That journey had taken courage and
determination. I feel sick with pity.

~

Many people are lucky enough to go through their whole lives
without having to think very much about people whose lives have
become so torturous that they would rather be dead, but for those
who do lose a family member, partner or close friend to suicide,
the aftermath is devastating and often leaves an ongoing sense of
damage. I have seen several adult survivors of parental suicide trying to come to terms with this cruellest of legacies, agonising over
questions that can never be answered, rage and self-blame welling
up many years later, pulling them back into the past. The questions
dominate their inner lives and ghost through subsequent generations, often not talked about, but sitting darkly and emanating fear.

What causes people to kill themselves? Earlier this week, I was
listening to the intrepid explorer Simon Reeves being interviewed
on *Desert Island Discs* on the radio. He talked openly about his very
dark state of mind during his teenage years: 'I just couldn't face
life, couldn't face existence.' Deep depression and suicidal thinking
had him hovering the wrong side of the rails of a bridge with an
intent to jump. Something drew him back and, through a mixture
of lucky breaks and determination over the next few years, he was
able to turn things around. His life had clearly hung by a thread,
but now embodies the life-affirming curiosity and passion that
make his travel programmes such a pleasure to watch.

As a psychiatrist in a personality disorder unit, most of the
patients I worked with had taken one step further than Simon

Reeves and made their first suicide attempt before I had even met them. One of our main concerns when we assess a suicidal patient is how much responsibility they can be expected to carry for themselves. If they are suffering, for example, from psychosis or a severe depressive illness that has altered their experience of reality, we are duty-bound to step in and protect them. This is likely to mean detaining them against their will while we treat their illness. Even then, it may not be possible to prevent them killing themselves, sometimes because of failings in the system, sometimes because they are just so determined to die. Often both. I remember well the horror we all felt when Jiten, a reputedly brilliant mathematics student, killed himself. He suffered from Cotard's syndrome, a type of severe delusional depression where the patient believes his body is rotting. Jiten was convinced he had terminal cancer that had already eaten away some of his organs. He experienced severe pain and believed there was worse to come. Despite many doctors' efforts to persuade him that there was nothing wrong with him physically, as well as various attempts to treat the depression, his belief was unshakeable, and he ended up hanging himself in the ward toilet.

~

Like most psychiatrists, I remember my first suicide: the details are still clear after nearly forty years. It occurred during the second six months of my training rotation and illustrates how difficult it can sometimes be to know just what is going on in someone's life, whether they are ill, what's going on in their head.

Jean was a woman in her early forties, a farmer's wife with two school-age children. Much of the time, she seemed very 'ordinary', teaching the other patients how to make scones in the day-hospital cookery group, and talking at length about her sheep. At other times, she had that haggard, preoccupied look of someone deeply depressed and would pace in an agitated fashion around the room. She had been admitted to hospital after taking an overdose, explaining that she had wanted to die because she'd just discovered her husband was having an affair. She'd had no previous contact with psychiatric services.

Jean's husband seemed, superficially, a nice enough chap, and adamantly denied the affair – such conflicting narratives are not unusual in a marriage, but the overdose clearly made it psychiatric business. We needed to know if she was just a very unhappy woman reacting to her husband's betrayal or someone in the grip of a serious psychotic disorder.

Was she suffering from delusional depression? She didn't present with the classic signs of what we labelled then as endogenous depression. There was no early-morning wakening or diurnal mood variation. True, there was a sense that the agitated pacing and hours spent crying marked a difference from her usual down-to-earth character. But severe depression tends to envelop the whole personality, without respite, while Jean was able to spend a happy hour or two baking scones or chatting to her children.

Could this be a paranoid delusion consistent with a diagnosis of schizophrenia? Following an era of casual overdiagnosis that had put psychiatry in disrepute, labelling someone with schizophrenia had become a rigorous technical process, taken very seriously. Crucial to the diagnosis were 'first-rank symptoms', two of which had to be present for a positive diagnosis. This was questionable in

Jean's case: her only symptom was a fixed belief that her husband was having an affair.

Morbid jealousy syndrome can indicate an underlying mood disorder, schizophrenia or, in rare cases, organic pathology such as a brain tumour or Alzheimer's disease. It is sometimes referred to as Othello syndrome, particularly in men, as violence towards their 'unfaithful' spouse is a high risk and often has tragic consequences. Jean, as is the tendency of women, had turned the violence inwards onto herself in the form of an overdose. Of course, we don't go around labelling everyone who has a disputed affair in their relationship with morbid jealousy; neither is it our job to turn private detective. The diagnosis is made by scrutinising the mental process through which the assumption of the affair was reached for evidence of thought disorder. A grey area indeed, you might be thinking. But when you meet people with a clear-cut example of this diagnosis, the depth of their delusion jumps out at you.

A year or so later, I was to meet such a person in my membership exam. This man was my 'long case', meaning I had an hour in his company to extrapolate his story and examine him, before presenting my findings to the two examiners and answering their questions about diagnosis, treatment and management. Stanley was in his sixties and was completely convinced his wife had started having an affair with her GP two years previously. The reason he was so sure was her new habit of coughing and clearing her throat, clearly a sign of guilt. She'd arrived home from work one day (she worked in a shop next door to the surgery) and coughed in such a way that he suddenly knew 'without a shred of a doubt' that she must be having an affair. She'd quickly denied anything was going on, but he was so convinced of the affair that he'd made an appointment to see the rather surprised GP to confront him. He'd also turned his study into a laboratory, with a microscope that had belonged to one of his sons to examine her clothes and handkerchiefs for 'evidence'. My mind boggled, but he was quite unable to tell me what he was looking for, just kept saying: 'It's all there – clear for all to see.' Then he proceeded to show me his 'investigatory notes', an A4-sized notebook full of cuttings from the local newspaper about the GP practice, going back over twenty years, all 'evidence of the affair'. The writing inside the notebook looked like gobbledygook to me, but he explained he'd written it in code 'just in case'. Of course, he couldn't explain either the code or the rationale for using such a code. I asked him what he planned to do to his wife and he shook his head sadly saying he didn't want her to die, but he might have to 'find a way to make this happen', 'for her own good', 'if she doesn't repent'. He denied having tried to hurt her, but the examiners told me he'd already tried to strangle her.

Jean's morbid jealousy, if that's what it was, was not in this league, but her process of deduction was odd. Of course, this was before the days of giveaway texts and emails, and Jean's evidence was mostly based on smelling another woman's perfume on her husband's clothes and finding threads of wool that didn't belong to her – a bit of a cliché, but no reason to disbelieve her so far. She would also examine his boots in great detail and use this information to discount his account of his day. When he visited her on the ward, she refused to speak to him, focusing instead on the two children, with whom she seemed to chat quite happily. More worryingly, she'd inappropriately taken one of the nurses aside before a visit and asked her to go through his pockets. Most significant, as with Stanley, was her absolute conviction that she was right despite the lack of hard evidence. Jean was completely unable to reflect on the relationship and what might be going on: there was no narrative, just the fact of the affair and a belief that her life was ruined.

The ward staff were split on whether the affair was real or not. The consultant thought she was mentally ill but some of the nursing staff – particularly the men, interestingly – sensed bad vibes from the husband and felt protective of Jean. The concept of gaslighting wasn't around in those days, but I guess that would capture what they were thinking. I was in the middle of these conflicting perspectives and uncomfortably on the fence, tending to steer clear of the 'affair' if possible in my chats with Jean and talk about other things. Our main topic of conversation was her ailing elderly mother who so relied on her help. She didn't want to appear in the approaching ward round; she just wanted to go home. Was there anything I could do to persuade them to let her go on leave, she wanted to know. 'Please tell them how much my mother needs me – I'd give anything to go home for a weekend.'

I duly put her case to the team. The consultant was reluctant, but the nurses were supportive and he eventually agreed: Jean was given weekend leave, Friday to Sunday. I happened to be on call that weekend and was called to the ward on the Sunday evening. Jean had apparently returned saying the weekend had gone well, but she had developed abdominal pain and been sick a couple of times. She didn't look very well so I examined her to rule out an emergency such as appendicitis. I decided she'd probably just got a bug and, to be on the safe side, moved her to a side room to minimise the chance of her infecting other patients, writing her up for routine blood tests in the morning. I popped my head round the door later that evening; she was sleeping peacefully and seemed more comfortable.

Twenty-four hours later, Jean confessed to one of the nurses she'd taken a massive overdose of paracetamol on Sunday morning before returning – hence the pain, nausea and drowsiness. Paracetamol is a potentially lethal drug in overdose but if discovered soon enough an antidote can be given. It was now more than forty-eight hours after she'd overdosed and we'd missed the window of opportunity. She was immediately transferred to the medical team as an emergency but there was little they could do. She died ten days later.

I felt devastated. What was I thinking? I hadn't even thought to ask if she'd overdosed. And I had argued for her to have weekend leave. Those poor children would now grow up without a mother. The whole team was deeply affected, but while the nurses blamed the husband I was really angry with myself. I felt responsible for her death. I would replay the conversations obsessively in my head, round and round in circles. What if I hadn't kept her out of the ward round? What if I hadn't pushed for her to go on weekend leave? What if I'd been more sceptical and considered the possibility of overdose when she returned with abdominal pain?

The consultant did all he could to comfort us. 'It probably wouldn't have made any difference,' he reiterated. 'It might already have been too late to treat her when she got back to hospital. If she was determined to die, she would have found a way of killing herself whatever. She chose not to tell us, which suggests she was pretty determined to die – this was no "cry for help".' But I knew

I should have questioned whether her symptoms could have been caused by an overdose. And I also knew, from visiting her on the general ward and talking to the nurses, that Jean had been full of regret when faced with the reality of her imminent death. As far as I was concerned, it was an avoidable tragedy and I'd played a major part.

The consultant was right, of course: it is inevitable that some patients will choose to end their lives, and all psychiatrists, however good and conscientious, encounter this as part of their work. But it is a hard lesson. Each time one of my patients has killed themselves, I've been through this process of questioning my every action. Over time, though, it has gradually become less agonising. The emotional territory has become more familiar and I have learned along the way that the intense feelings in the immediate aftermath eventually pass, leaving a gentler, more philosophical sadness.

~

In the psychotherapeutic literature on suicide, there is the concept of a split between the self and the body: the suicidal act is seen as the self killing off the body. When I visited Jean a few days before she died, I was young and frightened and we didn't talk about how she thought of her death, or whether this thinking had changed. But I suspect, like many people contemplating suicide, she might have imagined it as a long, peaceful sleep, as if she could jettison her body but somehow still exist. There is evidence from talking to people whose suicide attempts have failed that at the point when they intended to kill themselves, they experienced their body as a separate object.[1] It seems many of them wanted to kill off their body but imagined, at some level, another part of them would continue to live on in a conscious but bodiless state. These beliefs were independent of religious affiliations or formal belief in an afterlife.

Such a split is also evident in some people who intentionally self-harm or mutilate their bodies while not intending to die. Over the years, I've seen a few patients who performed elaborate 'operations' on their bodies, dispassionate bloodletting rituals, for example, or intricate dissections of their limbs, torturous acts that split the sadistic and masochistic functions between self and body. At the other end of the spectrum, there are people who act violently towards themselves only when they're in a frenzy of emotion and often intoxicated. Sometimes, particularly in psychotic states of mind, the violence is an attempt to kill off their thoughts.

The relationship that self-destructive people have with their bodies (a proxy perhaps for a parental figure, or in Jean's case her husband) is full of twists and contradictions. I am often struck by the irrationality. During the pandemic, I was seeing a patient who lived with compulsive suicide plans in his head and indeed had acted on them in the past, but when he wasn't talking about suicide, he was obsessing how to keep himself free from catching Covid, apparently oblivious of any irony.

Some patients who deliberately cut or burn themselves talk about craving the physical pain because it rids them of noxious thoughts and feelings. We've already seen how some patients crave physical pain because it's easier to bear than mental pain. The emergence of endorphins in reaction to physical wounding suggests this attitude might be partly grounded in biochemical reality. Others talk about cutting themselves in order to let the evil or badness out, as if the act has a purifying function, the thought of exsanguinating reassuring. And yet others say the sight of blood makes them feel alive, describing self-cutting as a way of ridding themselves of the sense of numbness and deadness inside.

~

Many of the patients I see have a long history of suicide attempts and deliberate self-harm. It can be tempting just to see this as part of who they are, a component of their diagnosis. Tired and pejorative labels such as 'borderline', 'manipulative' or 'attention-seeker' superficially fill the gaps in understanding but I fear their use reveals us to be lacking in genuine curiosity, seemingly uninterested in what the behaviour means and what it's trying to communicate. After all – as I tell trainees – we all need attention and most of us can be manipulative when we need to be. The main difference is how good we are at it. Anyone who needs to cut holes into their arm or swallow a whole bottle of tablets to get attention is very desperate indeed.

I am always surprised at how little interest many psychiatrists have in finding out what is going on in their suicidal patients at the time. It's as if once the diagnosis is made and 'treatable mental illness' excluded, the job is done. But I've always found it helpful to take patients back to the lead-up to the critical incident, to the days and hours and minutes before they acted against themselves in this way. This is where we find the clues that will help us minimise the risk of further attempts, and this is where we can start to make sense of the subjective meaning in their behaviour.

There are key areas of enquiry I have in my mind. The first is why they started to harm themselves or attempted to kill themselves in the first place. There is often, for example, a link between this historical incident and the start of an abusive relationship. But the connection has not been made, either by the patient themselves or the health workers trying to help them.

Another important question is whether the patient's behaviour was intended to end their life or was really a cry for help. This seems to be taken more seriously by clinicians who might turn detective and ask about suicide letters and timings. An overdose, for example, timed a few minutes before their partner gets home may not be a genuine attempt to end their life and will almost certainly be a cry for attention or an act of aggression or retaliation towards their partner. Sometimes it's not clear if they wanted at some level to die. And even if it's an obvious cry for help, it doesn't mean they are not desperate and doesn't rule out that they might go on to take a fatal overdose in the future.

The 'body barrier' is a term that describes the survival instinct that prevents people from taking their suicidal or self-mutilating fantasies to the next step and physically acting on them. Simon Reeves, for example, was clearly in a pre-suicide state but he wasn't able to jump, and he stepped back over the railings to safety. Listening to him describe the event, he is clear it wasn't a rational process of changing his mind, more an instinctive fear pulling him away from danger. The important thing to know is that once this body barrier has been crossed a first time, it is that much easier to do so again. A prior attempt is the single most important risk factor for suicides in the general population. It is not difficult to see how such behaviour, if one survives, can become repetitive, a habitual response to the experience of drowning in emotion, almost a reflex way of relieving seemingly unbearable psychic tension or pain. The worry is that people with a long history of suicide attempts or parasuicide* tend not to be taken seriously when in fact the likelihood of a successful suicide becomes increasingly likely.

There are certainly people who carefully plan and execute their suicide, often going to lengths to distract or deceive those who might try to stop them. But it was not clear how many of the patients I had seen who later supposedly died by suicide had intended to end their lives. Letters for those left behind were rare. Often the patient had a long history of surviving overdoses and had developed a sort of carelessness towards their body, eventually dying from a cocktail of alcohol, illegal drugs and too many sleeping tablets or painkillers. Alcohol is involved in 35 per cent of completed suicides and presumably has a role in reducing the usual resistance to crossing the body barrier. I get very frustrated trying to impress on patients the very real risk of dying from a paracetamol overdose. The patients tend to nod along and humour me but, having survived such poisonings on previous occasions, the look they give me conveys that they know better. They sometimes seem no longer clear if they want to live or die, their body barrier worn down over time.

Yet another group of patients seems addicted to the risk of death, as if they are playing Russian roulette. The patients who routinely tie ligatures around their neck – a form of self-harm

----

* I use the term parasuicide here to describe seeming suicide attempts where the intention was not to die.

particularly common in institutions such as hospitals and prisons – seem to be in this category. Whatever the psychology behind it, such addictions are reinforced by the body's biochemical response to fear and pain and sometimes sexual excitement, as well as the particular social attention such behaviour attracts. Paradoxically, these patients talk about 'never feeling so alive'.

While it's important to distinguish between a serious suicide attempt and deliberate self-harm, sometimes this can be very difficult. It's true that self-wounding or cutting has become relatively common among teenagers and will often stop with a bit of understanding psychological support and increasing maturity. Most of them harm their body in an attempt to communicate intense distress but have no wish to die. Some deliberate self-harmers will continue to self-harm for years without ever intending to kill themselves. A minority, however, will progress to more serious, high-risk forms of self-harm, ligaturing and overdosing with frequent crisis visits to the emergency department, sometimes needing admission. I find that patients who have a long history of such events are often dismissed as 'self-harmers', with their intentional suicide attempts hidden within the general chaos of their presentation. For this reason, I try to judge each incident without being prejudiced by the history and make a point of asking if at any time they have genuinely intended to die, taking their account of this very seriously.

There are many prejudiced assumptions we can make that allow us to dismiss the seriousness of a suicide act. As always in mental health work, it's important not to make judgements about the intent behind a suicide based on our own view of the world. I've heard nurses describe an overdose as being unimportant because it 'followed a row with the boyfriend' (said with great disdain). But such a row could carry painful resonances with abuse or abandonment in a sensitive person with early experience of profound neglect or betrayal. I've seen many young women over the years where a row with a boyfriend has cut through any sense of precarious maturity and made them feel like helpless children, drowning in despair. Too often we judge such a reaction to be disproportionate, stick a label on them and prescribe medication. But every crisis is an opportunity to learn and start making sense of oneself if only we could set up the right sort of conversation.

With any puzzling behaviour, I try to identify both the immediate trigger and the underlying psychological trauma or conflict – what the trigger hooks into for the patient. Two young women, Lizzy and Ginny, survived – only just – serious overdoses a few weeks apart from each other. Both had recently finished intensive residential therapy – always a particularly vulnerable time as it is not unusual for a core childhood trauma to re-emerge. And both overdosed after their respective flats were burgled. But to have stopped asking questions at this point would be to have missed crucial information. Lizzy, who had been sexually abused as a child, was left feeling violated by the burglary. She felt assaulted, intruded on, and couldn't bear the thought that the burglar had been in her 'private place' which now felt 'dirty and spoiled'. Ginny was devastated by her burglary because her jewellery had been stolen, including a ring that had belonged to her mother. Ginny's mother had died when she was so young that her memories were vague and misty. The ring was of enormous importance because it was the only tangible item she had that linked her to her mother. Losing it had put her back in touch with the overwhelming grief she had felt as a dependent child.

Lizzy and Ginny illustrate how trigger events can induce a sort of emotional flashback to overwhelming traumatic events people have experienced as children. Neither of them was consciously aware of this link when they took the overdose, and the suicide act was more unconscious compulsion than a thought-through decision. It required a nuanced conversation and careful listening to work out what was going on for each of them, helped by the fact that my team knew them well. Being able to make the connection to their childhood gave Lizzy and Ginny a sense of control over the deluge of emotion so they could stand firm and break the link with self-destructive acts. Happily, with support over the next few months, both women went on to do well.

~

Mental health workers are evaluating suicide risk all the time. It is not a straightforward science. The work involves making difficult decisions, complex judgement calls that get easier with experience, but are rarely black and white. Attempting or becoming preoccupied with suicide is not always a symptom of an illness but, in any case, our patients don't fit neatly into diagnostic boxes: they are all unique and some of them have more than one diagnosis. Having said that, understanding the likely course of a particular condition can be of vital importance and is often counterintuitive. Patients with an elated mood and a diagnosis of bipolar disorder, for example, are at risk of suicide when their mood starts to come down – something that can happen very quickly. Patients with a depressive illness at the catatonic end of the spectrum are more likely to die by suicide when treatment kicks in and they are starting to appear better but have more energy to enact their death wish. Patients with a personality disorder have a tendency to deteriorate in an inpatient ward and can paradoxically do better in the long term if the psychiatrist can hold his nerve and manage them in the community – with the right sort of support available, of course.

The decision-making process becomes increasingly difficult as resources diminish, therapeutic choices become fewer and staff are stretched more thinly. The kind of repetitive box-ticking question-naires that are increasingly used to assess risk in crisis teams seem fatuous to me. As if many patients don't know what answers to give to trick the system; as if a patient intent on killing himself is going to readily admit his intent to the people with the power to restrict his liberty.

There is a lot of pressure to do increasingly comprehensive and time-consuming risk assessments. The problem is that most people we see as psychiatrists are at risk of suicide at some point, but only a small minority will go on to kill themselves. Identifying this smaller group and taking effective measures to protect them from themselves is far from easy.

Thoughts about suicide are relatively common in the general population. Many years ago, after my first husband left me for someone else, I had a recurrent dream that I had died in a car crash. The climax of the dream was always my ex-husband arriving at the scene, distraught with guilt. The dream was about revenge: making him see what damage he'd caused, making him suffer – very common themes in suicide. But I didn't want to kill myself and I didn't want to be dead.

Some of the doctors and nurses I've seen who have been working in ICU throughout the coronavirus pandemic have fantasies
of being dead. When we explore this, it seems more like a wish
to sleep, a wish to merge with, rather than fight with, nature. An
understandable wish to escape their present circumstances. But,
more worryingly, one or two of them find themselves imagining the act of ending their life, the thoughts coming unbidden,
deeply distressing and frightening. I'm alert to the risk and step up
my support: what I'm really on the lookout for is the possibility
of these suicide fantasies developing into deliberate, compulsive
imagining, and sometimes planning, the event. It is at this point
– the presuicidal state of mind – that we consider people as being
at imminent danger.

Whatever the background causes and the build-up that make
ending one's life seem a real possibility, people in a presuicidal
state of mind, including those who are psychotic, seem to have
key features in common, most obviously a preoccupation with
intentional suicide fantasies – often detailed plans. There is often
a profound sense of being trapped, of having no choice; and a
struggle with conscious or partly repressed hatred and revenge
that seems so overwhelming that putting an end to one's life seems
the only way out. Psychiatrists with their medical model, diagnostic categories and medication regimes are not necessarily well
enough equipped to work at the level that is needed with people
in this presuicidal state. Such work needs to be seen as a dynamic
process within a therapeutic relationship that invites reflection,
questioning, and is vigilant to subtle shifts in risk.

One of the reasons I have become somewhat disillusioned
with mental health services is the lack of understanding of the

importance of such an ongoing therapeutic relationship. Mental health patients in particular need a consistent relationship with the person or closely knit team trying to help them. A vital part of this ongoing relationship is careful monitoring of the person's mental state. Whenever I'm talking to a patient, I have a sense that, at some level, I'm doing a risk assessment, although this would not necessarily be explicit or obvious to the patient. The better I know a particular individual, the more confident I can be in my evaluation of the risk they pose to themselves and others; the better I know the patient, the safer the patient will be. This might seem like common sense, but it is no longer the way the UK mental health system works, nor indeed the way primary care works.

As many families and friends know, it is not easy sustaining a relationship with someone going through a particularly dark time, when you know their hold on life is tenuous. When I'm working closely with a suicidal patient, I can feel a dull ache in my stomach and I'm aware of a hovering jitter. I know their struggle with suicide may end in death and find myself carrying the risk around with me, willing the patient to hang on in there, 'holding them in the light', as the Quakers say. Alongside this, I try to create a neutral space where suicidal, even homicidal, feelings can be candidly explored, where a connection can be made that just might be meaningful enough to anchor them to the living. At the same time, I'm anxiously questioning if I've done everything I should, ticked all the boxes, made the right decisions. Yet another voice is urging a more philosophical attitude: I cannot ultimately be responsible for keeping this person alive and I'm certainly not responsible for all the suffering that has made their life so unbearable. It is a delicate balancing act.

~

The fear of suicide is always there for people working in mental health settings, sometimes uncontainable, and oozing, unwanted, into family life.

I remember years ago being at home on a Friday evening, waiting for visitors to arrive for the weekend. They had been held up for hours on the M69 because someone was threatening to jump from a motorway bridge. As soon as I heard the reason for the delay, I started to go through a list of patients in my head, wondering if it could be 'one of mine'. Quite a number came to mind.

There was Suzette who made a suicide pact with her boyfriend to jump off a multistorey car park. She couldn't jump when it came to it but is haunted by his screams as he fell to his death and the picture of him lying like a run-over cat on the road below.

There was Mark – but it couldn't be him because he was now disabled and in a wheelchair having sustained serious injuries to his feet and spine when he'd jumped off a railway bridge two years before.

There was Vernon, with a dual diagnosis of personality disorder and Asperger's syndrome. He was obsessed with bridges: cataloguing their design, when they were built, the name of the architect and taking pictures, often hanging precipitously from a ledge to get the right angle. He'd been referred on to us after being picked up by the police having climbed up with his geeky notebooks and expensive camera to the ramparts of a bridge in the middle of the night. The police were understandably suspicious.

There was Simran who had been regularly picked up wandering across the lanes of motorways, always claiming she didn't remember how she got there.

Molly's and Leah's favoured method of self-harm was to sit themselves on a main road and wait to see what happened, both of them having learned this behaviour a few months earlier from another patient who'd been on the acute ward with them and had since died.

And there were many others whom I didn't associate with roads or bridges but who could be overwhelmed at any time with the desire to end their life, to play their version of Russian roulette or overcome their sense of powerlessness with threats to self-destruct.

I told myself that there was no point in worrying but woke up in the morning having had a horrible dream of trying to rescue a baby sitting in the middle of a motorway. I felt badly rested and the first thing that popped into my mind, despite a houseful of visitors to look after: all those patients of mine with possible connections to motorway bridges. The worry niggled away in the background throughout the weekend.

It turned out eventually that the potential motorway jumper had no connection with me or any of my colleagues. It's always the same when someone seemingly crazed and destructive hits the headlines: I feel a sudden panic, a kind of physiological jerk as my threat system prepares my body for danger; then hours or occasionally days determinedly keeping calm, a fluttering of anxiety or a wave of nausea reminding me of the need to keep my worries under control.

Death by suicide is experienced differently from other bereavements. It's as if the victim's hopelessness and despair is left behind in the people trying to help. Most obviously this will be their friends and family but sometimes it's the clinicians who have seen them at their most vulnerable and know the secrets of their heart, who have been trying so hard to connect with them at the point when they take their own life. Almost every patient of mine who has killed themselves is etched in my memory. I can remember the circumstances of the death, what I was doing when I heard the news, the sense of cold horror or sometimes bone-weary resignation as the news became real. As with Jean, I often remember the last conversation we had, going over and over it in my mind, wondering if I missed something or said something insensitive.

I know I'm not alone feeling like this. One of my colleagues came to see me a few years ago to talk through the suicide of Karen, a mutual patient. My colleague had finally decided to discharge Karen from the acute ward as she'd been there for months and was getting worse rather than better. They'd had an honest conversation about the risk of suicide. My colleague was clear that she could not stay on the acute ward for the rest of her life and carefully drew up a care plan identifying a support structure for her in the community.

Despite all the emergency numbers she had in her bag, Karen walked straight out of the hospital to the river, where she took all her medication and then drowned herself, Virginia Woolf style, with heavy stones in her pockets. It was a death I was able to be relatively philosophical about as I knew two psychiatric teams, social workers and GPs had tried their very best over many years. I had come to the view that Karen could not allow people to help her, and I was also more detached as it had been over a year since

I'd had any contact with her. But my colleague was knocked badly by her death. She was upset, regretful, full of guilt and couldn't exorcise the thought that she'd used the phrase 'sink or swim' in their last conversation, replaying the dialogue they'd had over and over in her head.

There is nothing like a suicide for making you feel a failure.

~

While I was working as a senior consultant, I was asked to carry out a formal enquiry into the suicide of a patient who'd killed herself on the psychiatric intensive care unit. I was struck anew by the enormous cost to many of the doctors and nurses involved, not just after she'd killed herself – one or two were candid enough to describe a feeling of relief – but during the years before this, trying to keep her alive. This woman's high-risk behaviour had triggered decisions from the psychiatrist that had resulted in an increasingly restrictive regime: locked ward, seclusion room, no day clothes, and so on. But every restriction to her liberty amplified and reinforced her drive to self-destruct, the next suicide attempt becoming her sole obsession. One attempt – almost unimaginable – included a noose she'd painstakingly woven together over weeks from carpet fibres while in seclusion, forced to be creative as the clothes that she'd used as a ligature in the past had been removed. It was a horribly malignant vicious circle that no one seemed able to break. Sadly, such dynamics are not as rare as you might think. The staff I interviewed described their experience of the situation vividly and are quoted in the report:

'Every day, I'd wake up dreading that she'd kill herself during my shift.'

'You couldn't get away from her screams. The more medication we gave her, the worse she used to get. No one felt safe.'

'Her determination to die sucked all the energy out of me, looking back I was really quite ill.'

'It wasn't that you couldn't get through to her, but every time I thought I'd really connected with a more positive part of her, she'd follow it by doing something terrible to herself. It completely did my head in. In fact, I started dreaming about her – horrible, disturbing dreams that I can't talk to anyone about.'

'There was no space to think properly about the other patients, she obsessed us all, it was all we ever talked about.'

How could one young woman affect so many people in such a way? It seemed far too complex to think of her simply as a victim. Power and control can become slippery concepts in psychiatry and these horribly sado-masochistic dynamics create many victims.

~

I am always struck by the violence around suicide, the act of taking a life, the terrible traumatic mess it leaves behind, the torment lodged in the minds of those who tried to care.

Suicide was decriminalised in 1961, but it is still common to hear the phrase 'committed suicide' as if the law has been broken – which is why many organisations now recommend avoiding the term. In fact, if you live in Singapore, it is still a legal offence and you can be sent to prison for trying to take your life. We have come a long way since the eighteenth century when suicide was still seen as a crime against God and people who had killed themselves could not be buried in sacred ground. But in most countries the stigma lives on, discouraging people – especially young men

– from seeking help, and affecting everyone around, from family to professionals trying to help. In the UK, suicide is the only death in hospital that automatically goes to the coroner's court.

As mental health workers, we try hard to prevent suicide: listening, evaluating, advising, prescribing, intervening, sometimes using our powers under the Mental Health Act to detain someone against their will, hoping this will keep them safe until the despair has eased. These days, psychiatrists are often blamed when their patients kill themselves, finding themselves in a long persecutory legal process. It is almost as if *someone* must still be found guilty. Whatever the ethics involved, when society holds mental health professionals responsible for those who deliberately end their lives, it comes at a huge cost to the clinicians involved.

As my career continued, in addition to trying to console families of the deceased, I became increasingly aware of how many psychiatrists and other mental health staff were carrying this burden around with them. Left alone with private thoughts and feelings, they were silenced by a sense of shame, amplified by the fear of being judged by the law and exposed by a media only too happy to sensationalise the story and find someone to blame. The toll in terms of sickness rates, early retirement and low morale is significant.

It hasn't always been like this. When Jean killed herself in my first year as a trainee psychiatrist, I'd been helped through this by a very supportive team and consultant. This was an era when suicide was seen as an inevitable part of psychiatry. There had been an understanding that it leaves everyone with a difficult mix of sadness, guilt and anger to process, so two afternoons of reflective practice time had been scheduled for the team to share our thoughts and feelings. At one point, the psychologist in the team had challenged my 'stubborn obsession with failure' – a phrase I've never forgotten. It had been sufficient to free me up so that I was able to disentangle my feelings about Jean enough, at least, to attend properly to the other patients who needed to occupy my mind. If it was to happen today, such a suicide would trigger a persecutory legal process that could go on for months, if not years.

~

Jeremy Hunt, a previous Secretary of State for Health, talked about 'aiming for a zero per cent suicide rate – absolute zero tolerance'. Is this at all realistic? In contrast to the USA,[*] the suicide rate relative to the population size in the UK has declined by 31 per cent since 1981 but it is still the highest cause of death in men under fifty, and there is evidence that it may be starting to rise again.[†] It is difficult to see, however, how putting even more pressure on mental health practitioners is the answer to a problem that is deeply entrenched in society and highly correlated with social factors such as abuse, poverty, unemployment and, more recently, toxic social media. The suicide rate between 2017 and 2019, for example, in the most deprived 10 per cent of areas in England and Wales was almost double the rate in the least deprived 10 per cent.[2]

One of the most disturbing suicide statistics that I've come across recently is that the rise in suicides in Northern Ireland over

---

[*] In the USA, the suicide rate increased 33 per cent between 1999 and 2019.
[†] In 2018 and 2019 there was a statistically significant rise in the UK suicide rate (https://www.ons.gov.uk).

the twenty years following the peace process had been responsible for more deaths of young men than those killed in the Troubles. Resonance here with the famous finding by the nineteenth-century social scientist Émile Durkheim that the incidence of suicide decreases during a war — his hypothesis being that camaraderie and a sense of well-being improve when there is a clear external enemy in common and a strong sense of social solidarity.[3] In line with this argument, early data suggests that the male suicide rate in England and Wales was lower between April and July 2020 than the corresponding months in previous years. This decrease corresponds with the first national lockdown and the largest difference was in the first few weeks of the lockdown in April. It is generally agreed that there was a sense of the country pulling together at the start of the pandemic with, for example, neighbourhood groups springing into action to protect the most vulnerable, the Thursday evening ritual of gathering on our doorsteps to applaud key workers, and politicians uniting in sympathy with the prime minister who was very ill with Covid-19. Sadly, this Blitz-like spirit was short-lived and there is already some evidence that the suicide rate is once again on the rise.[*]

I came across another shocking war statistic — this time linked to the horrific trauma and grief experienced by a particular regiment (2 Rifles) fighting the lost war in Afghanistan: fifty-five soldiers from this one regiment died in active service and twenty-two took their own lives back home. The point is that suicide is a complex problem for society at large: it has a context way beyond

---

[*] There can be months of delay waiting for a suspected suicide to go to the coroner's court. This means there is a considerable time lag before reliable suicide statistics appear.

diagnosis and treatment and cannot simply be made the responsibility of mental health workers. The statistics bear this out: 72 per cent of those who died by suicide between 2002 and 2012 had not been in contact with their GP or other health professional about their feelings in the year before their suicide.[4]

Increasingly people turn to the internet, perhaps searching for support and understanding, perhaps so depressed they don't know what they're looking for. What they so often find is a world that normalises suicide: encourages, dares, models, demonstrates, idealises and provokes suicidal behaviour. I'm no expert on the internet, but I have seen at first hand the contagion effect, where psychiatric patients on inpatient units are drawn into a perverse culture of competition and fear around self-destructive behaviour. It is no coincidence that the incidence of suicides on wards tends to clump: one suicide increasing the probability of another. I remember a harrowing time early in my career where some patients on the ward – mostly young women – started to cut their faces. This horrible self-destructive behaviour seemed to spread from one to another, each wound worse than the last. It was heartbreaking to witness the damage. If this type of effect can happen on wards staffed by professionals, what chance for a desperately vulnerable young person journeying alone into the predatory jungle of the internet?

We need to wise up about suicide. In the UK, the depression rate in our children is the highest in Europe, and was rising even before the pandemic hit, so we need to get our act together quickly. This will not all be down to mental health services. Public health initiatives do help. The suicide rate in men in the 30–49 age bracket, for example, has reduced very significantly in the last thirty years, the improvement thought to be largely the result of a public health campaign raising awareness at primary care level and encouraging men to talk to their GPs about their feelings. There have also been several local public mental health initiatives in schools, aimed at developing social and emotional life skills, that seem to make a positive difference. If only such work was valued and properly resourced. A comprehensive mental health strategy across different government departments including education, housing, justice, defence, work and pensions, and the media would be a good start.

Of course, mental health workers like me will continue to do the best we can for our patients, targets or no targets, and resources permitting. But not all suicides – despite society's understandable but unrealistic expectations – can be prevented. Tragedies will continue to happen. Occasional mistakes will be made. It is right that we should be held – kindly and intelligently – accountable for the decisions we make. It is also important that we apply our knowledge and skills to the highest possible professional standards and constantly push to improve the care of those at risk of suicide. There is no doubt we could do it so much better. No suicide, though, can be fully explained and some can hardly be explained at all. Others can be understood only too well but the issues go far beyond mental health services.

9

GIVE SORROW WORDS

Grief is one of the most intensely painful of all human emotions; it's also one of the most intimate. Working in mental health has convinced me that unresolved grief plays a more significant part in psychiatric illness than is generally recognised, and that grief can have a distorting effect on the health of an individual, a family, an institution, even a country.

Prince Harry gave a candid interview in 2017 describing how he'd felt as a small boy as he walked behind his mother's coffin through London, full of grief as he was watched by millions of viewers. He felt he hadn't properly attended to his feelings at losing his mother at such a young age and linked this to emotional difficulties and problems with relationships he'd experienced as a young man. Simon Wessely, the chairman of the Royal College of Psychiatrists, tweeted in response that Prince Harry had probably done more good for the mental health of the nation in one short interview than he himself had done in his whole career as a psychiatrist.

When I look back to my teens and early twenties, I cringe at the thought of my insensitivity around bereaved people. I had friends whose fathers died suddenly while they were medical students or junior doctors. Our workplace made no allowances for such losses whatsoever and, as far as I can remember, our main input was to try to cheer them up by dragging them to the pub. It didn't cross our minds to encourage them to talk about their dead parent or to understand their need to sit quietly with their feelings. Years later, with the wisdom of experience, I know the pain of grief can feel like being beaten to a pulp in the early days, then a throbbing hurt that can gnaw away and leave one vulnerable for a long time. I understand the importance of supporting each other to bear such pain, holding each other up to withstand the storm of emotion that a bereavement can bring in its wake. And I understand the pressure to hold the feelings tight in one's heart, the fear of putting them into words. But there is a price to pay if we can't find the language to express such pain. This is summed up so perfectly in *Macbeth*:

> Give sorrow words. The grief that does not speak
> Whispers the o'erfraught heart and bids it break.[1]

I have become fascinated by the vagaries around our response to grief as a society, and often concerned at our discomfort with death and overt grieving. If only there was more understanding generally of the support that is needed: for example, better systems in our workplaces for responding to grieving employees, a

richer variety of rituals to draw us together and channel our feelings, and less reliance on the medical profession to box up and
'treat' the bereaved with medication.

The bulk of this chapter was written before the start of the
pandemic. Since I wrote it, many have lost loved ones to Covid-19,
and one of the cruellest things has been the way frightened, vulnerable people have been isolated when they are dying and most in
need of the loving presence of their family. The traumatic nature of
these deaths as well as the sheer number of what statisticians call
'excess deaths' makes it all the more important that we are able
to think and talk clearly as a society about death and bereavement.
It remains to be seen whether we turn away or can rise to this
challenge.

～

When my children were young and were asked what job I did, they
would reply, rather sweetly, that I 'worked with very sad people
to help them be happy'. Psychiatric patients don't in fact cry very
much – not nearly as much as you might expect. And, paradoxically, the work is more accurately described as helping people feel
sadness. This dawned on me slowly.

Years ago, while I was working in the therapeutic community,
I co-facilitated a group therapy session where Katie recounted the
story of her mother and brother being killed in a car crash when
she was eight. The telling was raw and interrupted by violent sob-
bing. Tissues were passed, sympathy expressed, and I wasn't the
only one struggling to cope with my own feelings as I tried to
reach out to her.

Later, it emerged that Katie had been left on her own after

the session rather than being encouraged to join the scheduled afternoon shopping trip. I think that for Katie this was a replay of what had happened after her bereavement. Her father, who'd been driving and injured in the same accident, was in hospital for months and Katie was left with her maternal grandmother who was too preoccupied with her own grief to think about her vulnerable granddaughter. Grandma had also blamed Katie's father for the accident, so Katie didn't get to visit her dad in hospital.

The shopping trip that Katie missed was described as 'hilarious' and 'a great laugh'. But why was everybody so unsupportive? The initial responses – 'we thought she'd like to be left on her own', 'we didn't want to stress her out' – seemed to be rationalisations. After we challenged them, we began to get closer to what was really happening.

One group member admitted he'd wanted to run out while Katie was talking; another that she'd had a strong impulse to cut herself after listening to Katie. For some, Katie's story had triggered memories of their own experience of loss or abandonment. Louise, whose mother was a heroin addict, had survived a wretched childhood in and out of foster placements and was able to say she felt jealous that Katie had at least some memory of a mother who loved her. She was ashamed to admit this but her courage in being so painfully honest was recognised and appreciated.

And then, Maureen, a thoughtful woman, slightly older than the others, said in a flat voice, 'I really despised Katie when she was crying. And I despise myself for feeling that.'

'What was it about Katie crying that made you feel like that?' someone asked.

'I just don't like it. Can't bear it. It makes me want to puke. It just doesn't feel right. I've never cried. Never. I just wouldn't. Not ever. Not even as a kid.'

'Perhaps you would like to be able to cry like Katie?'

Long silence while we all digested the implication of this question.

Maureen eventually muttered, 'Don't know.' Then a bit later, almost imperceptible, staring at the floor: 'I'll think about it.'

Sure enough, over the weeks that followed, Maureen began to share how she had been threatened and punished as a very young child for crying. I've heard variations of this story so often: the child crying because she's been hurt, then being hurt some more because she's crying, eventually learning to bear the pain in silence rather than risk a vicious circle of tears and further punishment. Or worse: children faced with raging, out of control or sadistic adults frequently fear that they are going to be killed. It is not difficult to see how this pattern can be passed down the generations. Suppression of crying doesn't have to be linked to physical abuse. It operates at a cultural level as well as a family level, although of course the two are interlinked. Don't most of us go through the ritual of apologising after we've had a good cry? And research shows that even the most socially aware and psychologically minded of us are not immune to the tendency to treat boys' tears differently from those of girls.[2]

Some parents feel rage at very young babies crying. I don't mean here the common-enough exhausted rage felt after hours of coping with a crying baby and sleepless nights when we are tired and at the end of our tether, but a more fundamental abhorrence of crying itself.

There is a very important and interesting area of psychosocial theory and scientific research known as attachment theory. The main idea is that the quality of our early bonding with others establishes a pattern on which our future ways of experiencing ourselves and connecting with others is based. Attachment theory suggests that we are shaped by early experiences of our carers' ability to meet and respond to our needs and feelings. We can grow up mainly secure in our relationships with others, able to manage anxiety, frustration and neediness – or indeed excitement and joy. Or we can develop a tendency to be unhelpfully entangled, wary or inconsistent.

Gradually, Maureen was able to cry a bit herself, albeit in a small, strangled way, but enough to soften the hate and envy she felt towards people who were lucky enough to be able to feel and express their grief.

It's not easy to sit with people who find crying so complicated, so conflictual, so unbearable. I've seen people who associate crying with being sick or incontinent, people who feel they are being strangled, people whose muscles go into spasm. Occasionally, when I'm sitting with such a person, I have a flicker of these physical fears myself, an example of what psychoanalytic therapists call projective identification, a kind of primitive communication that runs unconsciously between people, deeper than words.

Often an episode of crying in therapy will be followed by acute anxiety, an expectation of punishment or abandonment, a need to check that I have not been damaged by their tears, a need to apologise profusely. For some, this anxiety is so intense that they drop out of therapy; others pre-empt this drama by dropping out before this dreaded point is reached. Perhaps most painful of all is working with people who glimpse how damaged they are but have no hope that this can change – the potential catharsis of facing their worst fear, too threatening, too dangerous. Sometimes, just respecting this and sharing the pain has to be enough. Occasionally, it's a starting point.

~

Doctors encounter death and engage with loss and grief throughout their working lives. It is an integral part of their role and medical schools are increasingly aware that it needs to be prominent in the curriculum. To be comfortable with such work also requires a degree of self-knowledge and capacity for introspection.

As part of my paediatric placement as a medical student, we spent half a day with a child psychiatrist. We knew through the grapevine that she was a child survivor of the Holocaust, that most of her family had been killed. She told us she wanted to spend the afternoon helping us to remember what it felt like to be a child, that this insight would help us to be good paediatricians. What was it like for the children we were working with on the wards? Had any of us been admitted to hospital as children?

Perhaps knowing what we did about her tragic childhood helped us be more open with our feelings than usual, but what followed was one of the most memorable learning sessions in my six years at medical school. Four of our group had had their tonsils removed in hospital in the early 1960s, at a time when visiting, even by parents, was still rigidly controlled. Three of them described this as their first memory, so vivid and traumatic had the separation from their parents been. The fourth had been a bit older and had been so frightened by the old Nightingale Ward, the strange hospital smells and the scary matron that he'd tried to run away.

It reminded me of the time my little sister, Angela, was taken to hospital with severe pain and a high temperature, one of my first memories. I'd arrived with my parents for visiting hour, only to find that the two-visitors-per-patient rule was being strictly applied even on the children's ward, so I'd been left with a colouring book in the reception area. I sat quietly for a while watching other patients come and go, at first fascinated and then rather frightened as one woman who looked very ill was whisked past in a wheelchair at a run. Looking back, it was probably the first time I'd been separated for more than a few hours from Angela and suddenly I felt scared that something awful might happen to her. Perhaps I was also anxious and wanting my parents. I knew that if I tried to walk up the corridor, I would probably be stopped, so I decided to walk around the outside of the building, hoping I would see Angela through a window and could climb through. My parents eventually found me in the hospital grounds, looking up sadly at the huge austere Victorian building that seemed to my four-year-old self to go on forever, craning my neck up to the high windows, desperate to see a little girl waving from them.

There were about twelve of us in that group with the child psychiatrist, all with poignant memories. By the end of the afternoon I had learned that one of my peers had a younger brother with Down's syndrome and went back home at weekends whenever he could to help look after him. Another had an older sister who'd died of leukaemia when she was eight. Such stories are common in the lives of doctors and often determine their choice of specialty. Sometimes they are aware of this and it might even be part of their personal statement in their application to medical school. But it's surprising how often the link has not been made.

Over the years, I've helped a few doctors uncover an underlying wish to make loved ones from their childhood better and understand more clearly how this plays out in their work. There's even a term for this: the self-assigned impossible task.[3] The point is that if this wish sits unrecognised and unacknowledged behind their motivation to make the patient better, they are thrown back to their original grief and helplessness every time a patient deteriorates or dies – a common-enough situation in the day-to-day life of a doctor. The here-and-now situation is sad enough anyway, but if yearning and grief about the past is howling just beyond awareness, it all gets to feel very desperate. If those early feelings have not been acknowledged and understood, present-day grief and failure get pushed away, and they drive themselves ever harder. The result is often burnout.

I remember attending a psychotherapy conference early in my career. One of the speakers, as an aside, made the comment that we were all here because we'd had depressed mothers. I remember shaking my head in disbelief. It didn't ring true for me. What a crazy assumption! But the thought niggled away at me.

Years later, in my own therapy, I was able, painfully, to re-imagine the experience of my early infancy. My mother had given birth to a dead baby, two months premature, when I was eleven months old, a bereavement that was hardly talked about and probably resonated painfully with the unmourned loss of her father when she was a child of five. What had that been like for her? And what had it been like for me? She wasn't depressed in a way that

175

was picked up or worried about by other people but, in the 1950s, this would have been unlikely. Had I been aware of her desperation and grief that she was so good at hiding from the world? I can imagine myself anxiously witnessing her staring darkly into space. Maybe I'd had some awareness of her pregnancy and then her terrible emptiness.

There is plenty of evidence that young babies have much more awareness of these things than we might imagine. Our early months, rarely part of our later memories, can be formative. I'd always felt a huge sense of responsibility for looking after people, making them happy, even keeping them alive. It's probably my biggest strength but also a vulnerability, something I need to watch out for in myself. For a while, I guess, my mother must have looked to me to lift her out of her grief. So here you have it: here was my self-assigned impossible task. This dynamic that I could be so astute about in others was deeply buried in my unconscious, preverbal memory, and took me years to uncover in myself.

While death is the most profound and final separation we bear, we can experience severe grief with other forms of loss. Where children are concerned, the long-term impact of separation is mitigated if there are adults around who understand the grief and can sensitively help the child with their feelings. This was not the case with one of my patients, George, who grieved terribly the loss of his family and beloved home when he was sent away to boarding school. Boarding school syndrome, as it has been described by my colleague, Joy Schaverien,[4] is sometimes the underlying reason for people breaking down in later life and seeking therapy.

George had been duly referred to the outpatient psychotherapy department where I was allocated to see him. By this time, 1991, I had three young children. Leaving the bustle of ward life behind me for the time being, I was putting myself through the rigours of psychotherapy training, spending most of my time in intense and closely scrutinised one-to-one conversations behind closed doors. A year or so later, while I was still seeing George for his weekly sessions, my husband left our marriage, and I was catapulted into a personal state of grief and fury. Perhaps this heightened struggle with my own sense of loss gave George's journey a particular poignancy.

Being sent away to school at the age of eight had profoundly affected George. He hated to cry and would visibly pinch himself and pull his hair to stop himself crying in therapy sessions. Being the eldest of three children close in age didn't help. He felt he'd been cruelly uprooted from what sounded like a rather idyllic early childhood on a farm in Devon. He was mildly bullied by the other children at school, but it was the homesickness that he couldn't bear – literally a sickness that caused him to vomit and sob convulsively for hours. He just couldn't understand why his parents had sent him away. At first he clung to the idea that his mother would realise she'd made a terrible mistake and he would beg her every evening on the phone to rescue him. He missed everything at home: his bedroom with its familiar toys, the cosy farmhouse kitchen with its Aga and basket of kittens, the pear tree in the garden with the tree house that his uncle had built for his sixth birthday. He missed the comings and goings of the farmworkers who'd been in and out of the house for as long as he could remember, the tractors and the combine harvester, which had their own personalities and names he'd given them, and Ricky the sheepdog, whom he'd named and raised from a puppy. And most of all he missed his parents, his brother and his baby sister.

To start with, he'd been encouraged to have long phone calls home, his mother breaking off to let him talk to his brother and even the baby, then patiently answering all his questions about the farm, comforting him as he desperately sought reassurance that every animal, tree and machine was as he left it. But when his mother tried to finish the call and say goodbye, George would start to cry, begging her to pick him up and take him home. At the end of these calls, he was usually physically sick. Then he'd persuade himself that he hadn't explained things well enough, that it was his fault in some way, that next time he'd do better and get his mum to understand how bad things were. As well as the loss of everything familiar, he just couldn't understand why his mum, who seemed upset herself on the phone, didn't come to rescue him. He could never let go of the feeling that something else had happened, that sending him away was part of a bigger plan that he didn't understand and was too young to be told about.

After a few weeks, his housemistress took him aside and told him sternly that he must stop crying on the phone because it was upsetting his mother and the other children. She produced a star chart with promises of reward when he managed not to cry but also threatened that phone calls would be limited and possibly stopped if he didn't change his ways. George knew that he couldn't stop crying completely but took more care to hide himself away. His habit of pinching himself and pulling his hair stemmed from this time.

'Let's all give George a clap because he's managed a whole day without crying,' his house mistress proclaimed in evening assembly. Even at the age of eight, George could see through the crude behavioural training. He became increasingly isolated, secretive and cynical.

Eventually, he gave up the idea that his mum would respond to his unhappiness and settled to a state of resigned despair. His parents were warned that periods of leave might be unsettling for him so they were cancelled. When he finally returned to the farm, he couldn't relax and enjoy it for the thought that he would have to return to school at the end of the holiday. If grief is the price of love, George had determined that he wasn't going to love. He made a principle of never showing or sharing how hurt and vulnerable he felt, until, many years later, his wife having left him, he had a breakdown and started therapy with me.

~

George's struggle with grief over the loss of his home, over the life he'd had before being sent away to school, closely mirrors the traditional four-phase model that health workers are taught. In this model, the first phase is one of shock, emotional numbness, acute distress and disbelief. This stage can be understood as our way of protecting ourselves from the acute impact of a reality too painful to bear. This soon gives way to the second phase, a preoccupation with the loss that can include yearning, searching and anger. In George's case, his attempts to etch the details of his family and home into his mind would be seen to reflect this phase. As the reality of the loss is accepted in the third phase, the agitation subsides and profound sorrow and despair take over.

The model suggests that these depressive symptoms tend to peak at about four to six weeks, and gradually subside, but pangs of grief may occur at any time. They may be triggered by situations – for example, a piece of music playing, or most obviously in George's case phone calls – that evoke memories of the loss.

As time passes, the intense pain of early bereavement begins to fade, the depression lessens and it is easier to think about other things. This is the final phase and, as energy is invested in other relationships, normal activities and the future, it can be thought of as some sort of resolution – in George's case, more accurately, a pseudo-resolution. Typically, the model suggests that people recover from a major bereavement within one to two years.

This way of thinking about loss can be very useful for those grieving and those caring for them, but it can be applied too rigorously. There is a strong argument that Western culture has overmedicalised grief. Both of the commonly used disease classification systems give a diagnostic label to persisting grief symptoms. The bereaved are increasingly encouraged to see their doctors, who usually prescribe medication in the acute phase and refer them for counselling if symptoms persist. By assuming phases of natural grief are clear-cut and conform to a prescribed timescale, we fail to understand the complex mix of context, character traits and individual experience that each of us brings to the grief. This risks pathologising a sizeable minority of the population. Both classification systems emphasise that the grief should be judged in the context of cultural expectation, but what if this itself is unrealistic?

It is important that doctors try to identify individuals who might need extra support and those whose grief might lead to serious mental health problems. But too rigidly defining what is 'healthy', overdiagnosing illness and overmedicating, seems to deny that grief, in many forms, is a normal part of being human and that the experience of loss affects everybody in different ways.

~

We tend to grossly underestimate how long it can take to recover from grief fully, whatever the cause. Precisely a year after my marriage broke up, when I was still struggling with waves of sadness, a close friend suggested that I should be over it by now and should start on some antidepressants. This friend was a GP, rather black and white in her thinking and brisk in her manner. I'm sure she felt she was being helpful, but in fact she left me feeling hurt and irritated. The break-up had been complicated, with lots of mixed feelings to work through, practicalities to sort out, and other people's feelings to think about. But it was grief that overwhelmed me. Despite having been a psychiatrist for several years, I was shocked by the intense pain of the loss and the crying that seemed to go on and on. I was grieving, not just for the loss of my husband, but for the life we had created together with our children. I'd lost shared hopes for the future, my sense of being part of a loving couple that trusted and knew each other well, my belief that love would make things come right in the end, the dream of a family unit that felt safe and provided emotional security for the children. That's a lot to work through.

I cried almost every day the first year and quite frequently during the second, usually in the car, the transition space between work and home. Was this abnormal? Having now watched several friends, colleagues and patients struggle through similar situations, I know it isn't. It is common to hear bereaved people say the second year is the worst, as the pressure on them to appear as if they're back to normal builds up and the gap between others' expectations and how they are really feeling gets wider. When this happens, we can feel alone with our feelings, anxious we are being judged and fearful that no one understands. Even worse, we can conform to the expectations of those around us, persuading ourselves that we have recovered, but losing touch with our true selves in the process. Thinking back to Prince Harry and what he went through after his mother's death, presumably this was part of his reality.

Keeping someone's grief in mind is not easy and I can be as neglectful as anyone else in this matter. Lives in the twenty-first century are lived at a hectic pace. It can be difficult even to step off the treadmill to attend a funeral, let alone to make space in our lives for a friend who's been bereaved. Sometimes, there's just too much going on, or grief is just too incongruous and badly fitting with what's going on in our own lives. Sometimes there are personal reasons for wanting to distance ourselves or just not feel it.

~

One of my early memories of school is when one of the girls in the class cried all day because her hamster had died. I seem to be someone who doesn't have it in me to bond intensely with animals and I distinctly remember, even at the tender age of six, thinking that such a fuss about a hamster was ridiculous. Years later, I was reminded of this when one of my early therapy training patients, Sandra, talked incessantly about her cat dying. My fellow trainees had a lot more sympathy for her than I did, and my supervisor explained rather sternly that it was the grieving process that was important, not just the overt object of the grief. I knew the mourning process was about other unacknowledged losses as well, but gradually came to realise just how important the cat himself had been to her. She'd suffered some awful experiences, had had little in her life that had been affirming, and had invested a huge amount of meaning and energy into her relationship with her pet. Although I could understand this in theory, I struggled to connect empathically with Sandra. After a few months, she dropped out of therapy as her mother's illness had worsened and she was needed to provide daily nursing. I felt sad for her but a bit relieved for myself. I certainly didn't count my sessions with her as a great therapeutic success and wasn't sure if I'd helped at all.

I was surprised when a year later Sandra phoned the department. In an unexpectedly direct manner, she told me that her mother had died six weeks earlier. She'd completed most of the practical tasks linked to the death but felt she needed some help getting in touch with her feelings. Would I see her for a few sessions? I felt touched. This lonely woman had understood herself enough to know she needed help with her grief and trusted that I could help her. She came to see me for another six sessions, talked mostly about her mother, and again left abruptly in a matter-of-fact fashion, having found herself a job. This time I was left more certain that it had been a useful, if undramatic, piece of work, and what's more, that it was probably possible only because I had spent all those hours with her talking about her beloved cat.

Nowadays, this type of pragmatic, timely intervention would be almost impossible in the NHS. We have a system obsessed with 'finished episodes', categorising the level of distress, and rating outcomes after each session. There is little understanding of the painstaking work involved in building a relationship with someone like Sandra who found it hard to make eye contact and put a name to her feelings. The system is so rigid that someone in Sandra's position would probably be told that she no longer qualified for specialist psychotherapy or at best that she had to start again at the bottom of the waiting list.

But grief doesn't fit our increasingly obsessional need to fit everyone into categories, rigid systems and tidy models of our cognitive and emotional lives. Models of grief, such as the phases described above, are condensed descriptions, best seen as a rough guide, an attempt to provide some sort of reassuring map for an experience that can ambush and frighten one with its intensity. Every grief is different. We can oscillate between the different phases, and resolution of the grief is not always achieved – indeed, in some people, for very understandable reasons, resolution is not the desired outcome. I'm thinking particularly of the experience of parents who have lost a child where it is entirely normal for a part of oneself to continue grieving. This can be very difficult in a society where death is a taboo and 'moving on' the expectation.

⁓

Over the years, I've worked with many patients who have lost children or have living children with a terminal condition; work I've found particularly emotionally gruelling. I've known two colleagues who suffered tragedies connected to their children: one lost her child in a tragic accident, the other had two young children diagnosed with a terminal neuromuscular degenerative condition. Just the thought of our colleagues' grief threatened at times to overwhelm our team although, of course, we tried our hardest to support them. They both eventually decided to move on to an area where the emotional contact with patients was not so intense.

In my independent psychotherapy practice I have seen several couples who have lost a baby, usually a stillbirth or a cot death. It is impossible to compare suffering but if you have been through a pregnancy and loved a very small infant, you will know that such feelings are like no other. There is such an intermingling of bodies and minds, one hardly knows what is oneself and what is the baby. Anyone who has been present at a birth or just watched one on TV programmes such as *Call the Midwife* or *One Born Every Minute* knows that the moment of birth can bring forth an outpouring of ecstatic emotion in everyone present, not just the mother. It is this, the sudden termination of such intense connectedness and joy, that can make losing an infant so terrible.

The experience of being with a close friend shortly after her baby son had suddenly and unexpectedly died is etched in my memory. The sheer physicality of her experience was harrowing: her body contorted in pain, breast milk leaking, spasms of tears, clinging to baby clothes desperately trying to capture the feel and smell of her little one. I was a mother of a small baby myself at the time and after the first few weeks we both tacitly decided to give each other more distance. I've always regretted not being more present for her; it was just too painful for both of us. At the time I simply couldn't imagine carrying on if I lost my baby. But being with my friend and other courageous souls as they grieve and recover enough to rebuild their lives has given me strength. I find I can now be a calm and steadying presence for individuals and couples coming to terms with such loss, although I feel their grief acutely at times.

Like my friend, the couples who come to see me feel there is no place for them as their peer group moves happily on to the all-consuming job of parenting. I hear the same stories over and over: the futile attempts to avoid baby shops and playgrounds and the pangs of acute physical and emotional pain they feel when they pass pushchairs on the street; the halting, embarrassed conversations, and fear that people are avoiding them; the achingly lonely experience of boxing up the baby clothes and other paraphernalia that had been such a joy to buy only a few weeks earlier; the heartbreaking discussions about what to do with the nursery. They frequently report cheery comments from others, such as 'it's good to see you back to normal' when they are in fact struggling to get through each day, struggling to concentrate and focus on anything other than the dead baby, still struggling with a world that feels empty and a future that has no meaning.

Coming from a generation who rarely knew the gender of our babies before birth, nowadays I'm struck by the degree of character already projected on to the as-yet-unborn infant. Modern couples have frequently named their baby early on in the pregnancy and seem to me to have bonded in a more specific way than I ever did. Some bereaved couples are very angry about the care they received around the birth, rightly or wrongly blaming doctors for the death. Sometimes the women are physically ill, struggling with wildly fluctuating hormones and other perinatal complications, their immune systems probably affected by depression. Some are keen to conceive again as soon as possible, while others feel they can never replace the baby who has died or risk a repeat of the same terrible grief. Self-help support groups have been a lifeline to some but others have found such groups intrusive or insensitive in some way. Sometimes the partners in a couple manage their bereavement in very different ways and feel angry with each other or even judge the other for not feeling so deeply; others feel their relationship is stronger because they have been through something so terrible together. What's very striking is the amount of gratitude they express to me for seeing them, for providing a space where they can be themselves and don't have to worry about the damaging effect of their feelings on other people. At some level they recognise, even at the point of extreme despair, that their future well-being depends on them being able to 'give sorrow words'.

~

People referred to psychiatrists are often unaware that grief is part of why they are there. They have not been able to recognise and articulate their pain and commonly present with severe mood swings, their losses long buried. Sometimes, drugs and alcohol have been used as a way of dulling the pain, but the self-medicating has become a problem in itself.

When severe grief hits a child and the impact has not been adequately understood and eased by adults, the trauma can affect the development of their personality. If we go back to George, his grief was frozen in time as the grown-ups around him had responded in a panicky and ultimately harsh way to the intensity of his agitation and distress. As a consequence, part of his developing personality had frozen and his wife, unable to get through to this frozen part of him (her words), had eventually left him. George eventually sought therapy at the age of thirty-three because he knew he was relying too heavily on alcohol and drugs. He complained that his life felt meaningless and knew he was in danger of losing his job and friends as well as his wife if he didn't do something about it.

The course of therapy wasn't easy. At the start, he didn't seem to take it seriously, missing a lot of sessions, always with a supposed good reason. I wondered aloud if he was still drinking away his feelings and, although he denied it, it emerged that I was right when later that week he sent me a drunken email in the middle of the night:

> *Dear Dr Campling, Please just give up on me. I can't bear being me anymore. I'm a hopeless shit. I fuck up everything I do. I would give anything to be dead and not have to suffer the torture that is my life any more. Please help me. Everyone else hates me. What's the point? Answer that. No doubt you won't want to see me now you know what a drunken liar I am . . .*

The email continued in a similar manner.

When he arrived at the next session, George looked bleak and dishevelled but was sober. He'd not slept the previous night and had clearly been rehearsing what turned out to be an apology for sending me such 'emotional rubbish' and a well-argued case for why I should continue to see him. Refusing to see him had not actually entered my head. It was in this session that I first noticed him pulling his hair out. Clearly, he had expected me to reject and abandon him and was fighting with himself not to cry. He had broken his own rule, sharing and exposing his fear and despair, albeit while drunk and in an email. From the look of him, he seemed on the edge of breaking apart and although I hoped this would be a turning point, I realised it was important to proceed very gently.

Over the next few months, George managed to attend regularly and the conversation between us became increasingly meaningful as the story of being sent away to boarding school emerged. Unlike some children, George had not felt much bullied or abused by his boarding school experience, but he'd clearly learned to detach from his feelings. He had a strong sense that the colour had seeped out of his world; literally, his memories and dreams of school were in black and white, while his early memories of the farm were in vivid colour.

George saw me weekly for about three years. The pattern of becoming acutely anxious that he'd damaged our relationship whenever he talked about feelings continued but became less intense, something he could recognise and eventually manage with a kind of rueful humour. Crying remained torturous to him. Although he was able to stop pinching and hair-pulling, he continued to feel his body tense up whenever he was in touch with loss and sadness. I was often alerted to how he was feeling by becoming aware of muscle tension in myself. I wondered if there was more anger around that he couldn't locate and articulate. In his mind, he'd hung on to a hope that he would one day be able to cry his heart out with me and that this would be a transforming, cathartic event. It didn't happen and maybe part of him felt angry with me for this. The last few months of our meetings were spent in a mood of profound sorrow: some of this grief for 'lost years' and a sense of how damaged and empty he felt; some of it sadness and anger that he couldn't continue in therapy with me and grief that the therapy seemed incomplete.

George seemed very vulnerable when he left, almost like a small child going off to boarding school. I was aware that he was much in my mind over the next few months, but he didn't attend follow-up appointments and I feared that he might have gone back to his old drinking habits. I'd been anxious and preoccupied with him throughout the period of his therapy, often talking about him with my supervisor. I'd always wondered whether his idyllic early childhood was as happy and as unproblematic as he'd remembered but attempts to open this up had never got very far. Should I have been more challenging? If I'd been more gentle, would he have felt more safe? These sorts of questions went round and round in my mind but I think my preoccupation was more to do with his vulnerability and dependency on me. It was as if I was somehow holding the tearful grief he couldn't manage.

Years later, I received a Christmas card from him, a short message and a photo of a newborn baby.

Dear Penny, It's been six years! I have a good life farming in New Zealand with my partner, Keri. We have a beautiful daughter, Izzy, nearly four years old. Our second daughter was born with a heart defect and died at three days old earlier this year. Keri and Izzy and I cry together. Thanks. Best wishes. George

10

HIDDEN HISTORIES

One of the reasons I decided to specialise in mental health was my love of biography, the complex conjunction of biology and experience, of luck and planning, that makes everyone's story unique.

When I was at medical school, we were taught that taking a comprehensive history was the most important skill in medicine, that astute follow-up questions and careful listening would give us the insights we needed to formulate our ideas and focus our thinking towards the most likely differential diagnosis. But there were signs even then that this was starting to change, and now, even in psychiatry, I worry that the importance of a detailed history has been degraded. Too often, mental health patients are not encouraged to talk about their pasts or to explore the underlying reasons for their disturbed behaviour. We look for quick and easy solutions to complex, deeply entrenched problems but so often this entails avoiding the hard reality of people's lived experience.

Patients' histories are invaluable. I have seen so often how a missing or neglected piece of information from the past brings a new perspective on the problem, allowing in more light, more coherence, more hope. Such histories often go beyond the individual's lifetime, stretching back to traditions, traumas and secrets that have been passed down in families and communities; hidden histories that are sometimes so traumatic or shameful they continue to have a ripple effect. What is it like living with a traumatised parent or grandparent but not necessarily understanding what's happened to them? How can you deal with the legacy of something like the Holocaust or slavery when it has touched your family long before you were born? Does it make a difference to your mental health if you come from a society where the history of trauma is talked about openly or is it better not to know? How can you learn to move past a generational trauma of which you're not even fully aware?

~

On the way back from picking the children up from school one afternoon, many years ago, I'd stopped at the playground, gently rocking the pushchair while chatting to two other mums, both of whom had girls the same age as my daughter. Judy was talking about her daughter starting her period the week before.

'Too young,' she said, 'It's not fair. What a burden for her. I wish it could have waited till she'd at least been at secondary school. But at least we were well prepared, she's had a sanitary towel in a pocket in her school bag since she was nine.'

Judy and I carried on chatting: about our own experience of having our first period, how old we'd been, why we thought girls were menstruating younger, and how awful it must have been for our grandparents' generation when these things tended not to be discussed openly. I told her my granny's story: how she'd been told by her mother, in a mysterious knowing tone that was impossible to question, to 'look out for blood when passing water'. For years, she'd been very anxious every time she saw a stream, lake or river; she found herself scrutinising them, not sure what she was looking for, but feeling frightened nonetheless.

I was vaguely aware that Arushee, our other friend, had gone very quiet, which was quite unlike her, but I didn't think any more of it until she rang later in the week and asked if she could pop round for a chat. Over a pot of tea, Arushee told me she'd been shocked by the conversation about periods and found it disturbing. She hadn't even thought about her daughter's periods starting and now felt a bit odd about this. Arushee, a physiotherapist in the NHS, was one of the most down-to-earth people I knew, the sort of person who would help out in a crisis, popping round with food if I was ill and looking after the children at a moment's notice. This just didn't fit with the woman I knew.

She went on to tell me that she had no memory of starting her periods herself. Since the conversation, she'd been preoccupied with the subject. She must have been twelve years old, she'd worked out, an age that coincided with the family moving from Kenya to England. This was an awful time for them, so awful that, in the twenty years or so in between, she'd never had a conversation about it and never heard it referred to by anyone in the family. When she'd told her older sister the following evening about the blank in her memory, they'd both become very upset, the emotional impact of what had happened to the family in Kenya emerging for the first time.

In the decades after African nations started to achieve independence, the Indian populations across East Africa had increasingly found themselves the targets of persecution. It was particularly severe in Uganda, where in 1972 President Idi Amin expelled the entire population, giving them just ninety days to leave. Although the situation in Kenya was not as extreme, many still found themselves denied citizenship and were forced to leave behind fortunes built up over many years, and the prestige and comfortable lifestyles that went hand in hand with their wealth. They had to start again in the UK, their professional qualifications counting for little and their business networks decimated, struggling to find work of any sort.

Amid all this trauma, uncertainty and loss, I imagine Arushee's period starting must have seemed trivial and passed unnoticed, neuropathways closing down protectively as her family responded to the sense of overriding threat. The subsequent blind spot around this part of the family's narrative had, in turn, created a blind spot in Arushee around this particular developmental step for her own daughter. She might have failed to support her, just as Arushee's family had been unable to support her thirty years earlier. Now, triggered by our innocent conversation in the park, she had begun to reflect more deeply on a dark episode in her family history.

While Arushee was not in need of mental health services, I've seen a number of patients who developed distressing psychiatric symptoms at the point when their offspring reach an age that coincides with the age they were when horrible things started to happen to them. The traumatic childhood memories have been shut away for years, only to erupt into their consciousness as a particular developmental milestone – often expressed only in

a look, or attitude, or turn of phrase – echoes a toxic event so
many years earlier.

～

Living and working in Leicester, with its rich and diverse mix of
immigrants to the city over several decades, I became particularly
interested in the way that family history can affect mental health.
Joti was one of many patients where I wished I had access to a
detailed family tree.

I first met Joti when she was just seventeen, a year or two
after I'd become a consultant. She was petite, but had a boldness
about her, her chin tilting upwards in a habitual way, suggesting
defiance. Her eye contact was like that of a much younger child,
flitting around with an occasional unashamed full-on stare, appealing, hurt, intriguing. At times, she looked about ten years old, but
there was also a world-weariness about her, a sense that she was
old beyond her years. She was living in a hostel for the homeless,
had the telltale spots around her mouth that indicated serious
glue-sniffing, had already tried most of the illegal drugs available,
and was on the edge of prostitution. Her future seemed bleak.
Child and adolescent services, at this time, saw people only until
they left school; people like Joti left school at sixteen – an unfair
system if ever there was one.

It was hard to see how she would cope in adult services. I
hated to think of her on an adult ward but couldn't imagine her
coping for long in an intensive psychotherapy environment. Joti
lived in the present: spontaneous, impulsive, reckless. She found
it hard to be interested in other people's lives, rocking her chair
back and fidgeting like mad during the therapy meetings. We'd

accepted her into the therapeutic community knowing she probably wouldn't stay very long, but reasoning that we could try to keep her safe for a little while – out of the homeless hostel, away from predatory drug dealers and pimps – at least, giving a chance for her brain to mature a bit.

When we first met her, she was totally cut off from the experiences that had made her: seemingly unconnected to her inner world, unable to tell her story. She found our questions hilarious.

'What do you want to know that for?' she'd say if we asked her about her dad. 'I've told you I hate him!'

For Joti, being hated and hating someone was so normal it was hardly worth commenting on. The important thing was to put them behind you and move on. It was difficult to get any history at all from her, but we did establish that her family were Sikhs; that her dad – whom she said she hated – was unemployed, had an alcohol problem and regularly beat up her mum; that she'd grown up on a council estate on the outskirts of Leicester, the only Asian girl in her school, where she was the butt of racism, badly bullied and abused. She had little interest in discussing her family's history, but her story piqued my curiosity. Why, I wondered, did they live on a white council estate, when most of the Asian population at this time lived in a cluster around the city centre? She had no idea.

As predicted, Joti was out of her depth in the therapeutic community and left after a few weeks with Jake, a male resident she had befriended and who had come to the end of his therapy. We were anxious about what would become of her but felt, on balance, she'd had a good experience. The other residents had been protective and surprisingly patient with her. What's more, they'd persuaded her to have a coil fitted, two of the women accompanying her to the sexual health clinic. This was an artful piece of persuasion, given Joti had so little thought for the future, little sense of cause and effect and such an undeveloped capacity to protect herself.

As we'd hoped, Joti remained in contact with us, and while her life remained risky and chaotic, she managed to steer clear of the most damaging street drugs and prostitution. She came back for another stint in the therapeutic community about four years later. Older and wiser doesn't really describe this young woman, still only twenty-one and easily blown by the changing winds. But she was able to be a bit more thoughtful and questioning about her heritage.

It seemed the members of her family, fending for themselves in a white stronghold, on one of the worst estates in Leicester, were probably outcasts from the local Asian community. Not only was her father an alcoholic wife-beater, but Joti had a rather vague memory of an unpleasant scene at the temple when she was younger. This had ended with Joti and her mum being thrown out. In turn, Joti was an outcast from her family, too terrified of her dad to try to build bridges and therefore unable to question them about the family history. She thought they came from Uganda but wasn't sure.

'Idi Amin!' she responded excitedly in reply to a direct question. 'That's the man. I'm sure it was him.' Then less certain: 'Well, I think it was anyways . . . It rings a bell.'

Doing a timeline, it was pretty clear that the family had moved to the UK in the early 1980s, a good decade after most of the African Asians in Leicester had been expelled from Uganda. Joti thought her dad had enjoyed a good job in the government before they emigrated. It was something that her parents had often thrown at each other during arguments – arguments that so often ended in violence. Was it possible that Joti's father had worked for Amin's tyrannical government in Uganda? The same Idi Amin who'd described the Asian population as 'blood suckers . . . who'd killed the economy'. This would certainly explain why they were outcasts in Leicester.

Frustratingly, we were left guessing; Joti's story remained out of reach. With key questions about her family history unanswered, she was denied layers of meaning that might have been helpful to her developing sense of identity.

Having said this, Joti herself, like many of our patients, was ambivalent about exploring her history. Children can learn at a very young age that it is not safe to ask questions, that the answers are beyond their comprehension or too overwhelming to take in. Sometimes children glimpse such a level of pain, trauma and violence in their parents that they spend the rest of their lives trying to switch off their curiosity. Such suppression can be reversed and their interest in the experience of others rekindled in therapy. But, for some, this self-protectiveness has a lasting effect, their capacity for empathy, for identifying with another person's feelings, for satisfying intimacy, often limited to a degree that is disabling.

It's difficult to imagine how hard it must have been for so many immigrant families. I'd had a glimpse of this as a student many years earlier when my friendly neighbour Vanessa, a teacher at a local school, told me how shocked and moved she'd been by some of the vivid descriptions that her pupils had written for her about the horrors they'd witnessed in Uganda. One child wrote about leaving his grandparents to die; another being stopped on the road by a violent gang who raped all the women in the family; yet another saw his father shot and his mother becoming dangerously hysterical at the airport when her only remaining piece of jewellery, her wedding ring, was cut from her finger.

One thing that troubled Vanessa was how difficult it had been to follow up these revelations – either with the child on their own or with the class as a whole. Her guess was that the children had found themselves writing something that they were not used to speaking about. She'd wondered about the experiences of other children in the class, but when she tried to open up a class discussion about their experience leaving Africa, there'd been an uncomfortable silence. Some of them didn't seem to understand the question even though she knew many of their families had been exiled from Uganda.

Leicester is proud of being the first city of minorities – in other words, no ethnic group, including 'white British', makes up more than 50 per cent of the population. The original refugees from East Africa, many of whom already had links with Leicester through the textile and hosiery trade, now have children and grandchildren, even great-grandchildren, and make up about a third of the city population. What I've always found puzzling is that, on the whole, local psychiatrists and psychotherapists don't hear the family stories that were being picked up in Vanessa's English classes.

These issues are complicated and I'm aware of the dangers of making too many broad generalisations. There are obviously issues of race, culture and racism, of attitudes to mental health and psychotherapy, of religion, of family and community structures, of justice and reparation. But what I'm interested in here is hidden histories. Why are some histories passed down from one generation to the next while others become taboo?

~

There seems to be a consensus that in general it takes about fifty years or three generations before a severe collective trauma can be talked about freely. Think about the First World War: the generation directly affected was, in the main, unable to describe the utter nihilistic horror of trench warfare. But the damage was visible to all. As the many amputees and other wounded walked the streets, their determined silence, along with the stifled screams as many of them relived the traumas in their nightmares, conveyed the terror to their offspring, often at a level beyond language. This was not a generation who understood the importance of processing trauma, and maybe the horror was just too immense, every family affected, the loss of so many young men in their prime too overwhelming for a country to bear. Yes, Remembrance Day was instituted, and war memorials listed the names of those who had died but, beyond this, there was a widespread determination to move on and not dwell on the experience. They did what they needed to do at the time, but what a relief when novelists such as Pat Barker – who, interestingly, as a child shared the house with her wounded grandfather – started, at last, to find words to describe events that had haunted us for so long.

Nowadays, we are much more aware of the psychological effects of war and the way this can track down generations. The effect of the Vietnam War was well researched and showed a clear link with veterans' mental health problems. UK studies on PTSD in soldiers who fought in Iraq and Afghanistan show significant psychopathology and make a clear case for specially tailored clinical services. But, despite our insights into how difficult it can be to settle back into civilian life and relate sensitively to partners and children, our care of severely brutalised veterans and their families is still far from adequate. The nature of these faraway wars means there is little general interest in veterans' stories once they get home, not enough people to listen patiently and help them express and process the alienating experiences, not enough skilled therapists to imagine what it's like to feel so intensely frightened for months on end or to suffer the grief and guilt of seeing beloved comrades killed in action.

A handful of veterans sought help in the therapeutic community, but they were often too angry and resentful with the world to make much progress, their dependence on alcohol and other drugs already severe. There are specific services for ex-military, so if they came our way, they had often had previous therapeutic interventions that they'd been unable to engage with productively, and one or two of them had left the army in disgrace. A consistent finding in the research is that traumatic experiences can be particularly merciless on the mind if they hook into pre-existing deprivation and abuse suffered early in life. This was the case with the characters I'm remembering. It was virtually impossible for them to address what had happened to them on active service as adults without bringing up memories and feelings that belonged with their experience of being hurt and humiliated as children — memories and feelings they couldn't cope with revisiting.

Some of them were also very young when they'd first become soldiers. We are the only country in Europe that accepts sixteen-year-olds into the army, two years before we consider them mature enough to vote. One young man in the therapeutic community had realised it wasn't the life for him after the first few weeks but, being only sixteen, he could only be discharged if his mother signed the papers, and she refused to do so. I found this extraordinary. A cause for bitterness indeed.

More common in our therapeutic groups were women who'd been violently abused by partners who had done a stint in the services. Some of these men, I'm sure, had severe problems that predated their time in the army, but they all had clear-cut symptoms of untreated PTSD and seemed to be unconsciously trying to rid themselves of the sense of fear, humiliation and helplessness by making their partners and children experience these emotions. These women were sucked into relationships with men who were crying with fear one minute and sadistically raping or uncontrolledly beating them the next. Disentangling from such a relationship – sometimes escaping in the middle of the night with their children – was not easy.

One can start to imagine how such children would be affected by these circumstances: the repercussions of their father's behaviour creating a fearful and insecure environment, sufficient in some cases to have a long-term impact on the children's development – the veterans' trauma passing on to the next generation.

~

Some of the research on intergenerational transmission of trauma has been done on families of Holocaust victim survivors, where children and grandchildren commonly present with mental health problems. A study in an American child psychiatry clinic found, for example, that the grandchildren of Holocaust survivors were over-represented by 300 per cent in comparison with the general population.[1] Sometimes these offspring seem to carry the invisible weight of the trauma, despite not experiencing it first hand.

Much of the work on this was done in the early 1990s, roughly fifty years after the Holocaust, when 6 million Jews and people from other minorities were slaughtered. Since then, the term secondary traumatisation has become common parlance in the psychotherapy world to describe children being affected directly or indirectly by their parents' post-traumatic symptoms. There is some controversy about this, particularly among the Jewish community, and it is worth pointing out that patterns of resilience can also be passed down the generations. Sometimes these can be one and the same. For example, personal narratives and case studies of adults who came to the UK as children on the Kindertransport describe a typical defence pattern. From external appearances, they often seem to be surviving particularly successfully, but this is at the cost of cutting off from their emotional needs. As children they had to cope with overwhelming loss, danger, uncertainty, humiliation and hatred. Such extreme psychological injury and pressing survival needs forced them to function as adults at a very young age, cheated of their childhoods, uncomfortable with vulnerability in themselves, and sometimes in the next generation.

I have no experience of working with people directly affected by the Holocaust but I have seen a few children and grandchildren from such families. David, for example, had been a very successful violinist before catastrophic panic attacks paralysed his playing and abruptly put an end to his career. A CBT therapist had helped him manage the worst of the anxiety, but he emerged from these events feeling profoundly hopeless about the future and made two serious suicide attempts. When I first met him, I was struck by his obsession with violent death. Such thoughts seemed to pervade every waking moment, even though, by this time, he had resumed a career in his family business and was engaged to be married.

As our conversation developed, it became clear that violent death had been the 'unspoken known' in his childhood. David's father had come from Germany on the Kindertransport at the age of ten and found out years later that all his family left behind in Germany had died in concentration camps. As in so many families in the years after the war, these tragic events were never directly talked about, but somehow David grew up knowing the raw facts, although he couldn't remember quite how. By the time he started seeing me, his father had died, and his mother seemed to know as little as David did about the details of her husband's childhood. David didn't know what sort of family in England had fostered his father, whether they had adopted him after the war, whether he had been encouraged to retain his Jewishness or, like so many children, been enjoined to forget his origin and start his life anew. His parents' marriage and family life seemed to have been determinedly turned away from the past and focused on building a bright future for him and his sister.

One of the reasons for David seeking therapy was his horror at the idea of having his own children, something he knew his partner wanted, something he had been unable to talk about with her. The thought of being a father literally made him feel sick and he had no idea where this repugnance came from. He'd had a happy childhood himself, he told me, his parents doing everything they could to encourage the career he'd been so set on. He blamed himself for being a disappointment to them.

Eventually, he was able to acknowledge a sense of relief that he was no longer pursuing a career as a musician. He'd found being in the spotlight hard and the relentless practice regime stifling; and he was particularly relieved to be free of his father's vicarious interest, which he'd experienced as too intense. Shortly after this, he was able to confide that he had found physical contact with his father repugnant. He felt guilty that he'd not been able to be more affectionate towards him when he was ill and dying, but the repugnance went way back into his childhood. For as long as he could remember, he had lived in dread of the moment in the evening when his mother would instruct him, 'Kiss your father goodnight.'

'What's wrong with me?' he'd agonise, over and over, the tone more self-flagellation than curiosity.

David was difficult to work with, argumentative and prickly during the sessions, while, at the same time, his pain seemed to lodge right inside of me, something I was aware of throughout the week. Some people mistakenly think that psychotherapy is just about digging up the past. In fact, I have three stories in mind when I see a patient: their history, their present circumstances and, perhaps most important, the emerging relationship between the two of us. I visualise this as three sides of a triangle, all giving important information.

If it's true that patterns of thinking and feeling can be determined by experiences early in life, then these patterns should transfer into the present day and be expressed in some way in the relationship with the therapist. This is what therapists mean by transference. For example, a young boy who felt critically judged by a parent might be predisposed to reading things his therapist says as critical. If he's aware of how he feels, he might share that with the therapist, and they can discuss why he felt criticised on that particular occasion. But if he's not consciously aware of his feelings, things might get more complicated: for example, he might feel generally angry and resentful towards his therapist, or his anxiety might prompt him to miss a session or arrive late. The immediacy of the relationship between therapist and patient can make it a potent instrument of change. If we can catch patterns being repeated, there is the opportunity to think afresh about our habitual reactions and it might be possible to set about doing things differently.

David hated being a patient, he hated feeling vulnerable and, most of all, he hated letting me see his vulnerability and feeling the slightest stirring of need. Like his father before him, he had learned early in life to shut off emotions he saw as childish and weak. From the age of seven he was travelling from Leicester into London twice a week for music lessons, and practising the violin for hours a day, squeezing out any time for play or relaxation.

He routinely came late or missed therapy sessions, always saying he had important work that couldn't wait, impatient with my questions about this and suggestions that he was avoiding uncomfortable feelings. Eventually, we began to find a space where he could express some anger: he hated therapy, dreaded coming, why couldn't I be like his CBT therapist and teach him some life skills? He was constantly researching other types of therapy that he thought might be better and lecturing me about their value. He found it hard to let me do my job, hating it when I pursued something he'd said or made an interpretation about what I thought was going on. One day, I made a link between the repugnance he'd felt as a child towards his father and his resistance to being a father himself.

'I can't bear it when you say things like that,' he snapped. 'It's like you want to be one step ahead all the time.'

Round and round we went. He was hypersensitive to the mildest suggestion on my part that he was angry with his parents, meanwhile furious and critical of me. He told me I was airy-fairy and wasting his time, insensitive about his family background, constantly trying to get one over on him. It felt impossible for me to get it right. But most difficult was his resistance to talking about the Holocaust and the impact this had had on the family. There was no point, he said, because I wouldn't understand. It seemed as if he was making me feel just as his parents had made him feel. The Holocaust was not something that could be talked about. David would never be able to understand their experience just as I would never be able to understand his experience. And yet I was aware that David was conveying his desperation to me, perhaps in a similar way to how his father had, on some level, conveyed the immense suffering he had been through to David. I carried his pain around with me and the possibility of suicide haunted our sessions, just as death had haunted David's childhood.

Hard though it was, I felt from early on with David that I had a grasp of what we were working with. How can parents who've been robbed of their own childhood make space for vulnerability? How can a little boy growing up in the shadow of the Holocaust give enough weight to his own feelings? How could his feelings ever be expressed and affirmed? How could any loss seem important enough when compared with his father's immense grief at having his whole family wiped out in death camps? How do you express anger towards a father who's suffered so much? How can a father who couldn't even tell his wife what had happened to him and his family help his son find the words that might have lessened the fear between them?

But at that time, I was a relatively inexperienced practitioner. One thing therapists learn is that patients need to make their own discoveries in therapy. It is not enough for the therapist to have constructed a narrative that seems to make sense of things. Perhaps in David's case I was almost too curious about his story, assuming that he shared this curiosity. I was not sufficiently in touch with his ambivalence, his resistance to questioning his father's role in his life, and his fear of the rage that might emerge from under his overdeveloped sense of loyalty and duty.

He eventually moved back to London, saying he'd look for another therapist there. He didn't turn up for his last two sessions with me so there was no chance to say goodbye or review the work we'd done. This felt like a kick in the teeth. I was furious with him and cross with myself for feeling so strongly. My supervisor was calm. He thought David was probably more attached to me than he could acknowledge, that saying goodbye would have made him feel too vulnerable, that he still might be able to internalise something good from our supposedly therapeutic relationship. I wasn't so sure. Sometimes it all feels pointless and I wish I could just get out a prescription pad and not invest so much of myself.

I often think about David, wondering if he's dead or alive, wondering whether he was able to father children, wondering if he found someone who would look after his mental health in another city. Perhaps these thoughts are whispered echoes of how David's grandparents might have felt as they saw his father off during the Holocaust.

These days, the Holocaust is a topic that tends to be discussed much more openly but back then, twenty-five years ago, that was not the case. David didn't have access to his family history, to a shared narrative of trauma and, like Joti, he had learned to repress his curiosity. The horrors of the Holocaust loomed in his unconscious but without form, and he lacked the language that might have helped him link the beyond imaginable genocide to the actual lived experience of his parents. The repugnance that he described towards his father, and towards the very idea of fatherhood, was language of a sort – a coded clue from his unconscious that needed deciphering, but it was so imbued with confused shame that it was difficult to think about.

～

The famous psychoanalyst and founder of attachment theory, John Bowlby, wrote a deservedly famous paper entitled 'On Knowing What You Are Not Supposed to Know and Feeling What You Are Not Supposed to Feel'.[2] In the paper, Bowlby tells the story of a patient whose mother hanged herself when the patient was only three years old. She finally found out the truth about what had happened to her mother many years later, as an adult. Only when she was given the facts did she realise that she had known the truth all along. Children are alert to impressions, scenes and experiences and pick up so much more than we think they do. And in many cases much more than we want them to know. The least adults can do is help them verify the truth. Instead, many of us often actively disconfirm a child's observations and disapprove natural emotional responses to distressing situations, not realising that experiences, apparently forgotten, can continue to influence thoughts, feelings and behaviour.

I have a German patient, Clara, who talks about having 'divorced her parents' as a young woman. Apparently, this expression is common in Germany, but it was new to me. Both Clara's parents were notorious members of the Nazi SS during the war. Her story reminds me that trauma can be transmitted to the offspring of perpetrators as well as of the victims of atrocities. Clara grew up sensing that her parents guarded a terrible secret. She was somehow made to feel profoundly ashamed and guilty but had no way of understanding why, except to believe she was a particularly wicked child. Neither of her parents would talk about the war years but when Clara was admitted with depression as a young adult, her German psychiatrist suggested she do some research into their war record. As was the case with John Bowlby's patient whose mother had hanged herself when she was three years old, Clara's research confirmed what she had known deep down all along but had never actually been told. She described this revelation to me as a new beginning: having access to the cold reality of her parents' lives allowed her to finally shake off the feeling that she was responsible for something terrible and take action to distance herself from them and the murderous history they carried with them. For the first time in her life, she began to make sense to herself.

〜

Intergenerational transmission of trauma is complex, and can even become a lasting legacy woven into the fabric of society itself. For example, the concept has been used to add a perspective to why black Americans tend to do worse than their white counterparts in so many areas of life. Current racism, poverty and inequality are obviously key factors. But their ancestors' experience of slavery, racial violence and racial discrimination has had a lasting effect on their descendants. Cultural trauma such as slavery results in a loss of identity and meaning that affects generation after generation as the trauma becomes ingrained in society. For example, black children's internalisation of white people's reaction to their skin colour can be seen as a lasting trauma experienced originally by their ancestors.

In the UK, too, black British children of African-Caribbean heritage are less likely to do well educationally and socio-economically, and more likely – as we saw in chapter 5 – to end up in prison or detained under the Mental Health Act. There is some evidence to suggest that even if we attempt to extricate the impact of conscious and unconscious racism on diagnosis and perceptions of dangerousness, and control for factors such as unemployment and poverty, the prevalence of major mental illness in black ethnic minority groups seems to be higher than expected.

Perhaps more puzzling is the fact that the second and third generations – the offspring of African-Caribbean immigrants to the country – tend to suffer worse mental health problems than the first generation. Here intergenerational transmission may well play a part. The Windrush generation arrived in the UK in the early 1960s, full of hope, loyal citizens of the Commonwealth, excited about starting a new life in the 'mother country'. But they very soon encountered overt and often violent racism and discrimination. Jobs they were well qualified to do were denied them. 'Respectable' landladies turned them away because of their colour. Many of them ended up in squalid accommodation, earning a pittance doing mindless hard labour. Some were already parents, hoping to set up jobs and a home before the rest of the family joined them a few months later. But finding themselves so impoverished in the new country stopped this going to plan. How could this experience not have affected the way they brought up the next generation?

One of my patients, who came over to the UK when he was seven, had been left in Antigua with his granny before joining his parents. He found it hard arriving in this country, meeting up with parents he hadn't seen for four years and couldn't remember. He has few memories of his relationship with them over subsequent years. His parents worked shifts and so were often absent, but he remembers the pressure to stop speaking with an Antiguan accent, and being hit by them when he forgot.

It's easy to condemn such treatment of a child, but perhaps harder to explore what might lie behind it. How do you bring up a child in an environment you know to be racist? How do you protect them when you can't necessarily protect yourself? How do you bridge the years of separation? How do you stop your massive disappointment, humiliation and sense of betrayal, let alone the experience of being violently assaulted, being conveyed to the next generation? It is easy to see how trauma can be passed down the line.

The story of the Windrush generation erupted once more into public consciousness in 2018 after a Home Office scandal that resulted in some illegally being denied their pensions and sent back to countries they barely knew. We can only hope that the publicity will generate more understanding of these issues, both within the British Caribbean community itself and within the population at large.

~

Cultural history should be part of everyone's personal story: we need to know our place in the world. Joti had so much of her story missing that it was hard to make sense of herself. David knew the stark facts about his heritage but was unable to join up the dots; he'd inherited a profound sense of the horror of the Holocaust but not the conversations that might have helped him process such a legacy.

It is now about fifty years since large portions of the Asian population were expelled from East Africa. And true to received wisdom, there is a sense that conversations are starting to open up. The anniversary of Indian Independence has always been celebrated by the South Asian population in Leicester but in 2018, on the seventieth anniversary, there was much more media coverage of Partition than there had been in the past.[*] For some Leicester families, it was Partition that led them to start a new life in East Africa in the first place. The television coverage of this bloody episode in history was appropriately serious and spared us little, the number of deaths estimated at between 1 and 2 million, with 10 to 12 million people displaced. For some, I suspect it was the first time they were presented so clearly with the extent of sectarian

---

[*] Partition describes the process that split the Indian subcontinent along religious lines into two separate countries, India and Pakistan, with a tragic level of violence and loss of life involved.

bloodshed and the shocking role of British incompetence in the slaughter. Perhaps some people who watched these programmes found it threw a light on their personal story, giving a context for family trauma that previously had been shrouded in mystery.

One of my patients – Shamila, a psychiatrist herself, in her mid-thirties – is going through a phase of questioning everything she's previously taken for granted. Her grandfather has recently died and she wishes she knew more about his life. This was a family that talked a lot about Uganda, but Shamila always found the tone of melancholic nostalgia irritated her. It was as if nothing in her own life could compare. Since her grandfather died, however, she's much more aware of her heritage, of being part of the Ugandan Asian diaspora, wanting to work out what this means for her. She is planning a trip to Uganda, hoping to visit the places in Kampala where her family had lived and built up their textile business for over a hundred years before they were exiled. She is worried about what she will find. She has recently read an article suggesting that the wealthy Asian lifestyle in Uganda depended on exploiting the African population but doesn't feel able to ask her parents about this, so precious is their idealised view of the life from which they were uprooted as teenagers.

I believe the stories we tell ourselves matter and that the truth matters. I see part of my job as helping patients reconstruct a narrative of their lives that rings true – often painfully true. There are inevitably gaps in these narratives, gaps that require to be mourned, gaps that can sometimes leave people feeling fragmented and lost, like a map with vital bits missing.

Living and working as I do in Leicester, making sense of cultural, ethnic and religious history has been an important part of the work. I have had glimpses of hidden histories and secondary traumatisation, where parents' unspoken trauma has impeded emotional development in the children, and a vague but disturbing awareness of psychological pain in the family has not been met with a narrative that explains and makes sense of such feelings. If we can't think about the past, about distressing life events and disturbing relationships, we are likely to re-enact them in some way that is detrimental to the next generation. I see this in my own life, I see it in the families of patients, and I see it in organisations and society at large. Again and again, I witness how developing an attitude of enquiry and attention to their foundations enables people to become more effective architects of their lives.

11

A GLOBAL TRAUMA

Of all the crises that have threatened our lives and disrupted our ways of living over the last fifty years, arguably the most serious has been the Covid-19 pandemic. Frightened by the thought of dying or passing on the disease to others, we have had to huddle alone or in small groups, our links with family, friends and colleagues – including sick or dying loved ones – fractured. Everything from the early care of our toddlers and education of our children, to the security of our jobs and the economy to which they contribute, to our sense of belonging, in sports teams, choirs, religious groups or just our friendship networks, has been threatened.

I recently met an astute elderly woman, the mother of a friend, who talked about the Covid pandemic as being worse than the hardships of living through the Second World War. Metaphors of war have abounded during the pandemic, but I felt initially shocked that someone who had lived through the Blitz and lost loved ones would make such a comparison. True, such historical events have much in common, including the experience of death, loss, injury, damage, traumatic memories, and living in fear and uncertainty, but I think that at the heart of what she was getting at was the enforced isolation that was so specific to this particular collective trauma.

The effect the pandemic has had on mental health is wide and varied. People with learning difficulties and those with serious long-term mental illness have not tended to do well.[1] They have been more likely to become infected in the first place, and more likely to die from the illness, a sad example of us failing to provide effective protection for the most vulnerable. The mentally ill detained in hospital under the Mental Health Act have been particularly deprived. In our local hospital, they have not been allowed visitors, and any excursion outside the ward – even if it's to another hospital for a physical investigation – results in three days' quarantine in isolation, often delayed by another day or two, as they wait for the result of their PCR test. Others have presented with mental health problems for the first time during the pandemic and there is evidence accruing that some of them will have symptoms that are a direct result of the virus's effect on their neurobiological systems – part of the Long Covid syndrome.[2] What worries me and many others as much as anything is the inequality and the erosion of social capital that has been worsening for years in the UK and has taken a further hit with the pandemic. Poverty, unemployment, job insecurity and stark divisions within our communities all have an impact on our well-being and will tip some people over the edge. The data that links such factors with mental health problems, such as depression, anxiety, alcohol and drug misuse, and suicide, is well established, so we should not be taken by surprise.[3]

To be honest, I have never felt so overwhelmed by the need out there. I could work hundreds of hours a week if I so wished and all the psychotherapists I know are working at full capacity. Most of the work is very familiar, but sometimes I'm surprised by patterns and narratives that seem particularly linked to these times. The conversation with my friend's mother who had lived through the Blitz brought home to me the importance of really understanding the psychological experience the pandemic is putting us through and working out what makes it different from other apocalyptic events.

There is no doubt that more people than ever have been left struggling with mental health problems. But a word of warning. As a psychiatrist, I have become increasingly worried at how much we tend to focus on psychopathology and ignore the character traits and, even more important, the social conditions that enable us to overcome adversity. At the start of my career, the response to people caught up in a catastrophic event was to offer them 'treatment'. We now know that the human mind is evolved to protect itself and will, in most cases, gradually heal at its own pace. Trauma literature is full of examples of well-meaning people racing in to help but in reality making things worse. Of course, support should be available and easily accessible, but it is important not to pathologise prematurely or rush in uninvited.

Among the gloom of the pandemic, it is important to keep in mind the capacity of the human mind to find its way to a new spring, the opportunity for post-traumatic growth and for collective resilience.

~

The requirement to socially distance was one of the most difficult aspects of the pandemic, confining us, separating us from loved ones, and leaving many extremely isolated. As the lockdowns dragged on, I started to notice how many of my regular patients developed, for a time, symptoms of what I understand as separation anxiety: agitated pacing and searching behaviours; insomnia; intrusive, irrational, repetitive, frightened thoughts often linked to death anxiety. They seemed to lose the ability to soothe themselves, needing repeated consolation.

As with other animals, what we call attachment behaviour in infants is instinctive and serves to maintain proximity to protective adults, thereby improving the chance of survival. We know that infants separated from their primary carers experience anxiety and anger and, if this absence is prolonged, it will lead to helplessness, hopelessness and despair. As we grow older, we develop the capacity to hold people in our mind and become less dependent on physical proximity, but we are thrown back to more primitive feelings and behaviours as adults when we are under threat. With this pandemic, however, it was not just the heightened sense of threat but the reduction in factors that serve to protect our mental well-being that compounded our vulnerability: the deprivation of physical contact and affection; the reduction in everyday low-key contact that is usually taken for granted but offers a soothing background pattern to our lives; the loss of activities such as sport and music that give life meaning, motivate us and help regulate our mood.

During the war, trauma, loss and hardship were mitigated to some degree by the sense of camaraderie. The war bound people together, broke down social barriers, brought people closer in all sorts of ways, building up social capital in the process. I would have hated sheltering in a crowded underground station night after night during the Blitz, but maybe it would have satisfied my need for human contact – 'skin hunger', psychologists call it – more than the present situation.

Not so the pandemic, when loneliness and social deprivation were the reality for so many. I found I kept coming back to an evolutionary-based explanation when I was puzzled by people's states of mind during the pandemic. One of the reasons it took such a toll was that the behaviour demanded of us was counterintuitive: it went against our nature. Human beings are not designed to socially distance under stress. We are not evolved to live shut away alone or in closed-off nuclear family groups. While we agonised and rationalised and worked out how to obey the rules and keep ourselves safe during yet another socially distanced event, such as Christmas or a funeral, we were battling with a large part of our mostly unconscious brain that equates safety – indeed survival – with the opposite and urges us to huddle together, to visit and embrace our families, to share our food, to run protectively towards rather than away from each other. It was this exhausting struggle with our deeply embedded evolutionary programming that was unusual and had a distinctive impact on our mental health.

The pandemic has taken its toll across all walks of society. But here I want to focus on my work with front-line clinicians and their struggle to remain mentally healthy at a time of tremendous stress. It's hard to think of an environment that is less adapted to human well-being from an evolutionary point of view than an ICU in the middle of a pandemic: ultra-high-tech machinery, bright lights, constant loud noises and, most obviously, people dying without the comfort of their families. The sense of alienation can be profound. (Even before the pandemic, a significant proportion of the patients that had been on ICUs were known to suffer lasting mental health impairments known as post-intensive care syndrome.) And in the same way as psychiatrists are left to manage the mess of mental health problems on behalf of society, front-line teams in hospital were left to manage the ravages of Covid-19. In some ways, their extreme experiences throw light on the experience of the rest of us.

~

Priti, an intensive care nurse, is describing how difficult it is to get herself into work.

> It's like I have to psych myself to face each step. I wake up feeling tense all over and have to do my relaxation techniques before I even get up . . . Then I force myself to walk out the house and get in the car. I get to the hospital car park, and I can feel a sense of dread creeping all over me, like a sort of heaviness and horrible sick feeling, like I might puke. The worst bit is approaching the board telling us where we're going to be working. The thing about the board is when you look at it, you also get an idea of who's died since your last shift. A couple of times I've just looked at that board and could feel myself getting hot and shaky. Yesterday, I just collapsed in front of it, legs gave way, couldn't stop crying.

Priti is struggling with what is now being referred to as anticipatory traumatic stress disorder. This is a term I hadn't heard until recently but it is definitely a thing: a relatively common and distressing state of mind that is now visible in many of those working at the raw edge of the Covid pandemic.

'Once I'm there it's not too bad,' Priti goes on to tell me, 'but getting there, it's like my body's dragging me backwards. I've always been good at getting in on time, but now I'm quite often a few minutes late, so I get myself up and ready earlier and earlier, but it doesn't seem to make any difference.'

Jake puts it another way: 'It feels like there's a fight going on inside me. It's weird because I wouldn't say I hate my job, not even with Covid. But I have to kind of manage myself. It's almost like taking charge of another person, like I have to tell my legs to walk forwards. If I forget to concentrate for a moment, I find I've turned the bike round and I'm heading home without really making that decision.'

It's fascinating when different individuals emerge over a short period of time with such similar narratives, but what they say doesn't surprise me. Having worked with ICU staff since the start of the pandemic, I'm well aware of how deeply distressing the experience has been and continues to be. Of course, many of us feel ambivalent about going into work; Sunday evening blues or rising anxiety at the end of a holiday are commonplace. But this seems to be at a different level, an experience of reluctance almost beyond their control. From their descriptions, it sounds as if a primitive mechanism is working at a subconscious level instructing their bodies to turn around and head for safety. An example, surely, of the conflict between our deep-seated, evolutionary-driven protective mechanisms and our rational will.

～

It is early March 2020, before I have started my work with ICU staff, but two clinicians, Hilary and Maggie, have come to see me independently. Both are scared – really scared – by what they are observing in China and Italy. They are also scared by the lack of appropriate fear in those who will have a major part to play in protecting us. This is the week when the prime minister is televised happily shaking hands with hospital patients, seemingly oblivious to the danger and gloating about his lack of anxiety afterwards – gestures and statements of impervious stupidity that sent ripples of shock through the clinical community. Li Wenliang, the courageous eye doctor in Wuhan who first drew worldwide attention to the possibility of this disease emerging, is already dead from the virus, as are doctors and nurses in Italy. Our shock is well founded.

I've not met Hilary before. She starts by telling me how she had decided at the last minute to cancel the house party she had arranged in a farmhouse in Cornwall to celebrate a special birthday. This should have happened the weekend before, but she felt with Covid it was too risky. She'd been looking forward to the event all year and felt sad and disappointed, but what had really got to her was the angry reaction of some of her friends: 'Did you think about how *we'd* feel when you changed this plan?' one of them asked. 'It's spoilt it for all of us!' She felt really hurt and alone.

Hilary goes on to describe a Covid-19 planning meeting of her division in the hospital a week or two earlier. Unusually, almost everyone had turned out, so the room was packed and there was a sense of excitement in the air. Hilary looked around, thinking how young most of the doctors were. A gulp of cold realisation that she was one of the most experienced in the room made her tremble. The responsibility felt enormous, and she had to work hard not to cry at the thought of the avalanche of illness and death that might be coming their way. She was also troubled by the thought of a patient who died unexpectedly from respiratory failure a few weeks earlier. It seems possible to Hilary that Covid-19 has been around in the hospital since as early as January (a possibility denied by officials at the time) and yet there she was crammed up tightly with her colleagues in a room with no ventilation. 'There we all were, making these impressive plans. But it was like no one really believed it. No one was acting as if the threat was real.'

Maggie is younger, less experienced and, as a healthcare assistant, much lower down in the hospital hierarchy. She works on a geriatric ward and already there is an instruction to discharge as many people as possible. She is quite sure that Covid is already there on her ward but testing for the elderly is discouraged and the results take up to a week to come back to them. She tries to talk about her fears – for the patients, for her colleagues and for herself – but no one seems to want to listen. She notices how many staff at all levels have no idea how to take their gloves off safely and how many simply hang their masks around their necks. At this time there was no proper personal protective equipment (PPE) that came anywhere near World Health Organization (WHO) standards. She feels vulnerable, unprotected and more afraid than she's ever felt in her life. The worst feeling is that no one in authority seems to be concerned about her safety or able to see the danger. She is utterly disillusioned.

The two women are from different hospitals, different cities, different backgrounds, but both can see with unflinching prophetic insight how things are going to play out, even though the WHO hadn't yet named the new disease a pandemic.

Both Hilary and Maggie are consumed by a dread that they themselves will die. Both have personal responsibilities – Hilary for her disabled daughter and Maggie for a particularly vulnerable sibling. They know how their deaths would impact on their dependent loved ones and it is this thought that is unbearable, magnifying the dread and the acute awareness of their own mortality. Both know that the risk of dying is relatively small, but it is real; they have not come to me to have their fear dismissed and the last thing either of them needs is a lecture on statistics. Instead, we face together the pictures that fill their heads and their associations with the thought of catching the virus and dying. Hilary decides to make changes to her will. Maggie, who has few possessions, writes a letter to her sister, and makes arrangements for the care of her beloved dog.

Those two sessions in one week at the beginning of the pandemic will stay with me. With both Hilary and Maggie, the terror in the room was tangible, communicating physiologically, body to body. But I admired their capacity to face the threat of imminent and premature death so authentically. I felt privileged: at some level I'd received a gift, a cathartic experience that helped me face my own fear. In fact, it was the catalyst that motivated me to find out if I could be of any help supporting staff from the local hospitals.

Healthcare staff have died across the world from Covid-19 in large numbers. Since those early sessions with Hilary and Maggie, a lot of clinicians have talked to me about the fear of their own death, particularly during the first wave when few were properly protected. I can feel the relief in the room when I raise it: tears flow, muscles unclench.

Some people might find this strange, the idea that talking about one's death can be helpful, liberating even. We live in a culture that sees positive thinking as the answer to most things. We vote for politicians that take this to the point of denial – as if denying suffering, denying threat, denying complexity will make it all go away. The culture in the hospitals reflects this. The messaging is relentlessly positive: buddy schemes, free relaxation apps, lots of talk about resilience, mindfulness workshops, free streaming of jolly films. For a while I was co-opted to the Trust's Health and Well-being Committee, but it was only the chaplain and myself who wanted to address the suffering and fear around, and it didn't go down well.

People need to talk about how frightened they are, the fact their masks don't fit, the fear of having to care for 'one of their own' if they become critically ill. As a therapist, I am committed to creating a space where the truth can be told. It is an absolute core value: the idea that if we can find the courage not to turn away from the negative and distressing, we will be able to hold on to hope in a way that is more grounded, more sustainable, more real.

Much of my career has been spent trying to help people who from childhood onwards have had their cries for help misunderstood, neglected and suppressed, so that when we do eventually get to see them, it is necessary to work through layers of accumulated mistrust before we can reach their carefully guarded vulnerability. With a few exceptions, this is not the case with the clinicians, who tend to roll up their sleeves and get straight down to telling me what's troubling them. They like the fact that I'm a medic, that I can picture the units where they work, that I can just about follow their professional jargon, that they don't need to hold back or stop to explain.

Perhaps surprisingly, the fear these clinicians express of infecting other people is much more to the forefront of their minds than their own death. It was chilling – particularly pre-vaccine – to hear the lengths people were going to in order to scrub themselves clean. Some sent their children away; others stayed apart from their families, one in a mobile home on the drive. Many described the elaborate homecoming rituals: no contact until they'd stripped off, put the washing machine on and showered, disinfected their car, their keys, their mobile phone. Most slept apart from their partners.

As well as the fear of literally infecting their loved ones with the virus, there is a fear of contaminating them with the horrors they are witnessing. To talk to their families about what the work entails feels dangerous in itself: too traumatic, too graphic, just too damned much. I worry sometimes that the protectiveness they feel, their understandable reluctance to allow work to invade their homes, leaves everyone in the family on their own with their fears.

Stacey comes to see me because she is worried about Tammy, her nine-year-old daughter who's become clingy and won't sleep in her own bed. Tammy is suffering from nightmares, waking up screaming but unable to articulate anything that happened in the dream. Of course, in the middle of the pandemic, there are

228

children all over the country suffering from anxiety symptoms, but it seems likely that Tammy's behaviour is linked to worries about her mum, an ICU nurse.

As we talk, it gradually emerges just how strongly Stacey feels that Tammy should be protected from 'adult matters'. When she was a child, Stacey was over-involved with her own parents' break-up and remembers how anxious she felt about her mother's sadness. She doesn't want to burden Tammy with her feelings in the same way and has banned all talk of the pandemic in the house, thinking she can somehow shut away everything that she is going through at work and carry on as normal in front of her family. Paradoxically, this seems to be having the opposite effect, and Tammy is anxious, not just about herself, but also about her mum, whom she doesn't want to let out of her sight. Children are far more perceptive than we give them credit for, and Stacey is indeed showing signs of stress, however much she tries to hide it.

'I'm pretty sure Tammy's picked up much more about the risks of Covid than you think,' I suggest to Stacey. 'I wonder if it's possible that your reluctance to talk about what's going on might be making her more anxious?' We discuss how she might make it possible for Tammy to ask the questions that are on her mind and how she might respond. Children are so much more able to cope with the truth than we imagine. But, left alone, their limited understanding of the adult world means they can get tangled up with their own attempts to make sense of things. They need sensitive exchange with an adult to help them do that.

It is surprisingly easy for Stacey to encourage Tammy to talk about how frightened she is feeling – to put it starkly, her fear that Stacey will catch Covid from work and die. Stacey shows her a photo of herself in full PPE looking like an astronaut, a picture that Tammy is later to show proudly to her friends, explaining what everything is for and how it keeps Stacey safe. She continues to sleep in the same bed as her mum for a while, but the nightmares stop, and they make a plan for her to move back to her own bed during a week when Stacey is off work and will be able to spend some time settling her back into her own room.

Even in very loving families, it's so easy for things to go wrong between parents and children, for blind spots to turn into vicious circles of misunderstanding and dysfunction, and for life paths to be set askew. I'm hopeful that my relatively straightforward intervention with her mum will stop this happening for Tammy. It feels good to intervene early in someone's life journey before things have built up.

~

A few months into the pandemic, I agreed with one of the matrons to visit her unit. Generally speaking, I don't think it's necessary to have experienced what our patients have been through in order to be empathic and supportive; we can, after all, engage our imaginations. But this felt a bit different and I was struggling to visualise this extraordinary environment.

The infection rate was still frightening and no vaccines were yet available, but at least hospitals had now acquired proper PPE and were no longer having to push nurses into Covid-dense areas dressed in pyjamas and bin liners. Donning and doffing PPE was something I was hearing a lot about, and I was intrigued to observe these oh-so-intricate rituals. The aim, of course, is to avoid contamination, and the extraordinary concentration on the face of the helper spoke volumes. It was like watching an Indian bride being carefully and lovingly dressed for her wedding, but the artistry was infused with science and the possibly deadly consequences of making a mistake.

Once decked in their PPE, it is hard for these doctors and nurses to see or hear or make themselves heard. This leaves them feeling isolated and massively amplifies the sense of alienation. Some tell me they've got used to it, but for others PPE has become a major focus of anxiety. Many of them fear not being able to get to the toilet: women tell me how difficult it is when they're on their period and others admit to restricting what they eat and drink before a shift. The gear is horribly hot, sweaty and the tight-fitting masks are painful.

One young doctor, Zarina, particularly hated wearing PPE. The protective gear made her feel more like a character in an apocalyptic sci-fi film, dehumanised and alienated. She sometimes felt dizzy and, knowing that the mask and visor restricted her vision and that three layers of protective gloves made her clumsy, she worried that her clinical acumen was compromised, and she would make a big mistake. She described to me how she'd man-age a thirteen-hour shift, holding on to the mantra 'one step at a time', replaying the calm voice of her mother as she helped her as a small child tidy up her room. Not only did she determinedly block out the bigger picture in this way, but she broke down every medical intervention into tiny steps in order not to give up in helplessness and despair.

As psychotherapists, it can feel as if we need to come up with strategies and solutions, but very often it is the patient or client who will find their own way through. The more we can resist our impulse to rescue them, the more likely that they will dig deep and discover their own strengths. Zarina had come up with an excellent strategy, accessing a soothing and nurturing memory to get through the task ahead.

But it's sometimes more difficult to find a way to cope. I was asked to see Jane because she had gone frantic in a Covid-dense area, ripping off her hood and gown. I had expected someone a bit flighty, but she was in fact a down-to-earth motherly woman who had been nursing for many years. She was clearly mortified and bemused by her behaviour, which was completely out of character. As she talked, I suddenly wondered if she was describing menopausal hot flushes, made a million times worse by layers of plastic. It turned out that the menopause had caught up with her unawares as she'd been so preoccupied over the previous months with Covid and put her lack of periods down to stress. Sometimes an objective pair of eyes on a problem can see through to the common sense that understandably gets lost under such stressful circumstances.

Not that these healthcare workers need the excuse of the menopause or any other confounding factor to explain their behaviour. The fear of losing control looms so large that some of them are already on sick leave.

~

Kevin comes to see me after suffering a serious panic attack that has floored him. Unlike those whose panic symptoms are clearly directly connected to the distressing circumstances at work, Kevin's terror erupted in the supermarket car park of all places, the sudden escalation and force of the pain sending him crashing to the tarmac. By the time of our first session, he's been off work for a few weeks and has already had some basic CBT sessions with the hospital counselling service. Although the physiology of panic attacks is clear to him and he's dutifully learned some relaxation techniques, he is still sceptical, and seeks me out. He can't shift the idea that he really has suffered a heart attack, even though he was taken to the emergency department where the usual battery of investigations all came back normal. 'It's left me so ill,' he explains, his eyes appealing to me to take him seriously.

A panic attack can be seen as an acute physical expression of fear that is perhaps too overwhelming for the mind to tolerate. But the actual experience of panic can be traumatic in itself: the sudden unpredicted onset, the sense of one's whole body being out of control, a condensed experience of helplessness that leaves behind a heavy ball of anxiety long after the physical symptoms have subsided. The potential for escalation is obvious and my job is to help Kevin break this vicious circle. As we talk it through, it emerges just how terrifying the experience was. Kevin's been told it was 'just anxiety' but he was convinced by the magnitude of his symptoms that he was going to die. This traumatic aspect of the experience and the way it links to his ICU work has been ignored. I ask him to describe his last nursing shift. He needs a lot of coaxing but eventually tells me that a lot of the patients in the unit at that time were healthcare workers, one of whom he knew. What had really upset him, though, was the death of a man with two children exactly the same ages as his own. ICU staff are used to patients dying, but it is unusual in this day and age for people who were well a week or two earlier to get ill so quickly and deteriorate so rapidly.

'I couldn't get over the fact that he'd been perfectly well three weeks earlier. And it was awful, a really horrible death . . . I can still remember his eyes when he was first admitted to the unit and realised where he was. They seemed to be fixed on me and so full of fear, like every breath was killing him – he was begging me to do something.'

Kevin is now looking anxious, sweat on his forehead, hands tightly gripping the arms of the chair, but he battles on trying to describe the particular quality of respiratory distress. 'It was unbearable, every breath was so painful, and each breath – you couldn't quite believe he'd manage it. I could feel it starting to cut through me. It was like I was trying to find the breath for him.'

I recently sat with my dad as he died of heart failure and realised that I had to concentrate sometimes to keep my own breathing steady. It made me wonder if the nurses' panic attacks might be linked to the torturous, effortful gasping breaths of their critically ill Covid patients. It's so easy to unconsciously mirror the posture and breathing of someone in close proximity, the distress communicated from muscle to muscle, from lungs to lungs.

Working as a psychotherapist through the pandemic forces me to think a lot about fear. Like most of my patients, I have more nightmares than usual; weird and hellish, waking in a panic, my unconscious mind bubbling to the surface, a midnight message that I'm more frightened about what's going on than I realise. It is not just front-line staff and mental health patients who are struggling; the pandemic has affected us all.

~

January 2021, grim in so many ways, finds us in the midst of another lockdown. I am talking to Nilesh, a consultant who came to the UK from India, proud to work for the NHS, convinced it was the best healthcare system in the world. Sadly the pandemic has left him disillusioned, and he is now very homesick. He worries about his parents back in India – an uncle has already died from Covid – and spends some of his precious time away from intensive care doing online teaching sessions on Covid-19 to groups of doctors at his old medical school. Many overseas doctors who are part of a diaspora with family members scattered around the world found the travel restrictions emphasised how far they were from their families. Like Nilesh, they talk to me rather shyly about their loneliness and yearning for 'home'.

Aware of how isolated so many of my patients are feeling, I've started to hold face-to-face sessions in my garden under a makeshift shelter with a small heater. It is apparent to me that there is something dangerously depersonalising about working in the ICU during this pandemic, not helped by being locked into PPE for hours on end. I hope that sitting in the garden with a pot of tea between us and rugs on our laps will provide more human warmth than a Zoom call. It's highly unconventional but given the number of clinicians like Nilesh who choose this option, despite the freezing temperatures, I think my intuition on this one is right.

Another young doctor, Ellie, has come to see me because she is frightened that she is losing her humanity. Tearfully, she confesses that she can't remember any of the patients' names. It is unusual to be dealing with just one illness and Ellie is aware that she has developed a sort of resigned, rather impersonal attitude to the patients – 'just another Covid case' – with resonances of an industrial production line. It takes the death of a previously healthy seventy-year-old, a retired English academic like her own father, to crash through these defences and force her to face up to the grief all around her.

I knew she was not alone in this. Our minds tend to manage traumatic events by denying the true horror, repressing the most disturbing memories and associated feelings, narrowing down the wider picture. During the first wave, most patients arrived on ICU with a tube down their throats into their lungs or had one inserted soon after arrival. Patients were largely unable to speak and there was no family to speak for them. Many of the nurses have described how difficult it is when the small details that help us see the person within the patient are absent. The clinicians grieve for the families and blame themselves for keeping them at a distance even though it's beyond their control. Like Ellie, they worry that they can't remember the names of the patients. They watch their feelings becoming numb as they deal with one death after another. They wonder if enjoyment of the job will ever return. One or two ask me if I think they're bad people.

Ellie is only too aware that many patients are dying a frightening and lonely death. She does everything possible to help the families feel connected to the patients, even spending her time at home sewing pairs of little hearts for the nurses so that one can be placed by the patient and the other given to the family. She organises final goodbyes using iPads or relaying last words on the phone, but she is haunted by the desperate circumstances of these scenes of grief-stricken intimacy. The absence of family goes against everything she holds important.

I usually ask someone at our first meeting if they are haunted by a particular memory – a particular patient maybe or a horrible incident? Some describe a gruesome death or a patient that they particularly identified with. But, most often, it is the stark communications with the families that is described as most harrowing. Despite being experienced and skilled communicators of bad news, these clinicians find it deeply disturbing to have to convey to people they have never previously spoken to and never seen face to face that the patient, perfectly well a few days ago, is about to die. They were only too aware, particularly in the first year of the pandemic, that many of these family members were also socially isolated with no one around to give them comfort. Ellie describes one heartbreaking situation where she had to break the news through a small child, the only person in the household who spoke English.

～

For ICU doctors and nurses during the pandemic, the moral distress is graphic and immediate; it can express itself in many ways. Some of them are eaten up with anger and there are plenty of people to feel righteously angry with, from government ministers down to their friends and family who can no longer be bothered to wear masks and take other precautions to keep us all safe. Increasingly – and even more uncomfortably – they have to manage their fury with patients and their families, most of whom have not been vaccinated. Some of them just didn't get round to it; others have their minds set against the vaccine and are often mistrustful of the doctors and nurses trying to care for them. I'm told of a minister of religion who warned his congregation against

237

vaccination and ended up on end-of-life care; of a hospital porter who refused the vaccine and died of Covid; of a family where a brother was a victim of the virus but still the rest of the family refused to be vaccinated, and a few weeks later two more siblings were critically ill in ICU. 'Surely, that must count as delusional?' one of the consultants asks rhetorically. (Psychiatry is very clear that labelling someone as 'deluded' – expressing false beliefs – and 'psychotic' – being out of touch with reality – should take cultural norms into account – in the case of the vaccine, the beliefs shared with one's immediate community.) But I get his point and sympathise with his exasperation.

It's not easy to feel furious with the people you are caring for. Or the people you care about. Different attitudes to the vaccine or social restrictions during the pandemic have torn some families apart. A lot of front-line workers have been really upset by what they see as the irresponsible behaviour of their parents. The ambivalence when we feel both anger and tender protectiveness towards the same person can be confusing and is often at the root of a presentation of depression. More generally, anger can feel horribly consuming and has a way of spreading into relationships where it doesn't belong. It can also drive impulsivity and one or two people I've seen have had to work to rein in their road rage. But the people I really worry about are those who direct the anger at themselves, where moral distress manifests in despair and self-hatred, and where suicidal thoughts loom large.

Some people cope in the short term as best they can, then find their coping mechanisms take on a life of their own and tip into being self-destructive. Like many of her colleagues, Scarlet has tried to manage her feelings by keeping fit, but her running has got more obsessive and, as her weight has dropped away, she finds it harder to eat. I note she is wearing many layers of clothing, despite the summer warmth. Below the neckline, her collarbones stand out as a warning, stark and anatomical. I'm shocked at how thin she is. How is it possible that she is still working thirteen-hour nursing shifts? She confirms how little she is eating and tearfully describes the nausea and discomfort she feels after the tiniest of meals. Like so many people who are in the grip of anorexia nervosa, she seems strangely unconcerned about the risk to herself, smiley and well defended, not in touch with the emotional pain of the last few months. I encourage her to see her GP as she is clearly in need of a physical examination and blood tests. Unfortunately, there is a long waiting list to see the eating disorder team as referrals have rocketed during the pandemic, so I offer to continue to see her until the appointment comes through. I'm not surprised when she cancels our next meeting. Like so many people struggling with this condition, she is deeply ambivalent about accepting she has a problem.

Surprisingly few of the clinicians I see have taken to alcohol, although those who choose to refer themselves to me might not be typical of the whole staff group. Rufus came to see me a year into the pandemic, having qualified and started working as a nurse in intensive care only a few months before Covid-19 took over. During the first few weeks he'd been swept up in the sudden hive of activity. Everything was changing, new policies and guidelines introduced every few days, every shift a game of catch-up. Despite being a relative novice, as beds multiplied and the ICU spread its boundaries, he was often the most experienced around and was expected to take the lead. He found himself performing procedures usually done by nurses with much more experience and looking after disorientated clinicians deployed from other parts of the hospital. On one shift he had a consultant surgeon volunteering to help on a nursing shift but who was unfamiliar with ICU technology or jargon: 'I asked him to fetch something then realised he didn't know what I meant, let alone where to find it. So, I had to try to explain what it looked like, and I couldn't find the right words and I felt like an idiot. All the time I was panicking because the patient was getting worse and it all – the whole thing – it just felt all wrong, like I shouldn't be there, like I was an impostor.'

However difficult it was, Rufus found it easier to be at work at this early stage of the pandemic than at home. He'd not had a problem previously, but now found it impossible to switch off. News was breaking all the time – numbers rising, outbreaks all over the country, lockdown measures, government ministers ill with Covid, the prime minister admitted to an ICU in London, and front-line healthcare staff starting to die. Like many of his colleagues, he became addicted to 'doomscrolling'. The staff WhatsApp group also gave him no peace: full of the latest initiatives to beg, borrow or steal protective gear, letting him know which of his colleagues were sick, how many patients had been admitted and who had died. It felt easier to be rushing around trying to help at work than sitting at home trying to act calm in front of his wife and two small children. The two worlds just seemed too far apart. Usually a hands-on dad, he became increasingly irritable around his kids, starting to find toddler talk impossible and experiencing the baby's crying as intolerable.

He started pouring himself a glass of wine as soon as he got home, just to calm himself down. By the time he saw me, he was spending most of the time at home drinking whisky at the bottom of the garden, desperately trying to shut out the distressing scenarios replaying in his head and cutting himself off from his ordinary family life that had become both meaningless and unbearable. He was using alcohol as a medication to reduce his agitation and help him sleep but, like so many others, discovered that the magic it can work is short-lived. A year into the pandemic, he was at least aware that it was more of a problem than a solution. This gave us the chance to work on the things he was running away from and to help get his life back on track.

~

As the pandemic has continued, it has been interesting to witness how the different surges of cases and stages of the pandemic have impacted on the healthcare workers and their teams. My work with groups during the summer of 2020 at the end of the first wave found teams worn out and sensibly anxious about what the future would bring. They were aware of the cost to themselves, some struggling more than others, but in general most were proud of how they had stepped up to the challenge. There was a sense of a crisis managed well, talk of collective resilience and, on balance, a sense of post-traumatic growth rather than post-traumatic stress.

Sadly, this was not the end and there was no recovery time. At least three new variants were to emerge and dominate in the UK, all more infectious than the first. In the early months of 2022, a mind-boggling number of people in the UK were ill with the highly infectious Omicron variant. Over sixty hospitals declared a state of emergency because so many of their staff had Covid. Although many people were getting away with a relatively mild illness, the numbers in hospital were as high as they'd ever been.

Two years into the pandemic, with no end in sight, it is the exhaustion and hopelessness that stand out, fed by the impossibility of covering the staffing rotas properly and the grinding misery of not feeling able to do the job properly. There is a sense of things falling apart and NHS workers being left behind to cope as those with the power to help do nothing. It is very clear just how much the culture in hospitals has been challenged by the realities of Covid. True, there have been some trusts and team leaders who have been imaginative in promoting initiatives that relieve and reward their staff. But this is the exception. There is no 'plan' that gets anywhere near facing the reality of the situation. No real understanding that good healthcare depends on the carers being properly valued and well cared for themselves. Despite the ongoing pandemic, there is pressure to keep all the other specialties going as normal. The backlog of delayed treatment means many cancer and cardiology patients that are sent to ICUs are being operated on at a later stage in their illness, and therefore have a worse prognosis. Turning down these patients because of a lack of beds and staffing can be as distressing as the work with Covid patients.

Quite apart from the sheer number of deaths, the actual work is full on to a degree most of us find hard to imagine. The environment is extremely high-tech, brightly lit and noisy, and involves an almost impossible amount of multitasking. I find myself worrying about their overstimulated brains. There were a few minutes of dry humour in one of the group sessions I held during the summer when the subject of 'decision fatigue' was raised. 'There's got to be something wrong if you're asked what you'd like for supper and respond with a temper tantrum!' one consultant ventured.

Then with increasing confidence that they were not alone in their madness, they shared stories of their completely disproportionate rage at being asked an innocent question and pushed for a decision.

The shortage of specialist nursing staff is particularly desperate. Nurses who chose to work on ICU because they enjoyed the concentrated focus on a single patient find themselves supervising inexperienced staff, sometimes from other specialties, and having to spread their attention over a number of patients, racing – in many cases, trying but failing – to get through the list of things that need doing, constantly distracted by clinical emergencies. The gratification that came from knowing their patient was getting the best possible care is often absent; the sense of working sensitively with families to ease the trauma of critical illness and death still impossible in the present circumstances – although they try their very best.

Many have already left, and others are off sick. One woman I see drags herself into work to cover shifts, despite struggling with significant Long Covid symptoms. Surveys confirm that the majority continue to work despite significant symptoms of burnout. They know how stretched the service is and everyone knows of colleagues who are in a worse state than themselves. As the pandemic continues, the situation continues to get worse in many ways. Nursing on ICU is highly specialised and technical. As people leave, there are simply not enough nurses with the right skills for the job.

Annie, a senior nurse, told me recently that she no longer found it helpful to see friends: 'It feels like this experience has set me apart, I wouldn't know how to start to talk about it, but other things, ordinary things, just don't register.' Annie was particularly upset by the number of critically ill pregnant women who had given birth prematurely, the babies rushed to the special care baby unit while their mothers fought for their lives in the ICU. We know now that pregnancy makes people more susceptible to Covid-19 and that not getting vaccinated puts both mother and baby at risk. But, sadly, the government's messaging to pregnant mothers had been confused and many of these women chose not to have the vaccine, thinking they were doing their best for the baby. Annie wants to have a child herself and during the pandemic has had two miscarriages.

She goes on to ask tentatively what I think about her going on antidepressants. She is not the first clinician to ask me this question and it is often something I bring up myself, wondering if it might be a question in their mind.

'I've never thought of myself as someone who would take antidepressants – in fact I hate the idea – but I just can't see how I can stay in the job as I am. No one comes into nursing expecting to work like this. I try to remind myself that I used to love this job, but I don't imagine it's going to get better, so there doesn't seem to be any point taking a few weeks off and then returning to the same situation.'

Antidepressants can be a lifeline for many people prone to episodes of depression and I would never judge an individual for taking them. At the same time, I feel appalled at what this says about our society. It seems all wrong that conscientious public servants are reluctantly considering taking drugs in order to stay working in an environment where they are burnt out, over-stretched and can see no end in sight. Should individuals like Annie have to resort to medication in order to survive within a wider system that is failing her?

Sometimes I make comparisons with disaster work overseas where most charities have generous leave arrangements and carefully rotate their staff away from the front line every few weeks, mindful that the sheer volume of death and gruesome illness, the frustration at being able to do so little for patients and the moral distress at the far-from-ideal conditions push their workers to their limits. There has been no proper recovery time for our front-line staff and the ICU clinicians seem so deeply exhausted that at times I wonder how much I can help. All I can do is encourage these individuals to stand back and take stock of what they've been through, offer a calm space for them to disentangle and process their feelings of sadness, fear, guilt, disgust, helplessness and rage. I give them tips about how to manage their anxiety symptoms and their insomnia. I help them make sense of how they are feeling, perhaps making links to other issues in their lives. I reassure them that they're not mad. Often, it's a question of gently prompting them to talk and remind themselves of how traumatic the last few months have been.

As therapists, we hope that facilitating therapeutic conversations will help our patients own their story and find their voice, so it seems all wrong to me, on so many levels, that NHS trusts threaten disciplinary action on staff who speak out about their experience.

~

Witnessing the grim psychological suffering of previously healthy clinical staff has reinforced a crucial theme I've been coming back to throughout this book. Our society, our communities, all of us need to wake up to the fact that we cannot just think of mental ill-health as illnesses that can be mechanically treated like a cardiac arrest, cancer or Covid. Even those physical illnesses have psychological and social dimensions, but how much more is that true of mental health problems that are formed, triggered, shaped, sustained and made worse by the kind of society we create together. Stories from the front line bear out just how much impact our social environment and psychological stresses can have on our mental health and remind us not to box off mental health patients in a them-and-us sort of way.

This is not to take sides in the tired nature–nurture debate, which can unhelpfully encourage polarisation. We have moved beyond that in our understanding, well beyond it. Most psychiatrists would agree that mental health problems emerge from a complicated tangle of biological, psychological and social factors and some of the most interesting research at the present time is exploring the intricate ways these different factors impact on each other.

But what it boils down to is this: under the right circumstances, anyone can break under the strain. Our experience of the pandemic underlines this simple fact. The conditions we live in affect our mental health; frightening, alienating and exhausting times make us all vulnerable to breakdown. If we could acknowledge this, we would make very different choices – what we prioritise, the language we use, where we spend our money – both in the medical world and in society at large. This conversation needs to be had now, because while we won't be living in this pandemic forever, its effect on the mental health needs in the population and the culture within healthcare will be felt for many years. What's more, other global traumas are already brewing.

The reality is that mental ill-health is not only about the individual. It is often generated by and always expressed in the relationships between us. It is shaped by the societies and the environments we live in, and keeping politics out of this is impossible. Our mental health is always affected by how we treat each other, and how we organise ourselves as a society, and increasingly as a world.

MORALE

12

MORAL INJURY

M oral distress, which has been such a prominent feature of the
pandemic, is on a spectrum with another key term we're
hearing more about: moral injury. Moral injury is the result of an
individual encountering circumstances that force them to act or
tolerate circumstances that are contrary to their professional and
ethical values. It has been shown to be a major contributor towards
stress and can lead to impaired function and feelings of shame,
guilt, disgust and anger, sometimes leading to suicidal thoughts
and longer-term psychological harm. The levels of anguish and
the sense of alienation people experience distinguish it from other
mental health diagnoses such as PTSD.

I came across the idea of moral injury only recently. The concept originated in the 1990s in the writings of veterans describing
their experience of the Vietnam War and its legacy, but, as a recent
BMA survey shows,[1] it does seem to resonate widely across the
health professions – and has done for some time. I related to it

instantly and welcomed it with a sense of relief as it seemed to capture something I'd struggled with in mental health services for many years about the relationship between the individual clinician and the organisation. It laid bare the price that is paid when institutionally required behaviour fails to align with one's moral principles – such as having to intervene with a treatment that doesn't seem in the patient's best interest and may do them harm or being unable to care adequately for a patient because of lack of resources. Before this concept became common parlance, all severe work stress was subsumed under the concept of burnout, which hints, conveniently for the system, at individual weakness and a lack of resilience or, at best, overwork.

The concept now feels so obvious that it's difficult to believe I didn't have it to hand until recently. It would have been a useful framework to think about how I was feeling all those years ago at the Towers, a large inward-looking institution that dulled the sense of purpose, moral sensibilities and vision of many of its staff. The noxious circumstances were very different then, my ethical concerns as much about liberating as protecting the patients, but I now look back at the psychological unease I experienced during those months working in the asylum as a textbook embodiment of the moral injury spectrum, every cell of my body squirming at some of the situations I was drawn into.

~

Moral injury is much more likely to take hold in staff who feel disempowered. As a junior psychiatrist at the Towers I had very little sense of agency. I was expected to do what was asked of me, including the ECT lists three times a week. (ECT was much less

humane in those days than it is now and there was one particularly appalling psychiatrist who prescribed it for any patient who
cried.) I had to administer the electric shocks and had no say in
which patients were on that list.

If I questioned why a patient had been prescribed doses
of medication so much higher than was officially approved, an
amused look would pass between the rest of the team – a few
months at the Towers would open my eyes, they were sure. There
was a memorable fortnight when the consultant went on holiday
and the quiet but conscientious senior registrar covering for him
agreed with me to reduce all the medication to standard approved
levels. The ward staff sulked, and the consultant predictably started
to increase the doses again as soon as he returned. Our action had
a negligible effect on the long-term outcome for the patients.
Nevertheless, amending those drug cards was perhaps the only
real sense of agency I experienced during those six months and I
can still remember the spring in my step.

One way to disempower a member of the group, staff or
patient, is to keep them in the dark, not let them know what's
going on, refuse to clarify expectations. My experience at the
Towers was a lesson in such obfuscation. There were no induc-
tion sessions apart from what one could glean informally from
other junior doctors, no guidelines, no risk assessments; just a
sense of being thrown in at the deep end and expected to learn
from my mistakes. And it was never made clear who I was supposed to go to for help. This was very different from my previous
experience on the medical wards where the tight hierarchical structure of the medical firm was clear and senior doctors
always on hand. 'Referring upwards' in psychiatry seemed to be

a process surrounded in mystique and I hadn't a clue what was deemed appropriate. Whenever I did speak to my consultant for advice, he sounded so grumpy at being interrupted, I assumed I should have managed the situation on my own. On the medical wards, every junior doctor had a sort of ABC guide to common problems in the pocket of their white coat, full of practical information about how to do the job, including at what point to engage someone more senior. But there was nothing like that for junior psychiatrists; huge comprehensive textbooks, yes, but nothing that helped you get through the day's work or a night on call. Looking back, the lack of a sense of purpose, mission or agency had become morally disorientating: the experience had disrupted my confidence and expectations about my own and others' motivation to behave ethically. No surprise that I'd started feeling a bit depressed. I was full of self-blame, anxious about my judgements, my self-esteem plummeting – classic signs of moral injury, I now know.

It's always amazed me how much a change of team and environment can transform the way we experience not just the work but our very selves. Moving away from the antiquated asylum to the new unit at the General Hospital, I'd felt as if the cobwebs in my mind had been blown away. I rediscovered my values and remembered why I had decided to become a psychiatrist. Over the following years, I found my niche and developed my expertise. I had a growing sense of being someone who could make things happen, and a sense of running a service that I was confident served the patients to the best that our ability and the knowledge of the day allowed.

Of course, no system is perfect, and even then I was not

operating with as much time and resources and well-trained staff as I would have ideally liked. I'd had to learn to tolerate the odd mistake, to be pragmatic and to compromise and muddle through as well as possible. The nature of psychiatry is ethically complicated and requires decisions that are challenging and occasionally kept me awake at night. Working with uncertainty and philosophical dilemmas, however, is an acknowledged aspect of all medical practice. It was morally burdensome – but worlds away from causing moral injury.

Over the years, however, things became more difficult again. The first step in the decline was the introduction of fundamental changes to NHS funding arrangements that meant patients who didn't live in our geographical area could end up waiting years for their individual funding to be approved. Having interviewed them two or three times and written a long report advising that treatment in our service would be beneficial, I knew them quite well, and many of them had pinned all their hopes on the therapeutic community, where they knew we had a place for them. A few of them never made it: they languished for months on locked wards while their applications were knocked back over and over again, never quite making it to 'top priority' – then killed themselves before we were allowed to admit them.

It was just a few years later that we had to close all our beds and run exclusively as an outpatient department, after yet another round of cuts to the trust's budget. This didn't, of course, stop colleagues referring some of their most difficult patients to me, but I started to dread such assessments, knowing that for some of these desperate people there was nothing we could offer that would keep them sufficiently safe.

And so it continued: the gradual erosion of so many of the structures and practices that had allowed us to do our jobs effectively.

A friend of mine retired early at the age of fifty, a year or two before the pandemic. The final event that precipitated her resignation was having to send a fourteen-year-old patient, a child in the care of the local authority, over a hundred miles away to a secure unit run by the private sector. She felt it was no longer safe to keep her in her local CAMHS (child and adolescent) unit; there were simply not enough staff to contain her difficult behaviour. My friend was under no illusions. She knew that being isolated from family and friends would make the girl worse, amplifying her already deeply rooted sense of rejection, and had little faith that the private hospital would make her better. What's more, she knew that her unit would have been able to manage such behaviour a few years previously.

She felt terrible about resigning, but explained it like this: 'I just couldn't do the job properly any more. It wasn't safe. Constantly making decisions that I couldn't really defend. I'd stopped sleeping. Couldn't look patients in the eyes. Just all the time waiting for something awful to happen.'

She wasn't alone back then – and certainly isn't now.

～

Jonathon has taken off his glasses and is wiping his eyes. I'm uncomfortably aware that he may have been tearful for a while as it's easy to miss subtle shifts of tone when you're talking to each other via a screen. Jonathon is a consultant psychiatrist who sees me for supervision sessions once a month. Although we are meeting for supervision rather than therapy, it doesn't feel very different from the work I've been doing with ICU staff. Jonathon is overwhelmed by his work as a psychiatrist and it's got deep inside him.

He is in the middle of telling me a long, complicated story about a patient he feels very worried by. This young woman, Terri, has severe bipolar disorder. Much of the time she copes very well, taking good care of her three children on her own and holding down a job as a carer with the elderly. But when she's in a manic phase of the illness, she's very unwell indeed: disinhibited, grandiose, promiscuous and very chaotic and confused. Her last episode of illness was four years ago, when she went missing and was eventually picked up by the police, clothes ripped, running amok in a city hundreds of miles away. She didn't have a psychiatrist or a diagnostic label at the time and, for reasons that are difficult to understand, she did not get a psychiatric assessment after being picked up by the police and taken into custody. While she was ill, her children had been taken into care; she'd lost the job she loved as a nurse in the emergency department; she'd run up credit card debts of thousands of pounds; and gained a criminal record. Eventually she'd been referred to Jonathon's team, which had supported her through the next few months when she was seriously depressed and trying to come to terms with the mess her life was now in.

Four years on, she had seemed to be doing well, resumed care of the children and found herself a job as a carer for the elderly, but Jonathon had noticed a dramatic change in her at their last session two weeks before our meeting. Her face looked gaunt, she was hardly sleeping and Jonathon described her as 'literally bouncing up and down on her chair and speaking at double speed'. After altering her medication, Jonathon talked to her about the possibility of a hospital admission and was relieved that Terri had enough insight to agree this might be the best course of action. After she left, Jonathon put a call in to the school to see if they had any concerns about the children. He wasn't surprised to hear that the children had been arriving late, that the youngest seemed unusually unkempt and Terri had turned up to the school just that morning in pyjamas without a coat – in January.

Despite the medication increase, her condition continued to deteriorate, and Jonathon and the crisis team spent much of the intervening two weeks trying to find her a hospital bed, to no avail. There was not a single bed in her locality; shocking, but not uncommon these days. But, even more disturbing, there was not a single psychiatric bed to be found across the whole of the UK during that particular fortnight in January 2022.

Admitting someone to hospital should never become the default option and today's psychiatrists are very clear that keeping people out of hospital is better for some of them in the long term. But they also know that there are times when it is necessary to move them to a safe place to treat and monitor their illness, and, in some instances, to protect them from harming themselves or others. Paradoxically, the word 'asylum' comes to mind, but without its gothic overtones and frightening history. Asylum in the sense that we 'seek asylum from a storm', a place of protection and shelter, a haven from the stresses outside that might be making their condition worse.

Jonathon is by now clearly tearful telling me this awful story. Terri was let down by mental health services four years ago and now Jonathon feels that he is watching helplessly as the system fails her for a second time. Terri is now past the point of insight into her condition and will have to be detained under the Mental Health Act if a bed becomes available. Her children have once again been taken into care and Terri responded to this loss by threatening the social worker in an incident that escalated and involved the police. Jonathon is desperately upset for Terri but he is also wondering how he can continue to work as a psychiatrist under these conditions and constraints.

Jonathon is full of anguished guilt and I'm concerned he's in danger of falling into a dark hole himself. Jonathon is responsible for over six hundred patients. He works at least twenty unpaid hours a week over his full-time job. He supports a nursing team, badly depleted by vacancies and long-term sickness. The other consultant post in his catchment area has either been vacant or staffed by worryingly inadequately trained locums. Yet he is feeling he should have worked harder for Terri, that the situation is his fault, that he is a failure as a psychiatrist.

I know that Jonathon is a good psychiatrist; in fact, he is particularly empathic and conscientious, and his judgements are sound. Terri's scenario is shocking, but Jonathon is not to blame. He knows his professional duty to such a rapidly worsening patient is to bring her into hospital in order to keep her safe but is prevented from doing this by institutional limitations that chronically undermine – indeed violate – his professional standards. He is working in an impossible situation where his clinical intelligence, diligence and judgement are being thwarted by an inadequately resourced system. This is making him feel worthless and he is in danger of becoming seriously depressed.

My experience when I started as a consultant was very differ-ent from the impossible situation Jonathon finds himself in today. The sense of agency that consultants took for granted thirty years ago has been eroded over the intervening years. The problem pre-dates the pandemic; it has been deteriorating over three decades, but the strains and prolonged moral distress of the last couple of years have only served to highlight the limitations and failings of the system that lead to such anguish.

～

Healthcare workers are choosing to retire early in worryingly large numbers. When asked why, none of them blame the patients or the clinical tasks; it is always about the organisation. Many of them, like my CAMHS consultant friend, talk about the lack of resources that make the job so difficult and unsafe; another group – nurses particularly – cite the ridiculous and ever-growing moun-tain of red tape and paperwork they are obliged to navigate.

I have a young friend, Lowenna, who nurses on an elderly mental health assessment ward. Over her short five-year career, she has seen the staffing levels deteriorate, both in overall numbers and in the balance of qualified compared to unqualified staff. She often finds she is the only qualified nurse on the shift, in charge of the ward even though she is only a relatively junior Band 5. Meanwhile, there is such a shortage of beds for the elderly that only extremely ill and disturbed patients get to be admitted. Because it's a ward for old people, the patients are often physically frail, incontinent, immobile and have illnesses such as diabetes, so the demands on the nurses are many. Compounding all this, the culture is such that the volume of paperwork, and persecutory audits of the paperwork, increase by the day. Literally every bit of paper is audited by the trust's quality team every six weeks in preparation for the next Care Quality Commission (CQC) visit.

As Lowenna puts it, 'Every good nurse knows the importance of good documentation, particularly where there is potential for a serious untoward incident. It's drilled into us from the first day at university. But there's so much of it now that you can't see the wood for the trees and I'm always having to stay on after the shift's over to get it finished. You just wouldn't believe how pointless some of it is. The audit questions must have been dreamt up by someone who's never been near a proper ward.'

She explains that many of the targets and timescales are unrealistic: for example, if patients are given the drug lorazepam, they are supposed to have their pulse and blood pressure checked every fifteen minutes. But lorazepam is prescribed for acute agitation and fussing around taking agitated patients' blood pressure, when they don't understand what's happening to them, makes them more agitated than ever. Her senior colleagues know it can be counterproductive, but they shrug their shoulders and take a 'just got to do it' attitude, knowing they will be humiliated if their ward fails the audit.

Despite being a very conscientious nurse and not a rule breaker by nature, Lowenna is increasingly tempted to 'game the system' and lie. But it isn't the fact that the bureaucracy is more and more meaningless and time-consuming that really troubles her, it's what it means for the vulnerable elderly people in her care. It's not just that the bureaucracy distracts her from more important concerns; it's that, starkly put, the system often prevents her from doing what is best for the patient, squeezing out altruism and corrupting her priorities. Sometimes the shifts are so busy that they don't have the time to get the less mobile patients up and dressed. This happened one Christmas when she was in charge and she was still upset and feeling terrible about it when I saw her on New Year's Day.

Lowenna also feels responsible for the unqualified staff. One of them is off sick at the moment, having sprained her shoulder and had all her ribs broken while she tried to restrain a terrified, violent old man. The number of physical assaults on staff on psychiatric wards for the elderly is particularly high and could be massively reduced if the staffing levels were better. I ask Lowenna if the frequent violent episodes have made her frightened of the patients. She doesn't think so: 'not in a way that affects my relationship with them', but then she remembers she does have colleagues who are off with PTSD after being assaulted at work. Like Jonathon, Lowenna swings between rage at the system and tearful self-blame.

~

In mental health services in the twenty-first century, the situations that generate moral distress and injury are usually about what we can't do rather than the overt physical brutality that was common in the Towers. But neglect and cruelty are still intertwined just as they always were. It's just that the cruelty taking place is hidden – or not so hidden – in the community rather than behind the walls of the asylum. A friend who is a consultant in learning disabilities told me how secretly relieved she had felt when one of her very vulnerable patients broke the law recently and was sent to prison. At least he'll be kept safe and warm and fed in prison, she had found herself thinking. She's appalled at the thought but knows how difficult it's been to make him safe in the community.

Such situations are precarious for staff and even more dangerous for patients. Quite apart from the moral distress at not being able to act in the best interests of the patient, the doctors and nurses involved know that their necks will be on the line if things go badly wrong. Community care is shamefully under-resourced, leaving clinicians with very few options.

It is worrying how closely mental health services today resemble my early days in the Towers with regard to fair and just treatment for patients, and the impact on the moral compass of the staff. I suggest that the culture in contemporary mental health services can be as neglectful and dismissive of patients' needs, as blind to the individuality and personhood of the patients and, indirectly, as brutal as it was back then. Many mental health workers have been aware of this for years and continue to struggle with the knowledge that they are being drawn into some degree of compromise and collusion. The fact that moral injury is a normal response to abnormal circumstances is usually emphasised in the academic literature and has been an obvious feature of clinicians' struggle during the pandemic. But what if the circumstances have become normalised rather than being viewed as out-of-the-ordinary events? What if the circumstances have gradually been deteriorating over many years?

Repeated exposure to circumstances that jar with our moral code increases the likelihood of moral injury, but we also learn to turn a blind eye, knowing and not knowing at one and the same time that things are not as they should be. At worst, we grow weary of the cognitive dissonance and become frankly cynical.

It's vital that mental health services get a handle on this issue as the problems are widespread and an increasing number of mental health practitioners see themselves on the moral injury spectrum. Acknowledging this is so and how much needs to change would be a major step forward. Even without a huge injection of funding, there is plenty that could be done to reverse the situation. Tackling bureaucracy for one, and creating a more open culture where every member of staff feels able to speak out. Supportive supervision should be seen as integral to the job, however senior the clinician. This is not the case at the moment: Jonathon, for example, has to see me in his own time and at his own expense. More than anything, there needs to be a healthier balance between the responsibility mental health practitioners such as Jonathon and Lowenna hold for their patients and the authority they are granted by the system to make things happen. In other words, clinicians need to feel valued and empowered to act on their professional judgement on behalf of the people in their care. At the present time, they feel shackled by a shortage of resources and a culture that prioritises the demands of the system over the needs of the patients.

If we can't find ways to reverse this state of affairs, we have to live with the knowledge that mental health services as presently financed, designed and supported are failing many patients and violating the personal and professional values of many of its workers. The consequences for the quality of care, as staff, variously anxious, exhausted, angry, cynical or depressed, try to work together, are not hard to imagine. Moral injury, then, is not simply an individual syndrome, but a dangerously toxic characteristic of the system.

13

A SYSTEM OF EXCLUSION

Thirteen-year-old Sabina is taken to the emergency department with ugly scars crisscrossing her arms and legs. The cut she presents with this time is deeper than previous ones, a ten-centimetre trough in her thigh that needs a lot of stitching. Clearly there is something very wrong with this child that needs exploring urgently, but there is no chance of admitting her to the ward where some of the questions could be explored the following morning. The waiting time to be seen by CAMHS as an outpatient is over a year long and although there is a fast-track service, this is only for those in 'absolute crisis', defined as a suicide attempt. The young psychiatrist seeing her tries to explain the situation to the girl and her parents.

'What are you telling me?' Sabina's father asks angrily. 'Are you trying to tell me this behaviour's normal?' Then his tone becomes more conciliatory: 'Couldn't you just write down that she was trying to kill herself?'

This stark, but not unusual, example shows how the system excludes people, forcing them to get worse before they can access the basic care they need.

A shortage of beds is undoubtedly putting patients at risk; the statistics shocking, and the stories relentless. A severely disturbed teenager is sent over a hundred miles away from home. A paranoid father who's been assessed in the emergency department as psychotic and potentially violent is sent back home to his frightened family because the local inpatient facilities are full. A frail and confused elderly lady with dementia and a young man with severe psychosis are both discharged prematurely because the beds are desperately needed for other patients. I hear about bed occupancy rates – before the pandemic – of well over 100 per cent and senior nurses who spend their whole time shut away in an office trying to sort these impossible logistics and being blamed for these all-too-human, potentially tragic, situations.

~

A few years into my stint as clinical director at Francis Dixon Lodge, I became very aware of this dynamic after we had reluctantly made the decision to close the beds and run the therapeutic community as a day unit. This wasn't all bad as we were able to set up lots of outpatient groups and help many more patients, but we should never have had to prioritise one group of desperate patients over another. It meant we had nothing to offer the more severely damaged, highly self-destructive patients who clearly needed intensive residential treatment. We knew some of them were being abused by violent partners, drug gangs, pimps or even predatory parents, but we simply had nowhere safe enough to offer them the treatment they needed to enable them to turn their lives around. Their only hope was to commit a crime that might have given them access to forensic services and possibly led to the intensive inpatient psychological treatment that they needed.

These dynamics suggest a perverse flaw in the system that costs everyone. Quite apart from anything else, it is shockingly inefficient and ends up being more expensive for the taxpayer. And things are only getting worse: much of our mental health service is now based on a system of exclusion. Exclusion operates at every level, from wards to outpatient care to psychological therapies in primary care. A huge amount of energy is focused on keeping patients out of the system: devising exclusion criteria to restrict access; limiting clinical engagement by restricting length of sessions and duration of contact; and endlessly driving the bed numbers down even further. These are management 'solutions' to a problem of basic maths: the amount of need vastly outweighs what the service is equipped to provide.

The main resource in mental health care is well-trained clinical staff, but there are simply not anything like enough of them to provide a responsive, caring and attentive service, either on the wards or for the patients in the community. Relationships between clinician and patient in mental health services are all-important – not just the medium for delivering treatment, but very often the treatment itself. Such relationships take time and care to nurture. They cannot be squeezed into ever-tighter schedules. Even the most caring clinician cannot be endlessly stretched and in mental health services there has been a more-for-less policy in operation for decades.

As one psychiatrist puts it: 'We exclude based on postcode, diagnosis, complexity, comorbidity. Too much need, not enough need. Risk, lack of motivation, (no) readiness for change, any possible reasons to keep people out.' Writing angrily about the use of the term 'gatekeeping', she reflects on what this terminology says about the systemic attitude to our patients: 'Our services are fortresses; patients are intruders to be prevented from breaching our defences. There is a rot in the system that views beds as needing protection from patients.'[1]

One of the effects of the reduction in beds is that it is hard to sustain a therapeutic culture on our wards. The bar for admission is set so high now that most patients are very disturbed indeed, about two thirds of them detained using the Mental Health Act. As soon as they start to show some improvement, they are discharged so that a bed can be released for a more desperate patient. There have always been acutely ill, potentially explosive patients on mental health wards and occasional outbreaks of violence, but such patients used to be in the minority and are now the majority. Reducing the overall number of beds doesn't just affect admission and discharge decisions, it also has a direct effect on the stability of the ward environment. As bed numbers decrease, the concentration of acute illness increases, and the wards become much more difficult to manage safely.

Experienced inpatient staff know that the best way to manage new admissions is to take a low-key approach wherever possible, keeping a close eye and hoping they will respond positively to being in a safe, 'low-expressed emotion' environment. They also recognise that the patients on their way to recovery can have a calming effect on the more disturbed new admissions, by modelling the routines and activities that may help them settle. Front-line clinicians know, only too well, that the general therapeutic milieu can switch very easily into frenetic chaos if the acutely disturbed outnumber the others. Sadly, despite all the evidence to support this rather obvious fact, such knowledge doesn't seem to influence the thinking of many of those in charge, and the drive to continue cutting back beds continues.

~

The bed shortage is just one factor that makes it difficult to sustain a mental health service that is helpful rather than harmful to patients. If anything, scarce resources are even more of an issue in the community, particularly when the cuts to local authority and voluntary organisations are considered. Even within mental health, there are diagnostic groups, such as those with alcohol and drug problems or those who recurrently self-harm, that are particularly unpopular, more likely to be on the receiving end of negative messaging, more likely to be excluded from the help they need. These patients are even more at risk of being left to get worse before they present with an escalating crisis, with huge costs in the long run to the health service more generally and to society at large.

No accident that in many parts of the country drug and alcohol services have been contracted to organisations outside the NHS, often in a tendering process looking for a cheaper option. It is not unusual for the non-NHS organisation to make the consultant psychiatrist – the most expensive employee – redundant a few months after they've won the contract. The patients that

particularly suffer from such a split are those with dual diagnosis – people with a severe mental illness such as schizophrenia
compounded by a problem with alcohol and drugs. The unedify-
ing debates about which team should take responsibility for such
patients have been going on for as long as I've been a psychiatrist
and have got worse now that two different organisations are often
involved. Meanwhile, the patients who can be particularly high-
risk and difficult to engage are often abandoned or left for the
most junior staff member to worry about.

It is not impossible to imagine a very different sort of system,
where instead of stand-offs between teams, there is a more mature
attitude that starts with the individual patient's needs. All involved
would meet to work out how they could contribute their expertise, and how they might do this co-operatively and efficiently,
providing a network of care around the patient. When I was a
consultant, I chaired a managed clinical network that focused on
the most difficult patients that came under the umbrella of personality disorder. The network brought together the teams and
different organisations involved in supporting a patient, tried to
align or increase understanding of how the different systems operated, put on training events, and fostered the type of relationships
between professionals that make co-operative and flexible working
around a patient possible. This is particularly important in mental health, where social workers and probation officers, schools,
various charities, housing departments and the police might all be
involved with a particular individual. As with so many initiatives,
it worked well for a while but eventually fizzled out as the effects
of austerity hit hard and individual organisations became more
self-protective and inward-looking.

The awful sight of professionals squabbling to offload responsibility for their most difficult and vulnerable patients is now accepted as the norm in mental health. It shouldn't be like this. One thing is for certain: unless resources improve, and the culture of exclusion is challenged, such situations will only get worse and continue to take up far too much time and energy to the detriment of patient care.

I could go through every specialty within psychiatry giving examples of exclusion and the shocking shortages that feed such a culture. The point is that the situation has been deteriorating for years and everyone has been hit badly. New initiatives are often focused on providing a more inclusive service for a particular group of patients but they are often under-resourced from the start and set up to fail.

What's known as the IAPT service (Improving Access to Psychological Therapies) illustrates some of the problems. The original vision was excellent: patients with common mental health problems could be referred easily by their GPs, seen locally within a week or two, and offered a diverse choice of psychological therapies while avoiding the stigma and fuss of being referred to a psychiatric team. But before it was even launched, the original vision had been watered down to just one model of therapy, and the therapists had only minimal training. And now the service is so inundated with referrals that it involves a wait of months in many areas. Of course, local leadership makes a difference, but overall IAPT is hobbled by over-prescribed exclusion criteria, over-determined therapeutic conversations and demoralised therapists forced to account for every session with an exhausting amount of paperwork. There is little flexibility to tailor the service to individual patients and the outcomes have been mixed, and often disappointing.

At the other extreme from primary care are what's known as tertiary services. These are highly specialised services that need to be planned and managed temporarily by the Department of Health because they are aimed at a specific, and usually much smaller, group of patients that tends to miss out if left to fight it out for locally available resources. While I was working as clinical director of Leicester's personality disorder service, there was a nationally driven initiative to improve the care for people with this diagnosis, optimistically called 'No Longer a Diagnosis of Exclusion'. The initial result was a much more even spread of services geographically and some interesting service models. As so often happens, however, the long-term planning was poor, and central funding for the initiative was devolved locally after three years. But local systems as a whole tend to be starved of resources, so a previously well-funded service, no matter how successful it is proving, often ends up being depleted in order to support other services that are struggling. I've seen this happen many times: panic about a particular patient group followed by investment, with the money often being covertly diverted away from other services. Then it's all forgotten as soon as improvements begin to show. That first patient group becomes old news while a new group creates panic and the cycle starts again, ignoring the fact that no improvements can be sustained without continued funding. Such a whimsical investment pattern has lots of unintended consequences, creating envious relationships between local services and cynicism when the new service you have put your heart and soul into ends up being depleted for reasons beyond your control.

What has never happened during my career is a comprehensive spending increase right across mental health.

~

I've noticed in my current role as an independent psychotherapist that people requesting private therapy are sounding increasingly desperate. It's not uncommon for someone to approach me after waiting several months to see a psychiatrist, a situation that would have been unheard of a few years ago.

Mo found his way to me in a terrible state after being messed around badly by statutory services. His father had walked out on the family when he was very young, leaving him with his depressed mother. Mo had become the carer in the family, looking after his mother and his younger brother. At school, he'd suffered some racist abuse but also felt stigmatised within his own community for not having a father and having a mother who was 'mental'. He'd secretly worried that if anyone knew how depressed his mother was they might take her away and put him and his brother into care, so he was guarded and mistrustful of teachers and other grown-ups who might have helped. As a teenager, he felt even more of an outsider, burdened by his responsibilities and too busy with money worries to invest in the activities of his peer group. Now, at the age of twenty, he found himself increasingly depressed and lonely, and had dropped out of college because his concentration was so poor. He had been referred by his GP for assessment by the IAPT service – the irony of that name only too painfully explicit in his case. Asked if he was ever violent, Mo told them he'd once thrown his phone at the wall in frustration and broken it. This was interpreted as fitting the exclusion criteria for the service so he was told his case was too complex and sent away. After returning to his GP and waiting for a few more weeks, his referral was assessed by secondary care services (psychiatrists and other specialist mental health staff) who told him his problems weren't serious enough.

Such messages would send most of us a bit mad, but if you're struggling to overcome mental health symptoms, the impact can be devastating. Asking for help from his GP had been difficult enough, but then being rejected and left with nothing after months of waiting had left him feeling devastated. For a few weeks, he'd been hardly able to leave his bed, let alone his flat, his sense of worthlessness confirmed.

As he reflected later, 'No one got it, how difficult it was for me – admitting I had a problem and needed help for myself. I was desperate, never done anything like that in my life. I mean, I was asking for HELP, telling them I was ON THE EDGE and trying to be as truthful as possible. Then I got told they couldn't help me because I was TOO ON THE EDGE, but I'd told them that, and THAT'S WHY I WAS THERE ASKING FOR HELP IN THE FIRST PLACE!'

He'd left those assessments feeling there was something wrong with him as a person, that it was impossible to help him, his despair amplified. After a bumpy start, he did rather well in therapy with me. By the time he left, he was feeling a lot better about himself, and had managed to apply for and hold down a job and start a relationship. He could have done this much earlier and at much less emotional cost, if the IAPT service hadn't been so obsessed with exclusion criteria.

Patients such as Mo are at risk of falling through the gap between services with no hope of getting their needs met. Even worse, the failed engagement can be traumatising. In Mo's case, the experience hooked into deep-seated pain from his early childhood and the racial abuse he had suffered. As with many patients, Mo's experience of asking for help from the service had triggered previous experience of rejection and left him more vulnerable than ever. No patient should be blamed for not fitting into the system.

~

Even if you are accepted by the service, you are likely to be put on a very long waiting list. Anyone who has ever waited for an important hospital appointment knows how slowly the minutes pass. The waiting times mental health patients are subjected to can be unimaginable; some of them hardly know how they'll survive the next week, yet they are expected to wait, sometimes years, for the help they need to get their lives back on track. For many, this is a repetition of previous neglect, confirming that their needs are not important. Some of them mess their lives up badly while on the waiting list. Some kill themselves or get killed. Those who are eventually seen can arrive full of anger and mistrust, their negative experience of how the system has treated them so far colouring the therapy sessions, making it more difficult and sometimes impossible to help them.

Once they get to the top of the waiting list, the therapy is strictly time-limited by the system. In the USA, this is usually determined by private health insurance companies, but the system in the UK is no better; it is increasingly designed around financial constraints and the need to process as many people as quickly as possible. Neither system is based on realistic appraisal of the patients' needs. It is not uncommon to wait over two years for an eight-session course of weekly group therapy, an absurd scenario that should make clinicians cringe in shame. But of course the therapists that have to face these patients are not those responsible for this system. Most would prefer to tailor the work to the individual patient rather than treat them as if they are on a factory production line. Some of them know that what they are providing for the patients isn't sufficient, but without being able to take any other course of action they often succumb to blaming themselves for not being good enough therapists, a message that the system is only too ready to affirm.

In the UK, official guidelines[2] recommend a range of evidence-based psychological therapies, but they are often ignored. For example, young people with depression or anxiety are supposed to be offered psychological therapy as a first line of treatment, but the system in primary care often allocates GPs not much more than five minutes with a patient. Given the long waiting times for therapy and the pressure on their time, they are understandably quick to prescribe antidepressants at a first meeting. If the patient continues to get worse, the GP will feel pressure to increase the medication, maybe adding tranquillisers and sedatives, while the long wait to see a psychiatrist or access psychological therapy continues.

These situations are uncomfortable, frustrating and sometimes deeply distressing for the clinicians involved. For the patients, they can feel catastrophic. It's not easy to ask for help with mental health problems: the very symptoms one needs help with get in the way. Anxious people fear having a panic attack; depressed people must overcome their sense of hopelessness, helplessness and worthlessness; psychotic people are frightened and thought-disordered; people with dementia are forgetful and confused; and people with complex trauma will have trust issues born from years of being let down or betrayed by parents or others in authority. Even those of us who are lucky enough to be mostly well can recognise that when we're feeling vulnerable, we're extra sensitive to how people speak to us.

It's so important to get people's first contact with mental health services right. We should aspire to be welcoming, reassuring, encouraging, and treat new patients with sensitivity and kindness. The system promotes the idea that this is the case, but too often the reality is that patients leave feeling dismissed and rejected.

~

I wish I could say that such patterns of exclusion and neglect are entirely due to the lack of resources but, like so much of life, it is more complicated than that. Ultimately it is clinical staff who deliver these negative messages and we can't completely wash our hands of any responsibility in how we do so. Some will struggle with the moral distress involved in working in such a system. Others – and here I hope it is true to say a small minority – go along with it without question, self-righteously ticking off the exclusion criteria and prioritising bureaucracy over patient care.

It is a terrible thing to say, but I have seen many people made worse by the way they are treated when they try to contact mental health services. I fear that we are so used to excluding people in this callous system that we hardly notice the impact any more. If there really is nothing adequate that can be provided within existing resources, staff should explain this truthfully but sensitively to the patient in front of them, making it clear that it is a problem with the system and not with them personally. If the patient wants to make a complaint or see their MP, then all the better. This is what would happen in physical medicine in the UK. Yes, it is the sort of behaviour that trusts these days panic about and attempt to avoid. And sometimes they resort to scapegoating to avoid grappling with the real problem, even to the point of accusing individual employees of reputational damage to the organisation – and in some cases going on to discipline them. Such intimidation is hard to withstand but if the clinicians took a collective stance and supported each other so that an individual could not be isolated and picked off, there would not be much top management could do.

It should be said that there are teams in some trusts who are addressing the issues around engaging patients very effectively: early intervention teams for people with their first episode of psychosis, for example, and new primary care liaison teams. But outside such islands of good practice, many patients and their families have an experience of being pushed backwards by the attitudes and rigidity they encounter.

An under-resourced system fosters an attitude of self-protectiveness in its staff. The recognition of distress becomes distorted and the desire to help undermined. Rationing then becomes the norm but is never named as such; instead we find reasons – usually without an evidence base – to turn the patients away. Rejection and neglect become part of everyday work. Many staff new to the system are told this is just how it is, just as I was when I started working at the Towers all those years ago. The problems were very different, but the capacity of the institution to dull one's judgement and the defensive rationalisation is no different now.

The longer one works in a system that denies or makes it difficult for people to access care, the easier it becomes to defend such exclusion. To help themselves live with the situation, practitioners appropriate and weaponise concepts such as autonomy, self-help and independence, knowing at some level that they are turning a blind eye to their patients' vulnerability. If they were serious about building their patients' sense of autonomy, the first step would be to build a trusting relationship and learn to listen to them with respect.

When I started psychiatry, some of the consultants had an open-bed policy in an attempt to encourage patients to come into hospital sooner, before they reached crisis point and while they still had some insight. There was some useful research from rehabilitation services showing that if patients with long-term conditions have a good relationship with the service and know they can admit themselves if they need to, the number of admissions paradoxically goes down.

When the therapeutic community was operating as a day unit, I would sometimes arrange with a colleague for one of my patients who was struggling badly to have a bed for the weekend if they needed it. They were simply given the phone number of the ward. They almost never needed to make use of this arrangement, but just having the option seemed to take the panic out of the situation. It conveyed that we understood how bad they were feeling and that we trusted them to decide what was in their best interest. It also conveyed that they were deserving of attention and lessened the urge to self-harm. That is what I would call efficiency – but it's a very far cry from the situation today that has become inherently distrustful of patients and their needs.

The driver of the present resource-starved, micromanaged culture is supposedly financial efficiency, but there is nothing efficient about a system that makes patients wait until they are at crisis point. Clinicians are then forced into a role where they are constantly reacting to emergencies rather than providing the thoughtful, proactive care that would be likely to pre-empt and offset costs further down the line. The evidence in support of providing the right treatment first time round is overwhelming. Such a course of action might seem expensive in the short term, but the investment is likely to result in very substantial savings in the medium to long term. Most importantly, helping someone access the treatment that is right for them, as quickly as possible, is by far the most humane pathway for the patient.

Epilogue

LOSING OUR WAY

When I look back at mental health services over the last four decades, I see a few years of progress followed by a steady decline. The closing of the asylums – for better or worse – propelled us forward with a vision of what might be possible with a range of new medicines and therapies, and a significant shift in our attitude to patients.

I feel lucky to have started my career in that more hopeful era. It wasn't that care was uniformly good or held in high esteem. But those of us who chose psychiatry did so because we wanted to make a difference and we had role models who were passionate about making advances in the field.

The systems in place during those early years at Leicester General Hospital seemed to strike a good balance between the laissez-faire approach I'd encountered at the Towers and the suffocating level of micromanagement that exhausts and demotivates clinicians working today. Regrettable things did happen, as they always will in a place dealing with mental distress and disturbance, but the culture was such that issues could be addressed openly and sensibly. That was my experience anyway, and that of many of my colleagues. But the progress was not to last long.

I recently had reason to visit the General Hospital and decided to detour to the Brandon Mental Health Unit that had symbolised that new and hopeful chapter. Moving in back then, it had felt as though the norms for psychiatric care had been reset, with a significant shift in expectations and attitudes. I remember the building being alive with fun and laughter, anguish and tears, and exuding a sense of endeavour and camaraderie. It closed a few years ago, after less than three decades, and now I found the building boarded up, with warnings that trespassers would be prosecuted. Looking through a gap in the window, I saw it was still full of furniture, perfectly good desks, beds and whiteboards, all just sitting there abandoned. It was hard to shake off a sense of sadness.

So many of the new services we felt so proud to have set up all those years ago have been steadily cut. Therapeutic communities, where they still exist at all, have been reduced to a day or two a week, while most day hospitals and day centres have closed. Some argue that such places have a tendency to encourage 'career mental health patients' and become psychiatric ghettos. In the 1990s there was a push for what was known as the recovery movement, aimed at helping people back into 'normal' social networks and 'proper' employment as soon as possible after a psychiatric illness. But very few of its supporters would have approved of the contraction of the therapeutic facilities that could, for certain patients, be lifesaving, especially as the social infrastructure that community care and the recovery model depend on was crumbling at the same time.

In any case, rarely have these places been closed for ideological reasons; the driving factor has usually been money.

So we come on to the situation today, and the stark reality that far too many very vulnerable patients are neglected: left in miserable isolation, brutalised in the community, or sent to hospitals far away from family and community networks. And it's not as if we are finished with large institutions: we might have closed the large Victorian mental asylums, but our vast overcrowded prisons are full of people with mental health problems and learning difficulties.

Most of my contemporaries have retired disillusioned, and a quick look at recruitment and retention figures within mental health services paints a grim picture. When I started training in psychiatry, it was not uncommon for consultants to choose to work until they were seventy, with the whole organisation benefiting from their years of experience and wisdom. Nowadays, mental health workers tend to retire at the earliest opportunity, often in their early fifties, sometimes younger. Two young consultants I know resigned recently within three years of taking up their posts; both had been particularly promising trainees. As I write, 15 per cent of consultant psychiatry posts are vacant across England – rising to more like 50 per cent in some trusts – while covering nursing shifts, let alone filling nursing posts, is a constant nightmare.

How did we get into such a dire situation? Some of my generation look back to those solid old Victorian asylums and think we should not have closed them. Was our enthusiasm totally misplaced? There were certainly sceptical voices at the time but I don't think any of us championing the idea of community care could foresee just how badly local authority budgets and community services would be eroded.

Perhaps our biggest mistake was to project so much of what was bad about psychiatry onto bricks and mortar. It was almost as though we held the buildings themselves responsible for the regressive behaviour within their walls. We missed a precious opportunity to make sense of the brutal and neglectful behaviour that had been exposed, prematurely writing it off as a product of the institution rather than an uncomfortable truth about humanity. It can feel threatening to be up close with extreme mental distress, and such fear can make us cruel, regardless of whether we're inside an institution or embedded in the community.

~

Clearly one of the major problems for mental health services is the lack of funding. While this is an issue across many areas of the NHS, the truth is that physical health has long been prioritised over mental health when they should be seen on an equal footing – an aspiration that is often referred to as parity of esteem. Just think, for example, how much talk there has been about waiting times for cancer consultations since Covid, yet we don't even collect data about the time most mental health patients have to wait – often well over a year and with huge variation across the country. Since 2013, the NHS constitution in England has included a commitment 'to improve, prevent, diagnose and treat both physical and mental health problems with equal regard'. But despite strategies and legislation,* we continue to miss this by a long shot.

---

* The 'No Health Without Mental Health' strategy in 2011 was enshrined in law in the 2012 Health and Social Care Act.

It is hard to know where to start with examples of disparity. Sabina, for example, who we met in the previous chapter, is facing a wait of over a year to get the help she needs, while children with physical problems usually wait a few weeks at the most to see an appropriate specialist. What's more, while there are strict targets for children in the emergency department to be seen quickly, this does not apply to children with mental health issues. Sabina waited seven hours to be seen, the paediatricians adamantly refusing to admit her to the ward, where she could have slept through the night and been checked on the next day. The young psychiatrist who saw her had never done a CAMHS job and was working unsupervised. This is all so different from when, as a junior psychiatrist, I was on the same rota covering the emergency department in the 1980s. There were far fewer children with mental health problems presenting as an emergency, for a start, and when they did present, they were seen by a special rota of CAMHS senior registrars and consultants.

The 'burden of disease' is an attempt to quantify the impact of a particular condition, taking into account financial cost, mortality, morbidity and other indicators. In the UK, mental illness is estimated to account for 28 per cent of the burden of disease,[1] but only 13 per cent of NHS spending. Clearly, there needs to be greater investment. Just as important, there needs to be a change in mindset, so that mental health spending is seen as an investment in the future. There is no question that Sabina will cost the NHS money over the next few years as her self-destructive behaviour escalates, and no question that the price of neglect will also be picked up by other institutions such as her school, and maybe, as she gets older, the criminal justice system. With a recent report highlighting an ongoing and dramatic escalation in CAMHS referrals (an 80 per cent rise in the UK between 2019 and 2021[2]), it is more urgent than ever that we rethink how to address these issues.

How do we persuade our politicians that careful spending in the short term will mean financial and therapeutic gains in the long run? There are cost-offset arguments for investing in mental health patients of all ages, not just children, but too often decisions about resources are made in reaction to a clinical or financial crisis, rather than considered analysis. It is not unusual, for example, for specialist services in the NHS to be cut because of short-term financial pressures, only to end up increasing spending on referrals to expensive rehabilitation wards in hospitals run by private companies. The NHS spends £2 billion each year on outsourcing mental health care because it has too few beds. Such care is often substandard and has been criticised by coroners and inquest juries many times over the last decade for providing unsafe care.[3] This is the antithesis of careful investment.

When it comes to physical care, it is the more routine, easier operations such as hernia repairs and cataracts that are subcontracted by the NHS to the private sector; in other words, the patients who pose minimum risk. In mental health, on the other hand, it is the opposite: patients who are particularly problematic and are deemed a high risk to themselves and others. The comparison should alarm us: it is well understood that private companies are not as competent at handling complex physical operations as the NHS, so why do we assume – despite all the evidence – that they are better placed to care for patients with complex mental health needs?

One aspect of disparity, particularly close to my heart, is the low priority given to psychotherapy. It's as if there's a parity of esteem issue within psychiatry itself, with physical treatments – usually quicker and cheaper – prioritised over psychological interventions. This is often blamed – wrongly in my opinion – on the dominance of what we call the medical model (in broad-brush terms, how the profession conceptualises and approaches illness); but today's doctors are trained in a 'whole-person' approach to their practice in any setting and should be taking underlying psychological and social factors into account with every patient.

The failure to do this is frustrating and ironic given the advances that have been made in our understanding of psychological change and our improved ability to tailor therapy to an individual patient. Many psychological therapies are approved and recommended by official bodies (NICE in the UK) but the NHS constitution, through a technicality, does not entitle us to them in the same way as we are entitled to approved drugs. This is not just a matter of disagreeing about the best treatment plan. The disparity skews the whole approach: the questions we ask, the way we frame the patients' problems, the words we use, which research projects get prioritised, the type of relationships we form with the patients, and whose voice is listened to. One thing I am sure of: if we took the broader factors that underlie mental ill-health more seriously, we would take very different approaches and make different decisions.

～

The situation for many mental health patients has been getting worse over the past few decades, despite government rhetoric and worthy aspirations. For me, the pandemic has highlighted just how badly mental health services have lost their way. It's as if the inequity between physical and mental health services has been internalised, not just by patients, but by staff and the service as a whole. Like disadvantaged groups of the population who live with an inequality that is deeply imbedded in society, the years of discrimination have left mental health services feeling diminished, unable to see their worth and increasingly unable to assert their particular perspective and much needed voices.

When I meet up with ex-colleagues who are still working, they are baffled and furious that their organisations are still encouraging, indeed instructing, their clinicians to work remotely. As one of them puts it, 'This is supposed to be a specialty that prides itself on communication skills. How can we sit back complacently and delude ourselves that remote working is no different from being in the room with the person? It's a lie. We're only getting a fraction of the information. Why are we putting up with this? Our patients deserve so much more.'

While we need to value mental and physical health equally, we also need to acknowledge that they are not the same, and that mental health services need to find their own unique voice. The pandemic healthcare guidelines, while necessary in some guise, needed to be adapted by mental health trusts to balance the risks particular to their patients. Masks, for example, can be particularly antitherapeutic in mental health environments, where so many patients are confused or paranoid. One psychiatrist I know managed to get hold of some transparent ones to mitigate the effect of the mandated face coverings, but the trust management, so intent on following the NHS guidelines to the letter, wouldn't even agree to a discussion about their use.

At the beginning of the Covid-19 pandemic, one trust I know of turned one of its wards into an admission ward, where all newly admitted patients could be kept for a few days while they were tested for Covid. This might seem a sensible measure to contain the virus, but imagine being penned up in this way when you're in the throes of acute mental disturbance, already feeling disorientated and frightened. The staff tried as hard as they could, but it proved impossible to keep these patients safe, either from infection or from assault or inappropriate sexual liaisons: the level of disorder was just too high. Although the consultant psychiatrists and admission ward nurses took Covid very seriously and wanted to minimise the risk of infection as much as possible, they realised very quickly that the system was dangerous and not the right way to go about it. They suggested an alternative system of group 'bubbles' based on the system schools were using at the time. But all their warnings to top-level management and even the Care Quality Commission (CQC) were ignored. Eventually, two patients killed themselves. The psychiatrists felt strongly that these deaths were avoidable.

There is no point in bringing patients into hospital if the ward staff are protesting that they can't keep them safe. This reorganisation was not the result of financial pressures, but a rather black-and-white response to Covid guidelines that were not balanced by an understanding of what it takes to provide a safe and therapeutic milieu for mentally disturbed people.

Although the details of these incidents are specific to the pandemic, they seem very telling to me. They suggest a demoralised institutional culture that is clinging to the false comfort of rigidly following bureaucratic guidelines while losing the capacity to think independently, to assert that mental health services are different, and to advocate on behalf of its patients.

～

I worry that we have lost a vision in the UK of how a modern mental health service should operate and what it should offer. Of course there are exceptions but in general the reality is long waiting times, cancelled clinics, a shortage of beds, underfunded teams compounded by problems in recruitment and retention, increasingly cynical worn-out clinicians, an unsupportive persecutory culture that's quick to blame – and patients who frequently end up feeling excluded and retraumatised. Part of what drove me to write this book was alarm at the increasing gulf between the sheer number of people with mental ill-health problems and our capacity as a society to contain and manage them, let alone provide the conditions and the skilled help that are needed to facilitate healing. We should never resign ourselves to this state of affairs. We all deserve better.

Grief for what has happened to NHS mental health services on my watch, or rather my generation's watch, resonates to my core, to such an extent that it sometimes dims my sense of the good work that does happen with many individual patients. I can't let go of the thought that, collectively, we should and could have done something to stop the rot and honour the optimism we felt as the old asylums closed. Surely we could have found a way to collaborate and stand together as healthcare professions, insisted that the rhetoric around parity of esteem was made a reality, fought to make understanding and meeting mental health needs a priority for society, found a way to make our patients really matter.

Maybe a future generation will manage this better. Perhaps, as we continue to unfold the mysteries and intriguing intricacies of the brain and develop our understanding of the complex social issues affecting mental health, psychiatrists of the future will be more secure in their skills, less narrow and defensive in their thinking, less in thrall to pharmaceutical companies. Maybe, as different perspectives and approaches become more comprehensive and inclusive, mental health clinicians from different professions will find a way to work more collaboratively and waste less energy trying to prove one model or discipline is better than another. Maybe we can start to move forwards again, not backwards.

There was a lot of talk at the start of the pandemic about 'building back better' and I can only hope that Covid-19 and what is already being described as the 'secondary mental health pandemic' will give us the impetus to change attitudes and develop the breadth and depth of services at the scale that is needed. If the pandemic doesn't do it, the reality of climate change may eventually break through our defences and kick-start desperately needed conversations about radically changing our lifestyles and our society.

There is plenty to keep us awake at night, but hope for me comes from knowing that there is untapped potential. Mental health is the focus of a growing number of conversations and I have a sense that there is an appetite in the general population to learn and do more. We can wise up about psychological trauma – both avoidable and unavoidable – and its effects, develop better systems to prevent and cope with it, and become more respectful of each other's vulnerabilities. We can create education and work environments, and care systems that value and bring out the best in us.

We can build communities where the mental well-being of citizens is given thoughtful attention and where meaningful support is offered to vulnerable families and their impressionable children.

Of course, we could choose to turn away from such a project, and many of us will. But if enough of us were persuaded to set our minds in this direction then who knows what might be possible?

ACKNOWLEDGEMENTS

Thank you to the brilliant Olivia Bays and Pippa Crane from Elliott and Thompson: to Olivia for reading the book in the first place, taking a risk and pushing for it to be published quickly; and to both of you for your hard work and professionalism, your tenacity in getting to the bottom of what I really want to convey, and your willingness to help me shape such painful stories and contribute your incredible creative skills.

Thank you to all the people I have worked with over the years: to my teachers and mentors, Chris Whyte and Richard Jones in particular; to all my very special colleagues and the group members who worked with me through good times and bad at Francis Dixon Lodge and made it such an intensely enriching environment for all involved; to Joy Schaverien and many others for helping me through difficult times; to the clinicians who have shared their experience on condition they remain anonymous – you know who you are; and to all the patients who have had the courage to ask for help and trust me with their hurt feelings and their stories.

Thank you to my many friends who have been enthusiastic about this project: to Ann Boyle for making it happen; and to those who have read early drafts of the book and offered valuable suggestions, in particular Marie Bradley, Debbie Chaloner, Toni Fazelli, Kevin Ford, Alison Greengrass, Nick Humphreys, Jane Lawton, Liz Logie, Chris Maloney, Mark Theobald, Polly Tuckett; and my siblings, Angela Magor and Peter Campling.

Thank you to my grown-up children, Rosy, Beth, Patrick and Natasha: it's not so easy having a psychiatrist as a mother, but miraculously, you've done me proud.

And finally, a huge thank you to John for your love, support and encouragement; and for sitting there on the sofa, on tap as my personal wordsmith – maybe doing all those cryptic crosswords has a point after all!

NOTES

Introduction

1 C. Millard and S. Wessely, 'Parity of Esteem between mental and physical health', *British Medical Journal*, (2014); 349:g6821

2 MIND, 2022 https://www.mind.org.uk/media-a/6293/the-impact-of-coronavirus-on-mental-health-hospital-discharge-briefing.pdf

1 Out of Sight, Out of Mind

1 E. Goffman, *Asylums: Essays on the Condition of the Social Situation of Mental Patients and Other Inmates* (Pelican Books, 1961)

2 H. Middleton and J. Moncrieff, 'Critical Psychiatry: a brief overview', *BJPsychAdvances*, vol. 25, no. 1 (2018), pp. 47–54

3 Terrible Secrets

1 R. L. Palmer, 'The Dietary Chaos Syndrome: a useful new term?', *British Journal of Medical Psychology*, vol. 52, no. 2 (1979), pp. 187–90

2 P. M. Campling, 'Working with Adult Survivors of Child Sexual Abuse: Much can be learnt from what goes wrong', Editorial, *British Medical Journal*, vol. 305 (1992), pp. 1375–6

4 Experts by Experience

1 D. Clark, 'Social Psychiatry: The Therapeutic Community Approach' in P. Campling and R. Haigh (eds), *Therapeutic Communities: Past, Present and Future*, (Jessica Kingsley, 1999)

5 Locked In

1 M. Archinard, V. Haynal-Reymond and M. Heller, 'Doctors' and Patients' Facial Expressions and Suicide Reattempt Risk Assessment', *Journal of Psychiatric Research*, vol. 34, no. 3 (2000), pp. 261–2

2 https://www.gov.uk/government/publications/modernising-the-mental-health-act-final-report-from-the-independent-review

6 Who's in Charge?

1 K. E. Kram and M. M. Hampton, 'When women lead: The visibility–vulnerability spiral', in R. J. Ely, E. G. Foldy, M. A. Scully, and The Center for Gender in Organizations Simmons School of Management (eds) *Reader in Gender, Work and Organization* (Blackwell Publishing Ltd, 2003), pp. 211–23

7 Hope and Despair

1 R. D. Hinshelwood, *Thinking About Institutions: Milieux and Madness* (London: Jessica Kingsley, 2001), pp. 42–3

2 S. Davies, P. Campling and K. Ryan, 'Therapeutic Community Treatment for Personality Disorder: service use and mortality over 3 years' follow-up', *British Journal of Psychiatry*, vol. 182, S44 (2003), pp. 24–7

8 Facing up to Suicide

1 D. Campbell and R. Hale, *Working in the Dark* (London and New York: Routledge, 2017), p. 27

2 https://commonslibrary.parliament.uk

3 Émile Durkheim, *Le Suicide* (1897)

4 *Facts About Suicide* (2015), International Association for Suicide Prevention. https//www.iasp.info/

9 Give Sorrow Words

1 William Shakespeare, *Macbeth*, Act IV, scene iii

2 S. Cramer, 'The Fragile Male', *British Medical Journal*, (2000); 321(7276): 1609–12

3 V. Zagier Roberts, 'The Self-assigned Impossible Task', in A. Obholzer and V. Zagier Roberts (eds), *The Unconscious at Work* (Routledge, 1994, 2019)

4   J. Schaverien, *Boarding School Syndrome: The Psychological Trauma of the 'Privileged' Child* (Routledge, 2011)

10 Hidden Histories

1   P. Fossion, M. Rejas, L. Servais, I. Pelc and S. Hirsch, 'Family approach with grandchildren of Holocaust survivors', *American Journal of Psychotherapy*, vol. 57, no. 4 (2003), pp. 519–27

2   J. Bowlby, 'On Knowing What You Are Not Supposed to Know and Feeling What You Are Not Supposed to Feel', *Canadian Journal of Psychiatry*, vol. 24, no. 5 (1979), pp. 403–8

11 A Global Trauma

1   G. Fond, K. Nemani, D. Etchecopar-Etchart et al, 'Association Between Mental Health Disorders and Mortality Among Patients with COVID-19 in 7 Countries: A Systematic Review and Meta-analysis', *JAMA Psychiatry*, vol. 78, no. 11 (2021), pp. 1208–17

2   Y. Xie, E. Xu and Z.Al-Aly, 'Risks of Mental Health Outcomes in People with Covid-19', *British Medical Journal*, (2022); 376:e068993

3   M. Marmot, J. Allen, P. Goldblatt, E. Herd and J. Morrison, 'Build Back Fairer: The Covid-19 Marmot Review – The Pandemic, Socioeconomic and Health Inequalities in England', Institute of Health Equity, 2020

12 Moral Injury

1   British Medical Association, 'Moral Distress and Moral Injury: Recognising and Tackling it for UK Doctors' (2021); https://www.bma.org.uk/media/4209/bma-moral-distress-injury-survey-report-june-2021.pdf

13 A System of Exclusion

1   C. Beale, 'Magical Thinking and Moral Injury: Exclusion Culture in Psychiatry', *BJPsych Bulletin*, vol. 46, no. 1 (2022), pp. 16–19

2   'Depression in Children and Young People', NICE Guideline NG134 (2019); https://www.nice.org.uk/guidance/ng134

Epilogue: Losing Our Way

1   House of Commons 2020 https://commonslibrary.parliament.uk/mental-health-achieving-parity-of-esteem/

2   E. Lockhart, 2022 https://www.rcpsych.ac.uk/news-and-features/
    latest-news/detail/2021/09/23/record-number-of-children-and-young-
    people-referred-to-mental-health-services-as-pandemic-takes-its-toll

3   BBC *File on 4*, https://www.bbc.co.uk/news/uk-59964353; and D.
    Campbell and A. Bawden, 'Three Private Mental Health Hospital Chains
    Censured 37 Times for Unsafe Care After Patient Deaths', *Guardian*,
    26 April 2022

FURTHER READING
AND RESOURCES

This is not intended as a comprehensive bibliography, but a list of books and papers that I have found useful: some recent, some old favourites; some self-help, some memoir; some more academic than others; all of them interesting and readable.

Adshead, G., and Horne, E., *The Devil You Know: Stories of Human Cruelty and Compassion* (Faber and Faber, 2021)

Bateman, A. W., Holmes, J., and Allison, E., *Introduction to Psychoanalysis: Contemporary Theory and Practice* (Routledge, 2nd edition, 2021)

Blackwell, D., *Counselling and Psychotherapy with Refugees* (Jessica Kingsley, 2005)

Clarke, R., *Breathtaking: Inside the NHS in a Time of Pandemic* (Little, Brown, 2021)

Clarke, R., *Dear Life: A Doctor's Story of Love and Loss* (Little, Brown, 2020)

Filer, N., *This Book Will Change Your Mind about Mental Health* (Faber and Faber, 2019)

Greenberg, N., 'Managing mental health challenges faced by healthcare workers during Covid-19 pandemic', *British Medical Journal* 2020;368:m1211

Jones, K., *Asylums and After* (Athlone, 1994)

Montross, C., *Falling into the Fire: A Psychiatrist's Encounters with the Mind in Crisis* (One World Publications, 2014)

O'Donnell, D., *Memoirs of a Psychiatric Orderly* (Vintage Books, 2013)

Palmer, B., *Helping People with Eating Disorders: A Clinical Guide to Assessment and Treatment* (Wiley, 2014)

Pearce, S., and Haigh, R., *The Theory and Practice of Democratic Therapeutic Community Treatment* (Jessica Kingsley, 2017)

Schmidt, U., Treasure, J., and Alexander, J., *Getting Better Bite by Bite: A Survival Kit for Sufferers of Bulimia Nervosa and Other Binge Eating Disorders* (Routledge, 2nd edn, 2015)

Schwartz, A., *A Practical Guide to Complex PTSD: Compassionate Strategies to Begin Healing from Childhood Trauma* (Rockridge Press, 2020)

Shooter M., *Growing Pain: Making Sense of Childhood – A Psychiatrist's Story* (Hodder and Stoughton, 2018)

Taylor, B., *The Last Asylum: A Memoir of Madness in our Times* (Hamish Hamilton, 2014)

Treasure, J., *Skills-based Caring for a Loved One with an Eating Disorder* (Routledge, 2016)

Van der Kolk, B., *The Body Keeps the Score: Mind, Brain and Body in the Transformation of Trauma* (Penguin, 2015)

Yakeley, J., *Working with Violence: A Contemporary Psychoanalytic Approach* (Jessica Kingsley, 2017)

There is also useful information on charity websites, for example:

https://www.mind.org.uk
https://www.nspcc.org.uk
https://www.rethink.org
https://www.samaritans.org
https://www.survivoralliance.org
https://unseenuk.org
https://youngminds.org.uk